Handbook of Sustainable Development

Reflections on the book

"The Handbook of Sustainable Development offers a series of conceptual frameworks and practical guidance on how to engage with sustainable development in a corporate setting. I congratulate Professor Radha R. Sharma for presenting an excellent team of authors who come with each their expertise and contribute to make this book a repository of insight on how to further advance business in bringing sustainable development to the world. I wish you much success with your book."

Dr. Mette Morsing,
Global Head,
PRME,
United Nations Global Compact

"Beyond recycling, corporate social responsibility, and conscious capitalism, there is emerging a tsunami of creativity about our living context. How can we consider our environment in everything from plant placement to supply chain to packaging? Can we truly make the environment a primary stakeholder, along with investors, employees, customers, and suppliers? If you are curious, and for all of our sakes, I hope you are, read this book—several times. Your children's health and lives will depend on it."

Richard Boyatzis, PhD,
Distinguished University Professor,
Case Western Reserve University,
Co-author of the international best seller: *Primal Leadership*,
and the *Helping People Change*

Reflections on the book

"*Climate change is one of the biggest challenges before us in this 21st century. Perhaps the biggest. It will determine the fate of our children and grandchildren. In that context, this Handbook of Sustainable Development should be a very useful guide for organisations, all over the world. Management is about solving problems; not blaming and fault finding. Prof Radha Sharma, the editor of this volume and the many contributors have rendered a valuable service by offering approaches to analyse, plan and act on the various issues in sustainable development. The eleven chapters contributed by scholars from various universities and research institutions, together constitute a bank of ideas and approaches. Each organization and its management can keep referring to that chapter or section, depending on their specific sustainable development challenges, at any point of their planning for growth. That is exactly the purpose and value of a handbook.*

Dr Radha Sharma, the editor, has dedicated the book to two entities. The first is her family, this is not uncommon. The family of every author usually deserves such a tribute. Her second entity is more unusual and unique. She has dedicated the book also to — "The Supreme: Omnipotent, Omniscient, and Omnipresent". It is quite relevant. Global warming is so serious that the belated battle of humankind to save the planet needs Divine Grace to succeed. May that Supreme give us the strength to perform our Climate Dharma, Duty. I wish the book all success, through worldwide study, dissemination and action based on this practical handbook."

Dr. M. B. Athreya, Ph.D. (Harvard),
Padma Bhushan,
Dharma Pracharak

Reflections on the book

"Handbook offers an absorbing read of a raft of key issues around sustainability and development at intersection of multilateralism.

Painstakingly pieced together analysis of human existence within the ambit of environment and economics, the Handbook presents curated content and structural solutions in lead up to accelerated organisational innovations and transformational sustainability, for now and future alike."

Pooran Chandra Pandey,
Member of the Board of Trustees,
United Nations World Food Programme Trust for India

Handbook of Sustainable Development

Strategies for Organizational Sustainability

Edited by Radha R. Sharma

BEP

BUSINESS EXPERT PRESS

Leader in applied, concise business books

Handbook of Sustainable Development:
Strategies for Organizational Sustainability
Copyright © Business Expert Press, LLC, 2021.

First published in 2021 by
Business Expert Press, LLC
222 East 46th Street, New York, NY 10017
www.businessexpertpress.com

ISBN-13: 978-1-95334-942-2 (paperback)
ISBN-13: 978-1-95334-943-9 (e-book)

Business Expert Press Environmental and Social Sustainability for
Business Advantage Collection

Collection ISSN: 2327-333x (print)
Collection ISSN: 2327-3348 (electronic)

Cover design by Charlene Kronstedt
Interior design by S4Carlisle Publishing Services Private Ltd.,
Chennai, India

First edition: 2021

10 9 8 7 6 5 4 3 2 1

Dedication

To the Supreme: Omnipotent, Omniscient, and Omnipresent
and
My family
(Chandresh, Anu-Vishwa-Avni, Swati and Abhinav)

for their love
and
unconditional support

Description

Sustainable development has garnered the attention of the global community when United Nations created the Brundtland Commission in 1983 to suggest various ways to save the human environment and natural resources and promote economic and social development. Sustainable development is a way of organizing that an organization can function in the long term. The United Nations' sustainable development goals provide a framework to translate these into solutions through responsible business and investment by incorporating the ten Principles of the UN Global Compact into strategies, policies, and procedures and establishing a culture of integrity, expected to bring out transformative change and create an enabling environment for doing business globally. Thus, corporate sustainability, to a large extent, would depend on the capability of the firm to function over a long period with sustainable relationships with the stakeholders.

The *Handbook of Sustainable Development: Strategies for Organisational Sustainability* provides guiding principles and diagnostic tools for transformation, generates knowledge about sustainable organizational designs, co-creating value with multiple stakeholders, managing diversity responsibly, ecopreneurship with entrepreneurial bricolage, sustainable business model, developing positive synergy, sustainability reporting, and organizational transformation for sustainability, which are pivotal issues to be addressed in management education and corporate world.

Keywords

sustainable development; stakeholders; ecopreneurship; bricolage; CSR; diversity; sustainability reporting; sustainable organizational design; organizational transformation

Contents

Acknowledgments

Professor Dr. Mette Morsing, Head, PRME, UN Global Compact, New York, USA

Professor Richard Boyatzis, Distinguished University Professor and Professor of OB, Psychology and Cognitive Sciences, Case Western Reserve University, Cleveland, USA

Professor Cary L. Cooper, 50th Anniversary Professor of Organizational Psychology and Health, Alliance Manchester Business School, University of Manchester, Manchester, UK

Professor Dr. Stephan Stubner, Dean, HHL Graduate School of Management, Leipzig, Germany

Professor R. Edward Freeman, University and Olsson Professor, The Darden School, University of Virginia, Charlottesville, USA

Professor Ernst von Kimakowitz, Humanistic Management Network, Geneve, Switzerland

Professor Adela J McMurray, former, Director, College of Business Doctoral Training Centre, College of Business, RMIT University, Melbourne, Australia

Professor Wolfgang Amann, HEC Paris, Qatar

Professor Claire Simmers, Claire A. Simmers, Professor Emeritus of Management, Saint Joseph's University, Philadelphia, USA

Professor Agata Stachowicz-Stanusch, Canadian University, Dubai

Professor Charles Wankel, Professor of Management at St. John's University, New York, USA

Professor Mary Gentile, GVV, University of Virginia, Charlottesville, USA

Dr. Michael Pirson, Fordham University, New York, USA

Dr. Isabel Rimanoczy, Convener LEAP, PRME Working Group on the Sustainability Mindset, Fort Lauderdale, Florida, USA

Professor Claus Dierksmeier, Global Ethic Institute, Tübingen, Germany

Dr. Ben Teehankee, De Salles University, Manila, Philippines

Ms Shabnam Siddiqui, Executive Director, Global Compact Network India, New Delhi, India

Dr. V. M. Bansal, Chairman, New Delhi Institute of Management, New Delhi, India

Professor K. K. Aggarwal, Chairman, National Board of Accreditation, India

Professor Subhash Sharma, Director, Indus Business Academy, Bangalore, India

Professor Madhukar Shukla, XLRI, Jamshedpur, India

Late Mr. Kamal Singh, Former Executive Director, UN Global Compact Network, India

Preface

Introduction to Sustainable Development

Radha R. Sharma

"Sustainability" has a long history with multiple perspectives, but sustainable development garnered the attention of the global community when United Nations created the Brundtland Commission in 1983 to suggest various ways to save the human environment and natural resources and promote economic and social development. The Brundtland Commission developed the most cited definition of sustainable development as "development which meets the needs of current generations without compromising the ability of future generations to meet their own needs" (World Commission on Environment and Development, 1987).

The United Nations' sustainable development goals provide a framework to translate these into solutions through responsible business and investment by incorporating the ten Principles of the UN Global Compact into strategies, policies, and procedures and establishing a culture of integrity. This is expected to bring out transformative change and create enabling environment for doing business and unlocking market potential across geographies. Thus, corporate sustainability, to a large extent, would depend on the capability of the firm to function over a long period with sustainable relationships with the stakeholders. The question then arises who the stakeholders are.

Freeman (1984, 46) defines stakeholders as "any group or individual who can affect or is affected by the achievement of the organisation's objectives." There are various types of stakeholders mentioned in the literature (Benna, Abratta, and O'Leary, 2016). Clarkson (1995, 106-107) categorizes them as primary and secondary stakeholders. According to him, primary stakeholders are essential and engage continuously with the organization. They are in a reciprocal and an interdependent relationship, such as employees, suppliers, and customers, whereas the secondary stakeholders do not directly interact with the organization but affect or are affected by the organization such as professional associations, media, trade organizations, and so on. He posited that a stakeholder need not be only an individual but an organization as well, which can also be treated as an entity. In view of the importance of stakeholders in the organizational functioning, firms require appropriate systems to assess if they are addressing their concerns and are communicating effectively with the stakeholders for sustainable development.

Sustainable development is a way of organizing that an organization can function in the long term. The awareness about this idea developed as the result of industrial revolution and economic activities that had significant impact on environment and society in the second half of the nineteenth century. The cascading effects of globalization in the form of changing business environment, economic uncertainties, the economic meltdown, and the recent pandemic have brought about unprecedented challenges before industry and organizations across the globe and also in India. Management education, which prepares human capital for the industry, is expected to address some of these challenges along with intensifying competition, advancing technology, and accelerating complexity. However, the current management education is largely based on traditional capitalism where focus tends to be on profits and competitiveness rather than towards a balance among profitability, responsibility, social accountability, and sustainability. Hence, there is need for paradigm shift in management education to be more responsible and sustainable, which addresses the needs of the stakeholders in the normal as well as challenging times.

The Handbook of Sustainable Development: Strategies for Organisational Sustainability is an endeavor to provide a comprehensive perspective covering salient aspects of sustainable development in eleven chapters contributed by experts from various countries.

Chapter 1 on *A Manager's Role in Triple Bottom Line: Global Compact and Responsible Value Creation* by Steven D. Olson deals with the evolution of social and moral expectations about business and discusses the Guiding Principles and Assessment Tool that provide managers with the diagnostic categories and criteria for beginning that transformation.

Chapter 2 by Bhutani, Nair, Groen, and Dess discusses the science and practice of organizational design and offers frameworks for '*Designing and Developing Sustainable Organization*'. In Chapter 3, Beal argues that privileging profit maximization is incompatible with sustainable development; hence, there is need for *Generating Knowledge for Sustainable Development*. The purpose of the modern corporation is to create value; hence economic value, once created, flows to capital, consumers, and/or labor. In Chapter 4 *Corporate Citizenship for Responsible Management* Loza and Mion explain the concept of corporate citizenship and discuss its contribution to responsible, sustainable, and humanistic management. Chapter 5 by Griffin discusses the importance, and multiplicity, of corporate impacts *Focused on Co-creating Value with Multiple Stakeholders*. In Chapter 6, Bilimoria and Chantal focus on managing diversity responsibly. Chapter 7 by Rastogi and Sharma makes a case for *Ecopreneurship for Sustainability: Role of Entrepreneurial Bricolage, Design Thinking and Creative Self-Efficacy*, under resource-constrained environment. In Chapter 8 on *Walking A Tightrope Between Business & Sustainable Development*, Bandyopadhyay and Ray discuss the tensions between sustainability and market needs and highlight the role of social entrepreneurs in combining sustainable products and services with a viable business model. Chapter 9 on *Developing Positive Synergy* by Daniela highlights the importance of positive synergy in humanistic management, and flourishing relationships greatly needed in the present scenario. Chapter 10 by Chantarasap on *CSR Reporting* posits that CSR has transformed into CSR reporting, which has translated into sustainability reporting, the way forward for which is to look at the "Integrated Approach to Sustainability." Chapter 11 by Bachani throws light on the need for *Organizational Transformation for Sustainability* by offering a number of suggestions including tapping into the individual creativity as a source of ongoing advantage.

The hope is that the book will serve as a resource to students, faculty, and researchers in management education and to professionals and practitioners in the corporate world for promoting sustainable development.

A true teacher is a learner for life inspired by quest for self-actualization.

Radha R. Sharma
May 2021

References

Benna, S., Abratta, R., and O'Leary, B. 2016. "Defining and Identifying Stakeholders: Views from Management and Stakeholders." *South African Journal of Business Management* 47(2).

Clarkson, M. 1995. "A Stakeholder Framework for Analyzing and Evaluating Corporate Social Performance." *Academy of Management Review* 20(1): 92-117.

Freeman, R. E. 1984. *Strategic Management: A Stakeholder Approach*. Boston: Pitman.

World Commission on Environment and Development (WCED). 1987. *Our Common Future*. New York: Oxford University Press.

Foreword

R. Edward Freeman

University and Olsson Professor, The Darden School,
University of Virginia, Virginia, USA

The essays in this new volume provide some context on the idea of sustainable development and is a welcome reference for scholars and managers alike. "Sustainable development" is one of those contested ideas that admits of multiple interpretations. This is its strength so long as we can compare and contrast the details of differing modes. This volume will assist us a great deal in this effort to make the idea more appealing to a broader audience.

It is especially heartening to see the authors and editor deal with the importance of multiple stakeholder relationships in unpacking how sustainable development can work in the real world. With chapters on both entrepreneurial thinking and the role of citizenship, the book offers a broad perspective on the environmental movement and its associated idea of sustainability. Recent trends on co-creating value with multiple stakeholders, social entrepreneurship, cultural diversity, and others all play an important role.

The authors of these essays have gone beyond the usual gloom and doom scenarios that one often finds in discussions of sustainable development, and they have, for the most part, avoided demonizing business organizations as the main underlying cause of environmental degradation. Perhaps we are truly making progress. Despite a political conversation that often goes nowhere, scholars and executives are actually getting about the important business of designing our organizations so that our children and grandchildren will be able to flourish. This book contributes a great deal to this process.

CHAPTER 1

A Manager's Role in Triple Bottom Line: Global Compact and Responsible Value Creation

Steven D. Olson

A Brief History of the Evolving Social and Moral Expectations Regarding Business

As consensus statements rooted in declarations and conventions that are as close to universally accepted as humans can currently manage, the Ten Principles of the United Nations Global Compact reflect humanity's best, shorthand understanding to date of what our baseline priorities ought to be in all our commercial activities. The Ten Principles are grounded in the Universal Declaration of Human Rights (1948), the Rio Declaration on Environment and Development (1992), the United Nations Convention Against Corruption (1996), and the International Labor Organization's Declaration on Fundamental Principles and Rights at Work (1998) and were crafted to cultivate corporate contributions to the UN Millennium Development Goals (Nations, 2000). The adoption of the Ten Principles by some 7,000 businesses established a voluntary, global learning platform that focused managers' attention on the four areas of greatest ethical risk for the socially, environmentally, and economically sustainable operation of businesses and markets: human rights, workplace rights, environmental impact, and corruption (Kell, 2013; Kell and Levin, 2003).

These four areas delineate the types of rights that we have come to recognize that every human has and that every human must recognize for others (The Universal Declaration of Human Rights, 1948). As such, these rights sketch out the baseline expectations for socially responsible behavior that every company must meet. Rights, of course, logically and practically infer correlative and/or converse duties (The Foundation of International Human Rights Law, 2013; Knox, 2008; Küng, 1998; Saul, 2000; Suter, 2009). As The Universal Declaration of Human Rights obliges, "All human beings are born free and equal in dignity and in rights. They are endowed with reason and conscience and should act towards one another in a spirit of brotherhood" (Article 1) and "Everyone has duties to the community in which alone the free and full development of his (sic) personality is possible" (Article 29.1).

Correlative duties to respect the rights of others and converse duties owed by individuals to society, future generations, and the environment share a common presupposition, namely, that you cannot will for yourself the conditions and behaviors that respect your rights without also willing those conditions for others. The Ten Principles delineate what managers and corporations can do to create those conditions for themselves, their employees, and for the other entities, persons, and communities that they affect.

Just as the experience curve focuses managers' attention on the learning that they and the corporation must do to meet the industry's steady improvements, improvements that not only decrease cost and price (adjusted for inflation) but also increase quality and value, the Ten Principles focus managers' attention on the learning that they must undertake to keep pace with the evolving expectations regarding business (Hirschmann, 1964; Stern and Michael, 2006). The Ten Principles direct a manager toward four key areas in which they must continue to learn and innovate in order to meet evolving social expectations regarding human rights and moral value while at the same time decreasing the cost to produce and the price (adjusted for inflation) to consumers. Whatever else managers do in creating and sustaining value, they must make sure that they respect these rights and fulfill these responsibilities.

John Ruggie, a principal architect of the Global Compact, facilitated the subsequent global learning process around the elaboration of what respecting human rights entails for corporations. In his role as the

UN Secretary-General's Special Representative for Business and Human Rights, Ruggie led a global exploration of what it would mean for corporations, states, nongovernmental organizations (NGOs), and other actors to make our universally accepted duties toward other human beings a reality. His final report to the Human Rights Council (Guiding Principles on Business and Human Rights: Implementing the United Nations "Protect, Respect and Remedy" Framework, 2011) culminated 6 years of learning and elaboration on Global Compact's shorthand commitments to human rights, namely, to "support and protect the protection of international human rights within their sphere of influence" (Principle 1) and to "make sure they are not complicit in human rights abuses" (Principle 2).

By endorsing the Guiding Principles, the Human Rights Council formally signaled an end to "the era of declaratory CSR" (Ruggie, 2013). Corporations and other actors would no longer be able to get away with simply saying that they support human rights. They would have to prove it. The "Protect and Remedy Framework" and "Guiding Principles," together with the "Ten Principles," make clear that corporations and their managers have a duty "to respect human rights in terms of risk-based due-diligence" (Ruggie, 2013: 125), to remediate violations, just as they would any other area of business risk, and to communicate "a balanced and reasonable presentation of the organization's significant economic, environmental and social impacts, and enable[s] stakeholders to assess the organization's performance" (Making the Connection: Using the GRI G4 Guidelines to Communicate Progress on the UN Global Compact Principles, 2013).

The move from declaring a commitment to the UN principles to actually managing these rights and responsibilities through corporate mechanisms of risk and remediation marked a sea change in corporate practices. Though the "Ten Principles" were affirmed by statements of support from nearly every major business association, as well as several major transnational corporations and other actors, Ruggie found that in 2005 less than 100 of the approximately 80,000 transnational corporations—one-tenth of 1 percent—had explicit, due-diligence policies and practices regarding human rights! I think we can safely say that the vast majority of the world's corporations are failing in their self-acknowledged, socially expected duties both to know what their human rights risks are and to show what they are doing to address them (Ruggie, 2013: 120–122).

Combined with the State's duty to protect human rights and civil society's role in mediating between governments and corporations, the Human Rights Council also endorsed a vision in which corporations play a vital role in a system of "polycentric governance" (Ruggie, 2014; Taylor, 2011). By internalizing these universally accepted social norms and standards into their strategic and operating principles, corporations make universal rights and responsibilities a reality within their unique spheres of action and influence (Blitt, 2012). The vision of polycentric governance was cast as a solution to the "governance gaps" that have permitted transnational corporations to act unethically and unsustainably (Backer, 2012; Prenkert, 2014; Weiss and Thakur, 2010).

Directly or indirectly, knowingly or unwittingly, many corporations have been guilty of or complicit in the violation of universal rights and responsibilities toward humans and nature. In industry after industry—oil and gas, mining and minerals, chemicals and pharmaceuticals, consumer products, and financial services—corporations and their subsidiaries, partners, and suppliers have violated human rights and defaulted on their duties (Schwartz and Gibb, 1999). Some pointed to conflicts and contradictions in domestic and international law and pled innocence. Others pointed to the compliance of their own operations and pled ignorance regarding what their suppliers or vendors were doing. Both responses leave holes in our systems of governance and action. Neither response can be socially or economically sustained.

Polycentric governance proposes the most adequate, if still incomplete, solution to date (Abbott, 2009; Lenssen et al., 2008). The Global Compact Principles aim to establish the conditions of integrity that businesses must create within their organization and operations in order to partner with governments and NGOs to fulfill the UN Development Goals. The risk-based due diligence that Global Compact and the Guiding Principles require of businesses ensures that corporations fulfill the conditions that partnering with integrity requires.

Many corporations have already taken up this vision, making it part of their corporate strategy (Avina, 2013; Isdell, 2010; Jones et al., 2004;

Prahalad, 2009). For its part in realizing a risk-based, due-diligence approach to baseline CSR, the United Nations Global Compact modeled its "Ten Principles Self-Assessment Tool" on the "Human Rights Compliance Assessment Quick Check," a tool developed by the Danish Institute for Human Rights to flesh out the implication of the Human Rights Council's "Framework" and "Guiding Principles." Therefore, to understand what the Global Compact means for a manager's role in the triple bottom line we have to view managerial responsibilities within the context of this evolving vision of polycentric governance and risk-based due diligence.

Consensus—Conflict-Clarifying Principles

As consensus statements, the Global Compact Ten Principles and Guiding Principles are not free from conflict, but far from it (Hoover, 2013). An earlier attempt to go beyond the Global Compact Ten Principles in delineating corporate responsibilities for human rights, the "Draft Norms on the Responsibilities of Transnational Corporations and Other Business Enterprises with Regard to Human Rights," aroused sharp divisions between rights advocates and business organizations (Doing the wrong thing: Human Rights Activists Fall Out Over How to Deal with Companies, 2007). Many companies, managers, management scholars, legal scholars, and human rights organizations oppose some or all of Ten Principles and Guiding Principles.

The consensus thinking, reflected in Global Compact's Ten Principles, about a manager's role in the triple bottom line does not resolve challenge and controversies, it clarifies them. This conflict-clarifying and engendering feature of Global Compact is not accidental. It is, argues Nobel Prize–winning economist, A.K. Sen, an essential feature of "the general discipline of human rights" (Sen, 2005). When we recognize a right we acknowledge that if we can plausibly do something that would prevent that right from being violated, then we have a duty to do what we can. What might we do? Which rights are in play? How do we integrate the rights claims with other important claims in play? All of these questions remain open to debate and interpretation (Giacomazzi, 2005; Knox, 2008; Kung and Schmidt, 1998; McGregor, 2013). Their resolution into action stands as the hallmark of ethical learning.

To lay out an alternative paradigm for a manager's role and for the role of management education and training in the triple bottom line, we must first appreciate what it is about these principles that offend so many. I will briefly describe the provocative, learning-stimulating challenges and controversies that surround the Ten Principles. With an appreciation of these challenges in mind, I will then outline the emerging shape of the manager's role in managing with people and planet, as well as profit, in mind. Managing for the triple bottom line requires the ability to generate sustainable profit margins ethically. The evolving expectations reflected in the Ten Principles have emerged as the "curriculum" that managers will have to master in order to create and sustain triple-bottom-line value. In light of the emerging curriculum for value creation, I will close this chapter by describing the new competencies that managers and corporations will need to develop in order to equip themselves and their organizations to deal with the challenge of creating the triple-bottom-line value.

What's So Challenging about the Ten Principles?

The challenge of the Ten Principles starts with their emphasis. The Ten Principles weigh heavily toward people and planet. Profit, the main concern of modern management theory, is absent. The absence of explicit reference to profit among a manager's responsibilities makes most management scholars and managers nervous, if not downright suspicious or hostile. Most Anglo-American scholars and managers believe, wrongly, that both law and economic analyses require managers to maximize the wealth of shareholders (Stout, 2012). Due to the fact that it is both logically and practically impossible to maximize two variables at the same time, most modern management scholars and managers cannot and do not support any rights and duties, legal or moral, beyond that of maximizing shareholder wealth. They even fight many laws and regulations on the grounds that those laws and regulations violate the requirement to maximize shareholder wealth. People (Principles 1–6) and planet (Principles 7–9) have few friends and lots of enemies in modern management theory and in much modern management practice (Ghoshal, 2005).

Second, the "ought-ness" of the Ten Principles and Guiding Principles puts them, and any manager who adheres to them, at odds, conceptually and morally, with the central thrust of modern management theory. Most modern management theory, and by implication, management practice, strives and claims to be "value free" or "value neutral." While laudable in some respects, the striving for value neutrality has led to much methodological and practical mischief.

Methodologically, management scholars have pursued their vision of a value-free or value-neutral science by overemphasizing falsification as the most important criterion for rigorous knowledge (Van de Ven, 2007). We can say we know something significant, management scholars maintain, when we have established claims that have withstood the attempts of others to disprove those knowledge claims. Disproving a claim requires the ability to conduct an experiment to test it. This condition narrows the focus of management researchers toward variance studies that isolate independent and dependent variables, studies that therefore favor laboratory experiments conducted upon people who have no prior experience with the experimental conditions. All variables that can't be scientifically controlled, including values, are ruled out.

The knowledge such studies produce is intersubjectively rigorous, but the findings have very limited application. The findings apply only to situations in which such variables can be controlled. In addition, the findings only apply to people who have no experience with the variables under these conditions, that is to say, to beginners only.

A manager's need for knowledge, by contrast, arises only after extensive experience. Moreover, managers operate in a teeming sea of relative values (cultural, organizational, social, and individual), dynamic conditions, and changing variables (Klein, 1999). In seeking to create value for customers and to return reasonable rates of profit to owners and investors, managers are much more concerned with the problem of fixation than falsification (Klein, 2009). Precisely because they cannot isolate or control all the variables that play upon them and their actions, managers worry about getting stuck in ways of thinking and acting that are not producing their intended results. Management science offers little guidance in this respect. The very conditions that make modern social science "rigorous"—the "boundary conditions" of the research—render that knowledge largely unusable by managers.

The practical mischief wrought by management science's striving for falsifiable rigor and value neutrality is perhaps the most insidious of all. It blinds us to the value laden, moral concerns that are an ingredient in all management decisions. The quest for scientific objectivity and value neutrality suppresses or rejects all value-laden forms of description and analysis, all the while surreptitiously valorizing status quo structures, policies, and priorities. This simultaneous blinding and valorizing mislead many scholars and managers into opposing the Ten Principles as unnecessary, even illegitimate, add-ons to the value-free core of modern management science.

Here's how the misleading most commonly occurs. Managers and business organizations stake their claim to legitimacy and authority on the basis of their efficiency and effectiveness (MacIntyre, 1984). Our trust and reliance on them for so much of our economic and social lives is warranted, so the claim goes, because managers achieve our ends and purposes, our "values," whatever they might be, in an effective and efficient manner. We determine our ends (values), and managers and management science simply provide us with efficient and effective means (value free; Bellah et al., 2007). This sounds good, and it tilts toward a bias in our neurological functioning, but it's not true (Boyatzis, Rochford, and Jack, 2014).

First, efficiency is a relative value that requires the invocation of other values in order to be used as a criterion. For example, consider the act of efficient teaching. It might be efficient in the short run for me to do something myself and just let my students watch. Big lecture halls with one teacher and multiple-choice tests conducted electronically reflect this idea. But in the long run it might be more efficient to let my students do it themselves while I observe and comment on their performance. Small, intimate labs and clinics reflect this idea. Efficiency itself won't help me decide whether I should prioritize—that is, value—the short term or the long term. Efficiency also won't tell me *how* to teach, let alone *what* to teach. Those valuations have to come from somewhere else. And they do. They come from our values (Schwartz, 1992).

Second, effectiveness is also not value neutral because, like efficiency, it always presupposes some additional criteria. By itself, "effective" tells us nothing. We need to know "Effective for what end?" or "Effective for whom and for what purpose?" The answers to these questions are all value laden. There is no realm of human endeavor in which a value-free assessment of "effectiveness" exists (Taylor, 1989).

The implications of the practical mischief done in the name of value-neutral management and management science runs a wide gamut, from cigarette company executives cynically abjuring all moral responsibility for the impact of their actions in manufacturing, marketing, and selling harmful products, to transnational corporations adjuring all responsibility for human rights violations committed by their subsidiaries and partners (Wolgast, 1992). Supposedly value-neutral management and management science always advance some values, and therefore somebody's values, over other values and other persons' values. Supposedly value-neutral management and management science also always imply that the particular state of affairs under study—the status quo, as for example, in studies of the "efficient stock market"—is the ways things are and therefore how things "should be." Management theories are not "cameras"; they are "engines" (MacKenzie, 2008).

Note the connection between management science and management culture's understanding of a manager's role and the understanding of a manager's duties. Management science purports to tell us "how things are in the world of business." Managers define and justify their duties on the basis of their view of "how things are in business." Thus, management theory provides managers with a model of how reality is and managers take it as the model for what they ought to do (Geertz, 1973). A person's view regarding a manager's role relies on his or her theory of management (Olson, 2007). The triple-bottom-line "theory" of management implied by the Global Compact Ten Principles, and its implications for managers' roles, is what offends so many.

The management theory implied by the Ten Principles offends because it prioritizes a set of values on behalf of people and issues that modern management theory and practice has represented poorly, if at all (London and Hart, 2004). For that reason, the Ten Principles imply a different understanding of a manager's role and responsibilities. Specifically, the Ten Principles value:

- Radical human equality, which is entailed by international human and labor rights, many of which exceed the laws and/or practices of many nations and organizations, including industrialized ones.
- Abolition of all forms of child labor in favor of child development and education.

- Collective bargaining and worker's right to voice in the workplace.
- A bias toward those populations of humans within and across societies who are potentially or actually the most vulnerable to corporate harm and who are also the least likely to have effective means of seeking justice and redress for those harms.
- Environmental precaution.
- Environmentally friendly technologies.
- Active prevention and correction of corruption in all its forms.

The Ten Principles offend because they openly state a commitment to the underserved people and values that were addressed by the UN Millennium Development Goals. Some of these values, and at different times and occasions, perhaps all of them, will offend, or at least present challenges, to all of us, whether we are acting as managers or owners, regulators or consumers, shareholders or stakeholders. Traditional management principles shy away from such substantive commitments. The Ten Principles confront managers and scholars with the unfinished business of recognizing and respecting the rights of ALL people and nature (The Foundation of International Human Rights Law, 2013; Suter, 2009).

In short, I suspect that the real reason that managers and management scholars find the Ten Principles so challenging is because they are so very challenging! To fulfill them implies that a manager or scholar will have to think, value, and act more complexly. Complexity can be daunting for even the best managers and scholars (Senge, 1997). More details, interacting with greater dynamics, require higher levels of thinking (cognition), feeling (affection), and acting (conation). Developmental psychologist Robert Kegan argues persuasively that the "curriculum" of modern management presents managers with challenges already "over the heads" of most managers (Kegan, 1998; Kegan and Lahey, 2009). By adding to these challenges, Global Compact doesn't pave the way for easy acceptance and adoption, especially when careful analysis reveals that over a 10-year period (1985 to 1995) the top-half of the Standard & Poor's 500 created a mere 1 to 4 percent return on invested capital, while the bottom half actually destroyed economic value (Thakor, 2011). If managers are not proficient at creating sustainable economic growth and profits given their current ways of thinking and acting, then they're not likely to embrace readily duties that appear to make their work more complex or less profitable.

This very complexity, however, makes the Ten Principles so attractive to so many. If it is true that there is nothing as helpful to a manager's personal and professional development—cognitive, emotional, and conative—as the presence of robust contradictions within his or her own thinking, acting, and valuing, then perhaps managers and management scholars recognize that the Ten Principles summon them to internalize a set of conflicting values, beliefs, and actions that will spur them to develop greater managerial capacities (Kegan and Lahey, 2001). Furthermore, if such learning is at the root of the real sources of the core competencies and dynamic capabilities that enable competitive advantage, then the managers and firms that internalize these challenges gain a learning-curve and experience-rate advantage over firms that do not internalize them (Christensen and Raynor, 2013). Data analysis from the Edelman Trust Barometer Global Survey strongly supports this connection (Czarniewski, 2014).

Implications for Managers' Roles

Given the conceptual, axiological (values), and developmental challenges and opportunities presented by the Global Compact Principles, what are the implications for a manager's role? I will first lay out the range of consensus-suggested role requirements, derived from the Global Compact "Ten Principles Self-Assessment Tool" (hereafter referenced as "TPSAT," and for sections and subsections "MA.," "HU.," "LA.," EN.," and "AC.," referring respectively to the sections on "Management," "Human Rights," "Labor Rights," "Environment," and "Anti-Corruption"; Global Compact Self-Assessment Tool, 2015). Grouped under the three categories of People, Planet, and Profits, these role requirements reveal areas of risk, opportunity, and reward that reside within the sphere of influence of every manager and every corporation. These areas coincide with the Global Reporting Initiative's G4 Sustainability Reporting sections on "General Standard Disclosures," "Disclosure of Management Approach," and "Indicators" (Making the Connection: Using the GRI G4 Guidelines to Communicate Progress on the UN Global Compact Principles,

2013). Managers need to be prepared to manage both for the risks and for the rewarding opportunities these risks give rise to, as well as communicate them to stakeholders (Esty and Winston, 2009; Porter and Kramer, 2006). I conclude the chapter with a brief description of new and newly emphasized management competencies that managers will have to master in order to seize these opportunities and transmute them into social and economic value.

The Bedrock Requirement and a Managers' Self-Concept

The bedrock of the manager's role regarding people is the requirement to "support and respect the protection of international human rights *within their [the business'] sphere of influence*" (Principle 1, emphasis added). The concept of "sphere of influence" has had a contested legal and conceptual history. The most legally and practically sound conceptions of a business sphere of influence center on the corporation's capacities to influence human rights, workers, stakeholders, and the environment (Porter and Kramer, 2006; Ruggie, 2013). These capacities flow upstream and downstream from the company's value-chain activities—upstream to suppliers and partners and downstream to vendors and customers. In whatever capacities the corporation interacts with people along this extended value chain, it holds responsibilities toward their rights. Managers are responsible for conducting due diligence to understand the potential and actual risks to those rights (they are also responsible for remedying violations of them).

This "capacity-based" conception of the responsibilities that fall within a business sphere of influence can be usefully extended to all 10 of the Global Compact Principles, not just to the first nine principles that pertain specifically to human and workplace rights and the environment. Then I will take up the implications of Principle 10, anticorruption, the significance of which will be evident when viewed against the backdrop of the preceding discussions. In whatever way the corporation interacts with society and the environment, it has a responsibility to assess and manage the risks and remedy the violations delineated by the Ten Principles. These responsibilities form the basic stuff of management and the foundation for strategic, socially responsible corporate management (Esty and Winston, 2009; Porter and Kramer, 2006).

The debates surrounding the corporation's sphere of influence have played an important role in clarifying a manager's role and responsibilities. These debates, however, have not addressed the personal and professional motivation to act on the Ten Principles. Like other rights-based schemes, the United Nation's concept of sphere of influence only works if individual managers feel an obligation, whether internally or externally motivated or both, to act upon the Ten Principles (Gardner, Csikszentmihalyi, and Damon, 2001). Given the tiny fraction of corporations undertaking risk-based due diligence regarding the Ten Principles, this motivation has clearly been lacking.

Your view of your corporation's sphere of influence largely depends upon your self-concept and on your perceived efficacy—your own (individual self-efficacy) and on that of your relevant group (collective self-efficacy; Bandura, 1997). If you do not view your role or your identity as encompassing a duty to respect and remedy the rights and responsibilities outlined in the Ten Principles, then you are not likely to act upon them as a manager (Reed II and Aquino, 2003). At most, you'll comply. Furthermore, if you don't feel and believe that you and your corporation have the capability to effect those responsibilities, then you are not likely to enact them. This is especially true in settings where laws, regulations, and institutional structures that might support and encourage such enactment are weak or nonexistent. Global Compact was designed for these places especially.

Given the centrality of self-concept and self-efficacy in determining individual and corporate action, you will find it worthwhile to assess your own self-concept and self-efficacy regarding the Ten Principles. Have you bought a smartphone or computer? Purchased new clothes? Owned an automobile? Eaten fruit? Sugar? If so, then you're almost certainly implicated, personally, in the rights and duties outlined in the Ten Principles.

At root, these principles merely express organizationally and socially the universal value of life and human equality (The Universal Declaration of Human Rights, 1948). Like the spectrum of colors dispersed from white, visible light when it is passed through a prism, the Ten Principles and the human and environmental rights they include make visible the components by which we respect and protect the lives of others, all others, including our own lives. In respect to the value of our lives, all people are equal and the values and actions that protect and respect life and human equality properly qualify as moral values (Hoban, 2012).

The Global Compact Ten Principles invite managers to express their moral obligation to respect and protect the universal life value by extending the perimeter of their moral concern and ethical action out through their spheres of influence (Kidder, 2009). At the heart of the vision of polycentric governance stands the moral identity of managers as protectors and respecters of life. People, planet, and profits are the essential means of living out that identity.

People

The manager's role with regard to people starts with the direct impact that the corporation has on its employees. The list of managerial responsibilities to recognize and respect worker's rights through risk-based due-diligence details the elements necessary for a productive, profitable, and sustainable workplace (MA.1-5). Global Compact extends these elements up and down the global supply chain (MA.6).

These responsibilities begin with the health and safety and the working hours, wages, and leave times of workers. Work facilities and conditions must be "safe, suitable, and sanitary" (HU.1). Things that so many of us take for granted—good lighting, adequate space, adequate temperatures and ventilation, food, water, sanitation, and privacy—must be available to all up and down the supply chain (HU.2-9). Equipment, machinery, protective gear, and the training for using them must be regularly provided or affordable (HU.2.a-f). Employees must be informed and involved in their own safety issues (HU.3). The special needs of vulnerable populations such as temporary workers, "residential" workers, and pregnant women must be especially attended to (HU.1.h).

As a rule of thumb, managers can safely assume that any dependency creates a node of specific managerial responsibility. That is, any time a worker depends on some thing or condition to fulfill his or her job, the manager has a special responsibility to ensure its provision or fulfillment. Managers are responsible for ensuring that all these responsibilities are met, maintained, and tracked not only within their company but also within their supply chain (MA.2-4 and 6).

Hours, wages, the right to appropriate, life-protecting time away from work, and the contracts that detail these form the other bulwark of a manager's role regarding people (HU.4-6). Fair, livable wages that are both in line with industry averages and provide enough for workers to meet their basic needs and those of their dependents lay that foundation for commutative justice (HU.5). Workers who are paid fairly and "livably" are empowered to enter into their other commercial exchanges fairly and are less likely to engage in the "desperate exchanges" that characterize so many rights-denying relationships, such as undocumented labor, child labor, forced overtime violations, and usurious, predatory lending (Walzer, 1983). Control of overtime work—defined as work exceeding the global threshold of 48 hours—and its appropriate remuneration—minimum threshold of 1.25 hourly rate—as well as periods of rest—a minimum of 24 contiguous hours in every 7-day period—and family, medical leave must be ensured (HU.4). Security and privacy must be secured and ensured, especially by and from the very security and monitoring services that companies employ to fulfill those duties (HU.11).

Ensuring that these bulwarks in respecting the rights of workers are in place requires that managers develop an ability to "see around corners." That is to say, managers must anticipate the ways in which others in their company or among their suppliers and partners will try to cut corners with regard to the rights of people. For example, bonus and piece-rate systems can easily be manipulated to deny some or all of the rights detailed above (HU.5.f). Workers in these systems frequently labor at overtime levels without earning a living wage. Residential properties and employee dormitories create numerous dependencies, each of which requires due diligence, including the protection of privacy and the security (HU.9). Procurement practices, such as pricing, delivery times, and incentives, can all contribute potentially to rights abuses under conditions that any competent manager can foresee (MA.6.e). Pleading ignorance of such conditions is no excuse for rights violations (Duhigg and Barboza, 2012).

Workers' rights to associate freely and to bargain collectively must be recognized and honored, even if the company discourages or otherwise restricts the operation of independent trade unions (LA.1-2). Ensuring that workers have to associate freely and give voice to their work-related concerns is not only a manager's moral duty, it's also good for business. Two-way communication demonstrates respect and provides the rich, shared information that characterizes profitable, efficient operations and partnerships (Levering, 1988; Patnayakuni, Rai, and Seth, 2006).

Managers must ensure that no labor is forced or bonded and that all minimum age laws are complied with (LA.3-4). This includes ensuring that none of the subtle forms of forcing labor, like retaining identity cards and passports, are practiced inside the organization or among its supply chain partners (LA.3.a-k). Hiring, firing, and other decisions related to employment must be based on work-relevant criteria (LA. 5). Like two-way communication, management policies and practices that are free from discrimination are not only moral obligations, they are also good for business. The evidence from the practices of industry-leading firms strongly supports the performance- and profit-enhancing impact of having rigorous, work- and performance-related criteria for hiring and promotion (Smart, 2005).

The key factor that determines whether managers' responsibilities are fulfilled or not is the presence of policies and procedures for the engagement with, and fair treatment of, workers (Tyler, 2010). Do workers have a voice in the decisions, practices, and policies that affect their work? Do all workers have the right to work in an environment that respects and protects their privacy and ensures freedom from all forms of harassment, threat, and abuse? Do all workers have the right to report violations of their rights and seek redress without fear of retaliation? If they don't, then you can almost be certain that some portion of the workers' basic rights are being obstructed or denied, if only out of culpable ignorance. Finally, do employees perceive that the policies and procedures are fairly enforced, regardless of status and rank, and violators sanctioned? If they do perceive that procedural fairness is upheld, then employees will themselves comply and cooperate in respecting the rights of others. If they do not, their voluntary compliance will drop to low levels. Managers bear responsibility for ensuring that these conditions are fulfilled.

Moving out from the company itself to its capacity to influence and impact consumers and communities, the manager's role remains constant, that is, to ensure through diligent assessment and preparation that the lives and rights of consumers and community members are protected and respected, if not enhanced (MA.7-9). Wherever and to whomever its products and services extend, the corporation's managers have a responsibility to prevent harm to others and to prevent violations of their rights (HU.13). From product defects and improper usage, to complicity in rights abuses and violations of laws by third parties, managers bear a moral responsibility to ensure that consumers and communities are protected (HU.10-14). Managers may not plead ignorance regarding rights abuses committed by either their host country government or by their host country society (HU.14). All known and foreseeable abuses, that is, potential abuses, must be assessed. This requires managers to engage with their communities and consumers directly so that they can see for themselves what the conditions and issues really are and inform themselves deeply so that they can "see around corners" and anticipate potential abuses (HU.12.a and HU.14.a.3).

The challenge of undertaking an honest assessment of such risks should not be underestimated because it runs up against deeply ingrained psychological biases that afflict us all (Bazerman and Tenbrunsel, 2011). Managers will do well, therefore, to engage proactively with NGOs and other third-party human rights groups who can provide a measure of objectivity to such assessments, not to mention their expertise in remedying abuses. Such substantive interchange between businesses and NGOs forms a crucial link in the vision of polycentric governance.

Planet

The manager's responsibility toward the environment extends the moral responsibility for risk-based due diligence from people to the ecosystems of which they are a part and upon which they depend. As such, these responsibilities further extend the managers' moral responsibility to protect and respect the universal value placed on life. To protect and respect human lives and equality of all others, managers must attend to the biological and ecological dimensions of the company's sphere of influence in order to ensure that they are not harming the ecological bases upon which those lives depend (EN.1-2). The economy, after all, is a wholly owned subsidiary of the environment.

The principle of addressing the environmental impacts of the company's operations and products with precaution tilts the manager's responsibilities toward the ever-increasing environmental responsibility. Like all forms of risk, environmental risk also contains the possibility of reward. Those companies and managers who embrace these moral constraints not only fulfill their moral duty but also tap into an important source of innovation (Lovins, Lovins, and Hawken, 2007; Nidumolu, Prahalad, and Rangaswami, 2009). From wringing out costs and risks, the benefits of which can, and often do, drop straight to a company's bottom line, to increasing supply chain efficiencies and reducing material inputs and throughputs, precautionary environmental responsibility spurs innovations that would otherwise remain untapped.

Each of the interdependencies between a business and the environment creates not only a moral obligation and a risk but also a node of potential reward. Responsible managers attend to these impacts and reduce or remedy the harms they cause (Esty and Winston, 2009; Porter and Kramer, 2006). Strategic, responsible managers attend to these impacts and create value-enhancing capabilities. Global Compact Principles 7 through 9 direct a manager's attention to the largest and most important of those risks and opportunities. Greenhouse gases, the impact of which add directly and indirectly to reducing the resilience and productivity of the ecosystem services upon which we depend, tops that list (EN.3). In addition to reducing the risks associated with energy consumption, water use, waste disposal, and air emissions (EN.3-6), the Global Compact also directs precaution toward the conditions for sustaining productive, resilient ecosystems. The safe handling and use of toxic chemicals, protection of biodiversity, and sustainable use and management of natural resources (EN.8-10), all drive managerial focus toward life-protecting and enhancing practices.

As noted by experts and markets, none of these environmental responsibilities can be fulfilled without the use and development of environmentally "friendly" technologies (Pernick and Wilder, 2007). The technological reach of the company's sphere of influence extends the manager's responsibilities into zones of impact and potential reward that have historically been treated in "value-neutral" ways (EN.11). Our increasing recognition of the environmental impacts and potential impacts of our technology, for ill and for good, forms an ever-expanding horizon for innovation. Managers who take on this moral duty in a proactive way will join the ranks of companies who are doing well by doing good, whether "well" is measured in reduced cost and risk or top-line growth in revenues, goodwill, and reputation (Anderson and White, 2009).

Profits

By now it will be clear to the reader that the Global Compact's main contribution to the manager's role in creating and sustaining reasonable profits resides in the moral insistence that managers shore up the necessary but insufficient conditions for sustainable value creation—socially, environmentally, and economically. Taken together, Principles 1 through 9 outline the managerial roles and responsibilities that are required of businesses within their spheres of influence and which enable those businesses to play their role in the value-creating and sustaining system of polycentric governance. Management science and the history of management have also revealed these role responsibilities to be the basis for superior, sustained value creation.

None of the value-creating principles can be reliably fulfilled, however, without vigilant attention to Principle 10, anticorruption. The legitimacy of economic markets and the social license to operate that societies extend formally and informally to business corporations depend entirely on fair competition and the risk-weighted return on investments. Managers and businesses that engage in corrupt practices like bribery, counterfeiting, and bid rigging betray both the value-creating logic of economic markets and commit treason against every party to the social compact that makes market exchanges possible and justifiable. Economic value cannot be created and sustained unless those firms that have devoted their scarce time, energy, and resources to creating "core competencies" receive their just rewards. Fair markets make this possible. Firms who lack these value-creating competencies and therefore fail to create the level of social benefit and welfare that their superior competitors create cannot be allowed to cheat for their unfair share. Cheating through corruption distorts the internal meaning of markets themselves and perverts their public purpose (social welfare) for private gain.

Like parasites who feed of and eventually kill their host, managers who engage in corruption destroy both economic value and the conditions that create and sustain it. Corrupt practices undermine trust, the most basic emotion and the key driver of corporate and social value creation. The data linking corruption to value destruction are incontrovertible. Transparency International's 10 most corrupt nations in 2014 had an average unemployment rate of 17 percent compared to only 5.6 percent average unemployment among the 10 least corrupt countries. The 10 most corrupt countries suffered from an average inflation rate of 13.9 percent compared to the 1.3 percent average inflation rate in the 10 least corrupt. The total GDP of the 10 most corrupt nations amounted to a meager US$593 billion. The GDP of the 10 least corrupt nations totaled a staggering US$6.533 trillion. Corruption renders life and economic life nasty, poor, brutish, and short. The infant mortality rate of the 10 most corrupt countries is 13 times greater than that of the 10 least corrupt. For every 1,000 live births in the 10 most corrupt nations, an average of 40 infants die before reaching their first birthday. In the 10 least corrupt nations, only three infants in 1,000 die before age 1. If you want to protect the lives and rights of others, then fight corruption.

Managers bear the responsibility of ensuring that all the elements of ethical compliance and anticorruption are fulfilled: clear organizational policies regarding anticorruption; realistic training that prepares managers for the corrupting challenges to integrity that they will likely face; monitoring, investigatory procedures; appropriate governance oversight; and oversight of all agents, intermediaries, and supply chain partners (AC.1-5). Fighting corruption requires shared effort among the three sectors of polycentric governance (EN.6). Only through conjoint activity can governments, businesses, and nongovernmental watchdogs roll back the "black" and "grey" markets and corrupt practices that traffic in the violation of the Global Compact Principles.

New Leadership Competencies

The Global Compact Ten Principles cast the manager's role in the triple bottom line in bold relief. Against the backdrop of the Ten Principles and the International Bill of Rights and supporting conventions and declarations that inform them, the manager's role in creating and sustaining economic, social, and environmental value takes on moral urgency. Managers must fulfill their responsibilities, not only as an economic imperative, but also as an ethical imperative. Ethics and economics speak in one voice.

Managers who would speak and act in "one voice" face significant challenges. The systems, structures, policies, practices, habits, and values that produced violations of the Ten Principles will not be reformed easily. Technical solutions will only address part of the work that needs to be done (Heifetz, 1994). Managers will have to learn new competencies for novel solutions.

Renowned author and "futurist" researcher Robert Johansen argues that to make the future different from the past, managers will have to learn 10 new leadership skills (Johansen, 2012). Eight of those skills relate directly to the challenges evoked by the Ten Principles. They are described below. As you read them, ask yourself, "To what extent do I (and my fellow managers) possess these skills?"

1. The ability to see through messes and contradictions to a future that others cannot yet see. I (we) are clear about what we are making, but flexible in how it gets made.
2. The ability to turn dilemmas into advantages and opportunities.
3. The ability to immerse oneself in unfamiliar environments and learn from them in a first-person way.
4. The ability to see things from nature's point of view, to understand, respect, and learn from its patterns.
5. The ability to calm tense situations where differences dominate and communication has broken down.
6. The ability to bring people from divergent cultures toward positive engagement.
7. The ability to engage with, create with, and nurture purposeful business and social change networks.
8. The ability to seed, nurture, and grow shared assets that can benefit all players involved and allow competition at a higher level to emerge.

To the extent that you and your fellow managers possess these abilities to a great or very great extent, you are well prepared for the challenge of the Ten Principles. To the extent that you do not, your management curriculum is clear. Welcome to the new paradigm for managers.

Summary

Taken together the *Guiding Principles on Business and Human Rights* (2011) and the operationalizing of them in the UN *Global Compact Self-Assessment Tool* (2015) mark the end of the era of declaratory corporate social responsibility (CSR) and the beginning of a new era: "Operationalized CSR." By defining the social and moral obligations that are incumbent upon corporations and managers by virtue of their business operations and spheres of influence, the *Guiding Principles* and *Self-Assessment Tool* redress gaps in the governance, reporting, monitoring, and sanctioning of corporate behavior that have been created by globally integrated supply chains and the transnational operations of corporations. The voluntary nature of compliance with these principles, however, requires that corporate managers internalize these obligations, incorporating them into their "working self-concept," that is, their understanding of their roles and duties as managers. The working self-concept enjoined upon managers by the *Guiding Principles* and the *Assessment Tool* derive from the triple-bottom-line theory of management. This theory of management and of managerial responsibilities and obligations rejects the purportedly value-free, descriptive theories of modern managerial science and replaces it with an ethically prescriptive theory. The conflict between these two competing views of a manager's role and responsibilities presents managers and corporate actors with set of conceptual and operational contradictions. These contradictions can only be resolved developmentally, that is, by corporate managers transforming the way they think about and manage their operations. The *Guiding Principles* and *Assessment Tool* provide managers with the diagnostic categories and criteria for beginning that transformation.

Questions

1. What is your evaluation of the claim upon which the rights-based theory of managerial responsibility is based, namely, that you cannot wish for yourself the conditions and behaviors that respect you and your rights without also wishing those conditions for, and enacting those behaviors toward, all others?

2. Compare and contrast the view of a manager's role and responsibilities in your organization, both explicitly stated and implicitly enacted

and rewarded, with the triple-bottom-line theory of management that informs the Global Compact.

3. Do you find the specific categories and content of the ethical risk assessments contained in the Global Compact Self-Assessment Tool conceptually and managerially sound and useful? What evidence do you have that supports or critiques the claim that observing these obligations is "good for business"?

4. If "what gets measured gets managed," then what managerial measures could you put in place to manage the ethical responsibilities and risks of your business operations?

References

Abbott, K.W. 2009. "Strengthening International Regulation through Transnational New Governance." *Vanderbilt Journal of Transnational Law* 42, p. 501.

Anderson, R.C., and R. White. 2009. *Confessions of a Radical Industrialist: Profits, People, Purpose—Doing Business by Respecting the Earth.* New York, NY: St. Martin's Press.

Avina, J. 2013. "The Evolution of Corporate Social Responsibility (CSR) in the Arab Spring." *The Middle East Journal* 67, no. 1, pp. 77–92.

Backer, L.C. 2012. "From Institutional Misalignments to Socially Sustainable Governance: The Guiding Principles for the Implementation of the United Nations' 'Protect, Respect and Remedy' and the Construction of Inter-Systemic Global Governance." *Pacific McGeorge Global Business & Development Law Journal* 25, no. 1, pp. 69–171.

Bandura, A. 1997. *Self-efficacy: The Exercise of Control.* New York, NY: Freeman.

Bazerman, M.H., and A.E. Tenbrunsel. 2011. *Blind Spots: Why We Fail to Do What's Right and What to Do about It/Max H. Bazerman, Ann E. Tenbrunsel.* Princeton, NJ: Princeton University Press.

Bellah, R.N., S.M. Tipton, W.M. Sullivan, R. Madsen, A. Swidler, and Tipton, S. M. (2007). *Habits of the Heart: Individualism and Commitment in American Life.* Berkeley: University of California Press.

Blitt, R.C. 2012. "Beyond Ruggie's Guiding Principles on Business and Human Rights: Charting an Embracive Approach to Corporate Human Rights Compliance." *Texas International Law Journal* 48, no. 1, pp. 33–62.

Boyatzis, R.E., K. Rochford, and A.I. Jack. 2014. "Antagonistic Neural Networks Underlying Differentiated Leadership Roles." *Frontiers in Human Neuroscience,* 8.

Christensen, C., and M. Raynor. 2013. *The Innovator's Solution: Creating and Sustaining Successful Growth.* Brighton, MA: Harvard Business Review Press.

Czarniewski, S. 2014. "Trust in Economic Relations and Business." *European Journal of Business, Economics and Accountancy* 2, no. 3, pp. 22–28.

Doing the Wrong Thing: Human Rights Activists Fall Out Over How to Deal with Companies. (2007, October 27). *The Economist* 385, p. 86.

Duhigg, C., and D. Barboza. 2012. In China, Human Costs Are Built into an IPad. *New York Times,* 25.

Esty, D., and A. Winston. 2009. *Green to Gold: How Smart Companies Use Environmental Strategy to Innovate, Create Value, and Build Competitive Advantage.* Hoboken, NJ: John Wiley & Sons.

Gardner, H., M. Csikszentmihalyi, and W. Damon. 2001. *Good Work: When Excellence and Ethics Meet/Howard Gardner, Mihaly Csikszentmihalyi, William Damon.* New York, NY: Basic Books.

Geertz, C. 1973. *The Interpretation of Cultures: Selected Essays* (Vol. 5019). New York, NY: Basic Books.

Ghoshal, S. 2005. "Bad Management Theories are Destroying Good Management Practices." *Academy of Management Learning & Education* 4, no. 1, pp. 75–91.

Giacomazzi, M. 2005. "Human Rights and Human Responsibilities: A Necessary Balance." *Santa Clara Journal of International Law* 3, no. 2.

Global Compact Self Assessment Tool. 2015. https://www.unglobalcompact.org/resources/235.

Guiding Principles on Business and Human Rights: Implementing the United Nations "Protect, Respect and Remedy" Framework. 2011. New York and Geneva: United Nations, Office of the High Commissioner for Human Rights.

Heifetz, R.A. 1994. *Leadership Without Easy Answers/Ronald A. Heifetz.* Cambridge, MA: Belknap Press of Harvard University Press.

Hirschmann, W.B. 1964. "Profit from the Learning Curve." *Harvard Business Review* 42, no. 1, pp. 125–39.

Hoban, J.E. 2012. *The Ethical Warrior: Values, Morals & Ethics for Life, Work and Service.* Spring Lake, NJ: RGI.

Hoover, J. 2013. "Rereading the Universal Declaration of Human Rights: Plurality and Contestation, Not Consensus." *Journal of Human Rights* 12, no. 2, p. 217. doi:10.1080/14754835.2013.784663.

Isdell, N. 2010. "Connected Capitalism: How Business Can Tackle Twenty-first-century Challenges." *Thunderbird International Business Review* 52, no. 1, pp. 5–12. doi:10.1002/tie.20305.

Johansen, R. 2012. *Leaders Make the Future: Ten New Leadership Skills for an Uncertain World/Bob Johansen; Foreword by John R. Ryan.* 2nd ed., rev. and expanded. San Francisco, CA: Berrett-Koehler Publishers.

Jones, A., M. Linguitte, J.L. González III, J.L. Tongzon, S. Nakamaru, W. Frank, . . . M. Kawaguchi. 2004. *Corporate Social Responsibility in the Promotion of Social Development: Experiences from Asia and Latin America.* Washington, DC: Inter-American Development Bank.

Kegan, R. 1998. *In Over Our Heads: The Mental Demands of Modern Life.* Boston, MA: Harvard University Press.

Kegan, R., and L.L. Lahey. 2001. *How the Way We Talk Can Change the Way We Work: Seven Languages for Transformation.* John Wiley & Sons.

Kegan, R., and L.L. Lahey. 2009. *Immunity to Change: How to Overcome It and Unlock Potential in Yourself and Your Organization.* Brighton, MA: Harvard Business Press.

Kell, G. 2013. "12 Years Later Reflections on the Growth of the UN Global Compact." *Business & Society* 52, no. 1, pp. 31–52.

Kell, G., and D. Levin. 2003. "The Global Compact Network: An Historic Experiment in Learning and Action." *Business and Society Review* 108, no. 2, pp. 151–81. doi:10.1111/1467-8594.00159.

Kidder, R.M. 2009. *Moral Courage.* New York, NY: HarperCollins.

Klein, G. 1999. *Sources of Power: How People Make Decisions.* Cambridge, MA: MIT press.

Klein, G. 2009. *Streetlights and Shadows: Searching for the Keys to Adaptive Decision Making.* Cambridge, MA: MIT Press.

Knox, J.H. 2008. "Horizontal Human Rights Law." *American Journal of International Law*, 102, no. 1, pp. 1–47.

Küng, H. 1998. "Don't be Afraid of Ethics! Why We Need to Talk of Responsibilities as well as Rights." *Global Ethic and Global Responsibilities-Two Declarations*, pp. 104–22. London, UK: SCM Press.

Kung, H., and H. Schmidt. 1998. *A Global Ethic and Global Responsibilities: Two Declarations*. SCM Press.

Lenssen, G., D. Arenas, P. Lacy, S. Pickard, J.A. Arevalo, and F.T. Fallon. 2008. "Assessing Corporate Responsibility as a Contribution to Global Governance: The Case of the UN Global Compact." *Corporate Governance: The International Journal of Business in Society* 8, no. 4, pp. 456–70.

Levering, R. 1988. *A Great Place to Work: What Makes Some Employers So Good (and Most So Bad)/Robert Levering*. 1st ed. New York, NY: Random House.

London, T., and S.L. Hart. 2004. "Reinventing Strategies for Emerging Markets: Beyond the Transnational Model." *Journal of International Business Studies* 35, no. 5, pp. 350–70.

Lovins, L.H., A. Lovins, and P. Hawken. 2007. *Natural Capitalism*. Boston, MA: Little, Brown.

MacIntyre, A. 1984. *After Virtue*. Vol. 99. Notre Dame, IN: University of Notre Dame Press Notre Dame.

MacKenzie, D. 2008. *An Engine, Not a Camera: How Financial Models Shape Markets*. Cambridge, MA: MIT Press.

Making the Connection: Using the GRI G4 Guidelines to Communicate Progress on the UN Global Compact Principles. 2013. United Nations Global Compact and Stichting Global Reporting Initiative, p. 31.

McGregor, S.L. 2013. "Human Responsibility Movement Initiatives: A Comparative Analysis." *Survival* 26, no. 3, p. 201.

Nations, U. 2000. *The Millennium Development Goals*. New York, NY: United Nations.

Nidumolu, R., C.K. Prahalad, and M. Rangaswami. 2009. "Why Sustainability Is Now the Key Driver of Innovation." *Harvard Business Review* 87, no. 9, pp. 56–64.

Olson, S.D. 2007. The ethics of leadership: Construction of an analytical framework, with application to Ken Blanchard's theories of situational and servant leadership. (3264091 Ph.D.), Emory University, Ann Arbor. http://ezproxy.gsu.edu/login?url=http://search.proquest.com/docview/304746473?accountid=11226, http://www.galileo.usg.edu/sfx_gsu?url_ver=Z39.88-2004&rft_val_fmt=info:ofi/fmt:kev:mtx:

dissertation&genre=dissertations+%26+theses&sid=ProQ:ProQue
st+Dissertations+%26+Theses+A%26I&atitle=&title=The+ethics+
of+leadership%3A+Construction+of+an+analytical+framework%2
C+with+application+to+Ken+Blanchard%27s+theories+of+situatio
nal+and+servant+leadership&issn=&date=2007-01-01&volume=
&issue=&spage=&au=Olson%2C+Steven+D.&isbn=97805490
26747&jtitle=&btitle=&rft_id=info:eric/&rft_id=info:doi/ Pro-
Quest Dissertations & Theses A&I database.

Patnayakuni, R., A. Rai, and N. Seth. 2006. "Relational Antecedents of
Information Flow Integration for Supply Chain Coordination." *Journal of Management Information Systems* 23, no. 1, pp. 13–49.

Pernick, R., and C. Wilder. 2007. *The Clean Tech Revolution: The Next Big Growth and Investment Opportunity.* New York, NY: HarperCollins.

Porter, M.E., and M.R. Kramer. 2006. "The Link Between Competitive Advantage and Corporate Social Responsibility." *Harvard Business Review* 84, no. 12, pp. 78–92.

Prahalad, C.K. 2009. *The Fortune at the Bottom of the Pyramid: Eradicating Poverty through Profits.* 5th ed. Upper Saddle River, NJ: FT Press.

Prenkert, J.D. 2014. "Business, Human Rights, and the Promise of Polycentricity." *Vanderbilt Journal of Transnational Law* 47, p. 451.

Reed II, A., and K.F. Aquino. 2003. "Moral Identity and the Expanding Circle of Moral Regard Toward Out-Groups." *Journal of Personality and Social Psychology* 84, no. 6, p. 1270.

Ruggie, J.G. 2013. *Just Business: Multinational Corporations and Human Rights.* 1st ed. New York, NY: W. W. Norton & Company.

Ruggie, J.G. 2014. "Global Governance and 'New Governance Theory': Lessons from Business and Human Rights." *Global Governance* 20, no. 1, pp. 5–17.

Saul, B. 2000. "In the Shadow of Human Rights: Human Duties, Obligations, and Responsibilities." *Columbia Human Rights Law Review* 32, p. 565.

Schwartz, P., and B. Gibb. 1999. *When Good Companies Do Bad Things: Responsibility and Risk in an Age of Globalization.* Hoboken, NJ: Wiley.

Schwartz, S.H. 1992. "Universals in the Content and Structure of Values: Theoretical Advances and Empirical Tests in 20 Countries." *Advances in Experimental Social Psychology* 25, no. 1, pp. 1–65.

Sen, A. 2005. "Human Rights and the Limits of Law." *Cardozo Law Review* 27, p. 2913.

Senge, P.M. 1997. "The Fifth Discipline." *Measuring Business Excellence* 1, no. 3, pp. 46–51.

Smart, B.D. 2005. *Topgrading: How Leading Companies Win by Hiring, Coaching, and Keeping the Best People*. New York, NY: Penguin.

Stern, C.W., and M.S. Deimler. eds. 2006. *The Boston Consulting Group on Strategy*. 2nd ed. Hoboken, NJ: John Wiley & Sons.

Stout, L.A. 2012. *The Shareholder Value Myth: How Putting Shareholders First Harms Investors, Corporations, and the Public*. San Francisco, CA: Berrett-Koehler Publishers.

Suter, K. 2009. "The Quest for Human Responsibilities to Complement Human Rights." *Medicine, Conflict, and Survival* 26, no. 3, pp. 199–206.

Taylor, C. 1989. *Sources of the Self: The Making of the Modern Identity*. Cambridge, MA: Harvard University Press.

Taylor, M.B. 2011. "The Ruggie Framework: Polycentric Regulation and the Implications for Corporate Social Responsibility." *Etikk i praksis-Nordic Journal of Applied Ethics* 1 (2011), pp. 9–30.

Thakor, A.V. 2011. *The Four Colors of Business Growth*. Cambridge, MA: Academic Press.

The Foundation of International Human Rights Law. 2013. http://www .un.org/en/documents/udhr/hr_law.shtml, (accessed February 5, 2015).

The Universal Declaration of Human Rights. 1948. (A/RES/3/217A). http:// www.un-documents.net/a3r217a.htm, (accessed February 5, 2015).

Tyler, T.R. 2010. *Why People Cooperate: The Role of Social Motivations*. Princeton, NJ: Princeton University Press.

Van de Ven, A.H. 2007. *Engaged Acholarship: A Guide for Organizational and Social Research: A Guide for Organizational and Social Research*. Oxford, UK: Oxford University Press.

Walzer, M. 1983. *Spheres of Justice: A Defense of Pluralism and Equality*. New York, NY: Basic Books.

Weiss, T.G., and R.C. Thakur. 2010. *Global Governance and the UN: An Unfinished Journey*. Bloomington: Indiana University Press.

Wolgast, E.H. 1992. *Ethics of an Artificial Person: Lost Responsibility in Professions and Organizations*. Redwood City, CA: Stanford University Press.

CHAPTER 2

On Designing and Developing Sustainable Organizations

Divya Bhutiani, Padmakumar Nair, Aard Groen, and Gregory Dess

Introduction: A Framework for Creating Sustainable Organizations

Recently, management educators and practitioners have been faced with the challenge of finding new approaches and frameworks to develop skills and attitudes for designing organizations and business strategies that promote economic development without sacrificing future generation's ability to meet their needs. This corporate sustainability agenda has generated genuine interest in new organizational forms such as hybrid and social entrepreneurial enterprises. In this chapter, we explore practical, theoretical, and philosophical challenges of designing sustainable organizations. There are two major challenges involved in preparing practitioners for envisioning and designing sustainable organizations: (1) Ideological nature of sustainability debate and (2) the highly interdisciplinary nature of the topic sustainability. We address both of these challenges by introducing a comprehensive framework for understanding issues related to business sustainability. There are six dimensions to this sustainability framework. They are expectancy, ethics, economics, environment, energy, and essential materials. This comprehensive framework helps organizational designers address both the challenges stated above. One of the most important characteristics of our approach is bringing together diverse fields such as social psychology, ethics, philosophy, environmental science, strategy, organizational behavior, economics, materials science, energy technology, and climate science. Finally, we discuss the importance of developing a mindset of framing (or reframing) challenges and problems in practicing managers to passionately carry forward the sustainability agenda.

The timeless wisdom that "seed corn should not be ground" is an excellent metaphor for thinking about sustainability. Even though scholars and practicing managers alike share this piece of wisdom, there is no consensus on whether we are already on our path to grinding the last bag of seed corn. This lack of consensus is not only due to our inability to understand the intricacies of science of climate change or resource utilization dynamics but also due to the diverse ideological lenses through which we see and analyze these challenges. Another major difficulty faced both by scholars and practicing managers is the highly interdisciplinary nature of the topic of sustainability. Unlike other practice areas of management, a good understanding of business sustainability needs a fairly good knowledge in diverse areas, such as ecology, materials science, energy technology, and the physics and chemistry of climate change.

The fundamental objective of this chapter is to provide an overview of the topic of sustainable organizational design with useful frameworks and rigorous practical concepts to deal with the major challenges mentioned at the start. One of the key features of our approach is a careful blend of science, engineering, and management in such a way that nontechnical practicing managers will be able to appreciate and use it in actual practice. Our sustainability hexagon that consists of six pillars of sustainability will help modern organizations to not just imbibe sustainability in their entire value chain but also help those corporations who have partially adopted sustainability agenda to assess areas that are lagging behind. Furthermore, the framework we have suggested will help organizations to find more innovative and sustainable solutions for their business problems. We end the chapter with a brief summary including suggestions for corporations on designing and developing sustainable organizations.

An Interdisciplinary View of Business Sustainability

For the purpose of designing sustainable organizations we define business sustainability as "the ability of an organization to continuously create value without harming its present and future stakeholders." The amount of economic value generated without harming its stakeholders should at least equal the amount of social value created through the activities of the firm. An organization can be redesigned to be sustainable only if it exists in a sustainable ecosystem. Here the term *ecosystem* is used broadly to cover all stakeholders, resource availability, macroeconomic policies, consumer base, and the availability of appropriate technology and other factors of production. For example, the economic sustainability of a firm depends on its ability to sell its products and services, and this will depend on the affordability of the consumer base in that ecosystem. Affordability and attitude of the consumer base is an important determinant of a firm's ability to be sustainable.

Shareholder versus Stakeholder Perspective of the Firm

It is important to consider a stakeholder perspective when thinking about designing sustainable organizations. The shareholder perspective that the sole purpose of a firm is to maximize its market value (Jensen, 2001) and shareholder's wealth (Friedman, 1970; Sternberg, 1999) will not capture all the nuances of *why, what*, and *how* of business sustainability. One major problem with this shareholder view is that it is based on two questionable assumptions: (1) Negative externalities of the firm's activities can be quantified and paid for and (2) the firm operates in an environment of perfect free market competition. Both these assumptions are problematic, and the sustainable strategic management approach is an effort to addressing these issues. Stakeholder perspective, on the other hand, rejects the primacy of shareholders and suggests that businesses hold responsibility toward all those who contribute to value creation (Krishnan, 2009; Philips, 2003).

Sustainable Firm as a Negative-Externality Minimizer

The concept of externality was first introduced in 1920 by the famous economist, A.C. Pigou, who taught at the University of Cambridge. Negative externality is nothing but the sufferings of third parties who are not involved in the transaction between the producer and the consumer. It has been long recognized that measuring and quantifying negative externalities is not a simple task. Even when it could be measured, formulating an economically viable strategy to minimize these negative effects could be challenging. Pigou argued that the negative-externality problems could be solved by the imposition of a Pigovian tax (1920). The challenge here comes from the difficulties involved in effectively monitoring negative externalities such as air and water pollution by manufacturing industries, waste disposal, to name a few. We argue here that if a firm focused on reinventing itself to be a sustainable enterprise, it will automatically minimize negative externalities. For example, take the case of an automobile manufacturer who uses renewable energy for all its energy needs; negative externality associated with emission of carbon dioxide and other air-polluting particulates and gases will be totally eliminated. The more the company recycles metal, plastics, and electronic waste, the lesser its negative impact on the environment. All of these actions will move the company towards a state of sustainability, effectively minimizing its negative externality at the same time.

The Sustainability Hexagon

Our sustainability hexagon (Figure 2.1) has six pillars—expectancy, energy, ethics, essential materials, ecosystem, and economics—that every business should consider to imbibe a sustainability mindset in its entire value chain. Our approach looks at all the six pillars of sustainability through two thinking strategies: *framing* (Table 2.1) and *physical science thinking* (Table 2.2).

Expectancy looks at how managers view business sustainability and how convinced are they about the need to addressing the issue of sustainability. For-profit organizations are mostly run on the business acumen of profit maximization or increasing shareholder's wealth (Friedman, 1962) so much so that most businesses consider employing environmental sustainability measures as a cost burden on them which also utilizes a lot of their time and distracts them from their main goal of profit maximization (Friedman, 1970). As Stefan and Paul (2008, p. 45) noted, "Managers have long associated environmental protection with additional costs imposed by government, which in turn erode a firm's global competitiveness." **Ethics** demands managers to be able to decide what is good for the

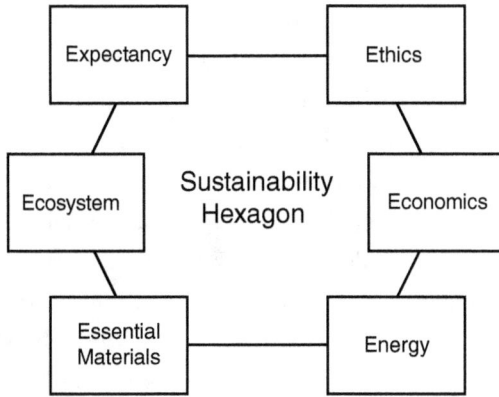

Figure 2.1 Sustainability hexagon

Table 2.1 Concepts and relevant questions related to framing

Framing	Expectancy	Ethics	Economics
"A structured way of thinking or an act of communicating" (Fairhurst, 2011).	How framing helps businesses and individuals to view sustainability in a wider context of practices (Barr, Gilg, and Shaw, 2011).	Sustainability as the right thing to do. Framing the question of sustainability using both utilitarian and Kantian ethical philosophies.	Value creation versus rent seeking. Framing the concept of "value" in multiple ways.

Table 2.2 Concepts and relevant questions related to physical science thinking

Physical science thinking (understanding the physical world)	Energy	Environment	Essentials
Gaining a deeper understanding of the material world around us.	How does a deeper understanding of energy systems help managers make organizations more energy efficient?	How does an in-depth understanding of the physical world help organizations protect the environment better?	How does an understanding of science of materials help managers overcome the scarcity of essential materials?

business and the society and be aware of the likely cost of doing the right thing. The dimension of **essential materials** questions the dependency of businesses on rare earths and other precious metals and minerals and whether alternate technologies are available to survive in the absence of these scarce nonrenewable materials. For managers, use of **energy**-efficient processes and finding nonpolluting energy sources is a key skill. On the contrary, businesses consider employing pollution control measures and stringent environmental policies to take care of the **ecosystem** as a cost burden on them (Stefan and Paul, 2008; Porter, 1991). Need for designing sustainable businesses demands awareness among businesses about their impact on the environment around them. Modern businesses are operating by utilizing resources beyond the carrying capacities of ecosystems (Gray and Milne, 2002). **Economic** sustainability demands that businesses should be cost effective. Managers should also develop skills to differentiate between rent-seeking and value-creating strategies. This pillar is most important, considering the fact that businesses should use the resources judiciously thinking about their own sustainability in the long run to be able to keep generating money for years to come.

Science and Practice of Designing Sustainable Organizations

There are multiple ways of thinking about redesigning organizations for sustainability. The starting point is defining of a sustainability vision (Figure 2.2). This step should start with a fundamental question that would help us define the purpose of our organization and a general question such as "what is a business for?" (Handy, 2002) is useful. This was the title of a 2002 HBR article by Charles Handy published in the aftermath of 2001 Enron crisis. Handy argued that the business of a business should not be just creating wealth for its shareholders but it should have a socially useful reason for existence. He further argued that businesses should measure their success broadly in terms of the outcomes for all stakeholders. A sustainable organization in this sense maximizes the benefit for all stakeholders. This idea of creating value for all will by default take care of aspects such as environmental impact, energy usage, essential material usage, and economic viability.

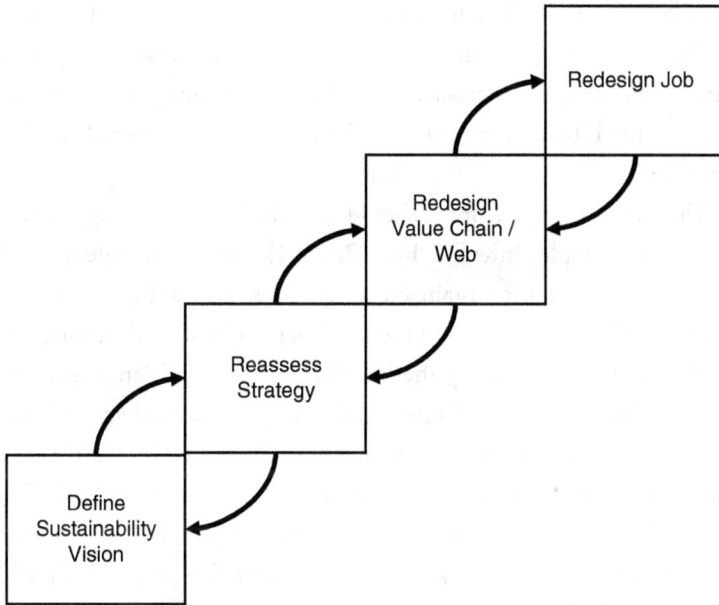

Figure 2.2 Organizational redesigning process

A sustainability vision is not a *green washing* statement. It should be meaningful and actionable. The vision need not always directly relate to green or environment; it should ultimately take care of concerns related to all the six Es of the sustainability hexagon. Vision of Johnson Matthey, a specialty chemicals company, states, "Our vision is to build our 3rd century through value adding sustainable technologies." Their sustainability vision has the following five elements: Social, Environmental, Health and safety, Governance, and Financial (Johnson, 2015). Their sustainability vision further states that "Sustainability is about making the right decisions for our people, our communities, our shareholders and, most significant of all, for the planet." This is a good example of a sustainability vision that is both meaningful and actionable.

Next step is reassessing the strategy of the organization. Here the story of Interface Inc., a $1.5 billion carpet-tile-making company, is a case in point (Box 2.1). The firm was founded in 1973 by Ray Anderson, who, in mid-1990s, redefined Interface's strategy to become one of the most sustainable carpet manufactures of the world. The corporation boldly states that "By definition, we are the world's largest designer and maker of carpet tile. For us, Design is a mindset and sustainability is the journey of a lifetime." The corporation further states, "The moral courage to do what is right, despite all obstacles. An abiding commitment to show that sustainability is better for business." This sustainability agenda helped Interface to transform into a truly sustainable enterprise.

This kind of strategic focus should then lead to redesigning the value chain. For example, Interface Inc. (Box 2.1) completely redesigned its value chain to be more sustainable. It includes but not limited to waste elimination in every segment of the value chain, elimination of toxics, use of renewable energy, closing the loop by recycling, efficient transportation, instilling a culture of sustainability in all stakeholders, and redesigning the business model for sustainability (Interface Inc., 2015). Key questions around redesigning the value chain should follow the six Es of the sustainability hexagon as discussed earlier (Figure 2.1). The primary goals should be reducing waste, minimizing fossil fuel usage, minimizing usage of essential materials and water, and maximizing the use of recycled and recyclable materials.

The final step in redesigning for sustainability is job redesign. There are several aspects to consider when redesigning jobs for sustainability: Availability of trained employees is the key. Instilling a positive attitude toward sustainability is very important as shown by the founder chairman, Ray Anderson, of Interface Inc. There should be total commitment from the senior leadership of the organization to make the transition from the traditional approach to business to one that lays emphasis on and is driven by sustainability practice.

Box 2.1 Sustainability Journey of Interface, Inc.

Interface, Inc. is a 1.5-billion-dollar global organization that stands as the world leader in producing soft-surfaced modular floor coverings. It was started in 1973 with only 15 employees and now it is among the *Fortune* "Most Admired Companies in America" and "100 Best Companies to Work For." The company holds a unique vision of being the first company to ensure that sustainability is in all its dimensions by 2020. The journey of Interface, Inc. towards sustainability started in 1994 when the company's business was booming marked by huge profits but the marketing team was often confronted by the customers for the company's environmental consciousness. Perturbed by such questions by the customers, the founder Ray Anderson decided to take his corporation on a bold mission to become "a corporation that cherishes nature and restores the environment." Ray Anderson defines the sustainability agenda that his corporation should achieve as the "Sustainability Mountain" and the pinnacle of it is the "Mission Zero" initiative which they intend to achieve by 2020 (Anderson and White, 2011). As part of this initiative, the company wants to remove all its negative footprints from planet Earth by the end of 2020. To achieve this, the company adopted a simple strategy to improve their energy efficiency and switch to renewable sources of energy. Since 1996, the corporation has successfully reduced its greenhouse gas emissions by 71% from 1996 to 2008; cut down the total energy usage in its global factories by 40% per unit of product; achieved 35% of its total energy usage from renewable sources and in 2014, four of its seven factories operated completely on renewable electricity. This huge success is supported by the vision of the founder and the strong support of every employee across all its manufacturing facilities across the globe.

This sustainability journey of Interface, Inc. was not a smooth sail at all with the for-profit business world being hyper critical of their sustainability business case. Despite being a successful profitable business, the adoption of sustainability initiative was seen with skepticism by other corporations. Even after the successful demonstration of being both financially successful and environmentally responsible, Interface Inc. still faces some resistance from its counterparts.

Anderson, R.C., and R.A. White. 2011. *Business Lessons from a Radical Industrialist*. Random House LLC.

Learning and Practicing Challenges for Practitioners

There are two major learning challenges we address in this chapter. The first and foremost is the highly interdisciplinary nature of the subject. In this chapter we describe techniques and strategies for practicing managers irrespective of their disciplinary background for addressing the challenge posed by the interdisciplinary nature of designing sustainable organizations. Our design and strategizing framework blends science, engineering, and management in such a way that it retains the rigor of good science and the applicability required for contemporary management practice. In this regard, "Physical Science Thinking" is essential for managers to gain a deeper understanding of the science required to redesign organizations for sustainability. Table 2.2 lists the key questions and concepts around which this can be done. A deeper understanding of the physical world will help the managers to answer the key questions related to the dimensions of energy, environment, and essential materials from the sustainability hexagon. Hence, a basic understanding of the physical world around them would in general help the employees to better understand the concept of sustainability, develop a positive mindset toward it, and, hence, easily implement it in practice. Hence, we suggest that corporations encourage sharing of interdisciplinary knowledge among its employees across all levels through job rotation.

The second major challenge comes from the inevitably ideological nature of sustainability debate. In order to address this challenge, we introduce two research-based techniques to help managers recognize the unique ideological lens through which they see and make sense of the world. These two techniques that form the basis of sense making in this context are *framing* and *theory of life* (ToL; Bhutiani, Nair, and Groen, 2014). Framing is "a structured way of thinking or an act of communicating" (Fairhurst, 2011) that can be used as an effective tool for learning and problem solving (Ihlen and Nitz, 2008) and help managers formulate innovative solutions for designing sustainable organizations by answering key questions related to the dimensions of expectancy, ethics, and economics of our sustainability hexagon (Table 2.1).

Figure 2.3 illustrates five different facets of framing: stakeholders, resources, history, outcomes, and ideology. For example, the sustainability challenge within an organization can be framed through broadening its stakeholder base. Say a decision on installing an emission treatment system will make more sense if the company considered the negative health-related impact on all the people living in that town rather than only looking at the pressures from official regulatory bodies representing

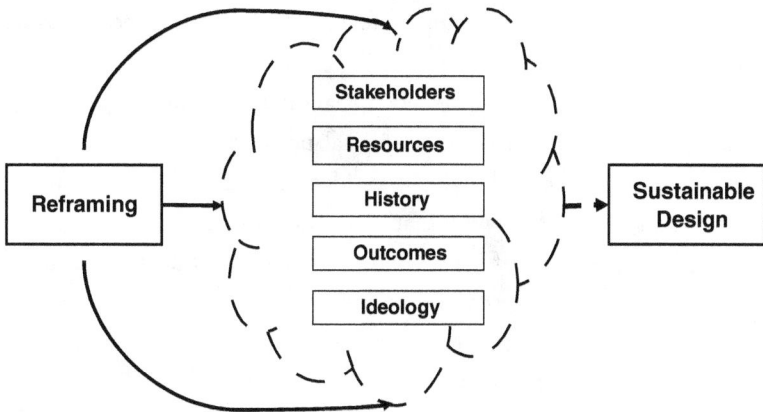

Figure 2.3 Reframing: an actionable framework

the government. In fact, broadening the stakeholder base from government regulators to all the people living in that town will give a new meaning to the efforts of the organization

Same way, framing of resource requirement or resource availability could be a useful way to finding solutions for problems involving severe resource limitations. Tesla's all-electric car is an interesting solution addressing two resource-related challenges in one innovation—scarcity of fossil fuel and platinum metal, an active element in the exhaust catalyst used in automobiles. Tesla cars require neither gasoline nor exhaust catalyst. Another example of framing resource requirement for innovation is the idea of microfinance; what traditional banks failed to achieve was effectively achieved by this. Framing in light of resource constraints helped not just to make the limited resource insignificant for the business but also afforded opportunities for innovative solutions and outcomes.

In certain situations, innovative solutions could be found by framing and changing outcome expectations. This can be best explained by the example of a state trying to minimize traffic congestion by constructing more highways and broadening existing ones. In fact, similar results could be obtained if a good subway rail system is constructed or when people are encouraged to work from home. Another example is minimizing the number of cars in the city by introducing a higher city road tax or by constructing a subway network to minimize automobile pollution. Lowering of pollution could also be achieved by introducing electric cars or imposing stricter emission and efficiency standards. In both these examples, framing the same issue by changing first-level outcomes helped to come up with multiple solutions.

Theory of life or *view of the world* is another useful concept to help managers make sense of their ideological positions with respect to the sustainability agenda. Rethinking one's ideology is an effective way to see problems and solutions in ways that were otherwise never considered. The ideology-based attitude of many conservatives toward the idea of anthropogenic global warming is a case in point. Many conservatives consider current warming we experience is cyclical and has nothing to do with industrialization and burning of fossil fuels. At the same time, most liberals believe that global warming is manmade and there is enough scientific evidence to support their views. It is natural that people have different views of the world, what we call one's ToL. In simple terms, ToL is the lens through which an individual sees the world and the filter through which he or she makes sense of the world. ToL can be understood using the schema theory which provides a framework for understanding how individuals interpret and make sense of external cues using predeveloped knowledge or belief structures (Bartlett, 1932). ToL can actually be considered a subset of mental schemas that people use to interpret and make sense of information relevant to problem solving or day-to-day decision making (Stein, 1992). These mental schemas are constructed while interacting with the environment in order to establish familiarity (Bartlett, 1932; Arbib, 1992) and are based mainly on beliefs, assumptions, schools of thought, and traditional practices and past experiences (Thorndyke and Hayes-Roth, 1979). ToL also helps to explain why same individuals behave differently under similar circumstances because of revision of mental schemas with greater exposure and experience. We have recently developed an instrument to map the ToL of individuals so that they can use it to make sense of their ideological positions (Bhutiani, Nair, and Groen, 2014). This ToL instrument can help managers develop the required skills for addressing the ideological challenges in the path to sustainable business practices.

Historical understanding can also help managers overcome sustainability challenges and formulate innovative solutions to challenging problems. For example, certain cultural practices can inhibit an organization's ability to transform and be sustainable. Traditional Indian organizations are highly hierarchical, where relatively older employees occupy senior management positions. It is important that younger professionals with a positive attitude toward sustainability agenda take leading roles so that they can drive the organization's journey toward sustainability. In situations like this, framing sustainability challenges with a deeper understanding of the historical context could help formulate more actionable transformation plans for the organization.

Summary

In this chapter, we have introduced several frameworks and tools to understand the challenges of redesigning organizations for sustainability. Two of the major challenges of instilling a positive attitude toward sustainability are the highly interdisciplinary nature of the subject and the ideological positions people take related to their understanding and view of the world. We have proposed that framing can be an effective technique to innovate for sustainable organizational design to overcome some of the challenges faced by modern organizations in adopting sustainable business practices. Managers should try to frame every problem related to sustainability issue using these five facets to come up with more innovative and sustainable solutions. In addition to framing, we have also suggested that a general understanding of the physical world can be useful for managers in understanding the need and ways of adapting sustainability in their entire value chain. For this, we have suggested job rotation within different departments of an organization as a useful tool to tackle the highly interdisciplinary nature of sustainability. Developing a sustainability mindset that is shared equally by every member of an organization along with full support from the top management is the first step in designing and developing sustainable organizations.

Questions

1. Explain the concept of reframing in the context of developing sustainable organizations.
2. Why is it important to understand the negative externalities of an organisation's operations when designing sustainable organizations?
3. Demonstrate the use of the 6E framework in redesigning the value chain.

References

Anderson, R.C., and R.A. White. 2011. *Business Lessons from a Radical Industrialist*. Random House LLC.

Arbib, M.A. 1992. "Schema Theory." *Encyclopedia of Artificial Intelligence* 2, pp. 1427–1443.

Bartlett, F. 1932. *Remembering*. Cambridge: Cambridge Press.

Bhutiani, D., P.K. Nair, and A. Groen. 2014, November 5. Theory of Life of Entrepreneurs: Are Social Entrepreneurs Different? Working paper presented at 11th Annual NYU-Stern Conference on Social Entrepreneurship, Boston, MA.

Cross, N. 1982. "Designerly Ways of Knowing." *Design Studies* 3, no. 4, pp. 221–27.

Fairhurst, G.T. 2011. "Leadership and the Power of Framing." *Leader to Leader* 61, pp. 43–47.

Freeman, R.E. 1984. *Strategic Management: A Stakeholder Approach*. Boston, MA: Pitman Publishing Inc.

Friedman, M. 1962. "The Interpolation of Time Series by Related Series." *Journal of the American Statistical Association* 57, no. 300, pp. 729–57.

Friedman, M. 1970, September 13. "The Social Responsibility of Business is to Increase Its Profits." *New York Times Magazine*, p. 33.

Gray, R., and M. Milne. 2002. "Sustainability Reporting: Who's Kidding Whom?" *Chartered Accountants Journal of New Zealand* 81, no. 6, pp. 66–70.

Handy, C. 2002, December. What is a Business for? *Harvard Business Review*.

Ihlen, Ø., and M. Nitz. 2008. "Framing Contests in Environmental Disputes: Paying Attention to Media and Cultural Master Frames." *International Journal of Strategic Communication* 2, no. 1, pp. 1–18.

Interface Inc. 2015, October 10. "The Interface Framework – Mount Sustainability and the Seven Fronts." http://www.interfaceglobal.com/Sustainability/Interface-Story.aspx.

Jensen, M.C. 2001. "Value Maximization, Stakeholder Theory, and the Corporate Objective Function." *Journal of Applied Corporate Finance* 14, no. 3, pp. 8–21.

Johnson, M. 2015, October 15. "The Elements of Sustainability," *Sustainability 2017*. http://www.matthey.com/sustainability2009/overview/elements-of-sustainability.html.

Krishnan, V.S. 2009. "Stakeholders, Shareholders and Wealth Maximization." *Journal of the Academy of Business Education* 10 (Proceedings 2009).

Lawson, B. 2006. *How Designers Think: The Design Process Demystified*. Routledge.

Phillips, R.A. 2003. *Stakeholder Theory and Organizational Ethics*. San Francisco, CA: Berrett-Koehler.

Pigou, A.C. 1920. *The Economics of Welfare*. London, UK: McMillan & Co.

Porter, M. 1991. "America's Green Strategy." *Scientific American* 264, no. 4, p. 168.

Stefan, A., and L. Paul. 2008. "Does It Pay to be Green? A Systematic Overview." *The Academy of Management Perspectives* 22, no. 4, pp. 45–62.

Stein, D.J. 1992. "Schemas in the Cognitive and Clinical Sciences: An Integrative Construct." *Journal of Psychotherapy Integration* 2, pp. 45–63.

Sternberg, E. 1999. "The Stakeholder Concept: A Mistaken Doctrine," *Foundation for Business Responsibilities, Issue Paper No. 4*. http://papers.ssrn.com/.

Thorndyke, P.W., and B. Hayes-Roth. 1979. "The Use of Schemata in the Acquisition and Transfer of Knowledge." *Cognitive Psychology* 11, no. 1, pp. 82–106.

CHAPTER 3

Generating Knowledge for Sustainable Development: The Case against the Corporate Objective Function

Brent D. Beal

The purpose of this chapter is to convince you to think differently about how large corporations are managed. This is not an attempt to make the case that corporations need to do a better job of avoiding imposing harmful externalities on third parties, or that corporations need to be more thoughtful, or more caring, or that the most effective way to maximize shareholder value is to make sure that all stakeholders are treated fairly. This is not, in other words, another attempt to state what I believe to be obvious, that is, that "the modern business corporation should recognize that, in this day and age, it can no longer hungrily pursue the single goal of profits to the complete neglect of its table manners" (McGuire, 1963: 144). It is assumed that this question has been settled: Yes, even corporations that are single-mindedly focused on profits need to be polite about it and recognize that they need to work with other stakeholders to achieve this objective. This chapter is not about this kind of "enlightened" approach to shareholder value maximization.

This chapter goes deeper than that. You are being asked to suspend disbelief (or at least intellectual resistance) for long enough to process the arguments outlined below and then to take a few minutes to think about where this line of reasoning leads and how it relates to sustainable development. Sustainable development is defined as "development that meets the needs of the present without compromising the ability of future generations to meet their own needs" (United Nations, 1987). Sustainability, as the term is used in this chapter, echoes common-sense notions of durability and longevity. Although the term implies a reluctance to despoil the natural environment in ways that may benefit us today, but impoverish future generations, it is also shorthand for efforts to find an internal systemic balance that contributes to the long-term health of our economic institutions and the social institutions in which they are embedded. The term "corporate objective function" in the title of this chapter is derived from an academic paper written by Michael C. Jensen in defense of the accepted notion that publicly traded corporations should be managed with the objective of maximizing shareholder value (or, as Jensen puts it, "firm value maximization," where firm value is defined as shareholder equity, and where shareholder equity is, by definition, a static measure of firm profits over time; Jensen, 2002).

According to Jensen, maximizing profits is the only "principled criterion for decision-making" that will keep managers from making inefficient tradeoffs and/or pursuing their own interests, thereby destroying economic value and ultimately short-changing both shareholders and society (Jensen, 2002: 11). Firms must have a yardstick with which to measure performance and an unambiguous single decision criterion by which to judge strategic decisions. More complex approaches that attempt to address competing stakeholder interests are inferior to a shareholder focus because these approaches "fail to provide a complete specification of the corporate purpose or objective function" (Jensen, 2002: 9). Although the term may be awkward, the phrase is loosely derived from simplistic mathematical modeling involving single-variable functions. In this context, according to Jensen, it is a practical impossibility to simultaneously maximize more than one variable at time. Shareholder value maximization, according to Jensen, is not only an acceptable yardstick and decision criterion, it is "unambiguously the preferred goal among available alternatives" (Sundaram and Inkpen, 2004: 359).

Contrary to Jensen's assertions, the purpose of this chapter is to explain why, in many contexts, the application of a single corporate objective function is likely to lead to inefficient tradeoffs and self-reinforcing systemic imbalances that have the potential to threaten our economic and social institutions. Although there is widespread acceptance of the notion that firms need to address the needs of all stakeholders—referred to above as "enlightened" shareholder value maximization—the reason often given for this acknowledgment is, ironically, that doing so is the most expedient route to maximizing shareholder value. A quick perusal of textbooks used in undergraduate and graduate strategic management courses unambiguously demonstrates that shareholder value maximization (and its associated narratives and justifications) is one of the foundational assumptions of the field of strategic management.[1]

If firms are to pursue a course of sustainable development, however, an "enlightened" approach to shareholder value maximization isn't good enough. To see why this is the case, the following three premises are offered: (1) The purpose of the modern organization is to create economic value; (2) economic value, once created, flows to one or more of three societal groups: capital, consumers, or labor; and (3) transferring value from one societal group to another is not the same as creating economic value. Using these premises, it is argued that the corporate objective function (i.e., shareholder value maximization) is fundamentally incompatible

---

[1]For example, see the following popular textbooks: Barney, J. B., & Hesterley, W. S. (2012). *Strategic management and competitive advantage: Concepts* (4th ed.). Boston, MA: Pearson; Baye, M. R. (2009). *Managerial economics and business strategy* (6th ed.). New York: McGraw-Hill Irwin; David, F. R. (2013). *Strategic management: A competitive advantage approach* (14th ed.). Boston, MA: Pearson; Dess, G., Lumpkin, G. T., Eisner, A. B., & McNamara, G. (2012). *Strategic management: Creating competitive advantages* (6th ed.). New York: McGraw-Hill Irwin; Grant, R. M. (2013). *Contemporary strategy analysis* (8th ed.). Chichester, West Sussex, United Kingdom: John Wiley & Sons Ltd.; Hill, C. W. L., & Jones, G. R. (2013). *Strategic management: An integrated approach* (10th ed.). Mason, OH: South-Western Cengage Learning; Hitt, M. A., Ireland, R. D., & Hoskisson, R. E. (2013). *Strategic management concepts: Competitiveness and globalization* (10th ed.). Mason, OH: South-Western Cengage Learning; Wheelen, T. L., & Hunger, J. D. (2012). *Strategic management and business policy: Toward global sustainability* (13th ed.). Boston, MA: Pearson; Pearce, J. A., & Robinson, R. B. (2011). *Strategic management: Formulation, implementation, and control* (12th ed.). New York: McGraw-Hill Irwin; Thompson, A. A., Peteraf, M., Gamble, J. E., & Strickland, A. J. (2012). *Crafting and executing strategy: The quest for competitive advantage* (18th ed.). New York: McGraw-Hill Irwin.

with the principles of sustainable development. At the end of the chapter, three reasons are offered for why this is the case. Before we get to that, however, each of these three premises needs to be addressed in more detail, and a possible exception to this conclusion needs to be acknowledged.

Premise 1: The purpose of the modern economic organization is to create economic value.

There is little disagreement about how economic value should be defined. Jensen, in his article on the corporate objective function, provides a workable definition: ". . . value is created—when I say 'value' I mean 'social' value—whenever a firm produces an output, or set of outputs, that is valued by its customers at more than the value of the inputs it consumes (as valued by their suppliers) in the production of the outputs" (Jensen, 2002: 11). A leading textbook on the economics of strategic management provides essentially the same definition: "Economic value is created when a producer combines inputs such as labor, capital, raw materials, and purchased components to make a product whose perceived benefit B exceeds the cost C incurred in making the product" (Besanko et al., 2010).

For present purposes, there is no need to complicate these relatively straightforward definitions. To determine if an organization has created economic value, first add up the subjective value of all the resources required to produce a given product or service. Include everything: intangible and tangible resources, the cost of capital, variable costs, fixed costs, entrepreneurial, physical and administrative labor, intellectual property, and so on. If it helps, imagine all these resources piled in a heap on the 50-yard line of a football stadium. Now, imagine meticulously assigning a value to each of these items and adding these values up to get a total. Once you have a number for the value of all inputs, do the same for all the products and/or services produced using these inputs. Again, if it helps, imagine all these products and/or services in a giant heap on the 50-yard line of a football field. Just as before, assign a value to each good and/or service and add all these values together to get a total. Subtract the former (the value of all inputs) from the latter (the value of all outputs); the difference is the economic value created by the firm. Note that the value of both inputs and outputs is subjective. In an exchange economy, in cases where the inputs and outputs represent private property, this value will be, more or less, the "market" price for the input or output in question. In many cases, however, particularly when public or collective goods are involved, the process of valuation becomes much more difficult.

The purpose and appropriate governance of the modern corporation has been debated in the United States for more than 150 years (Bradley et al., 1999; Sundaram and Inkpen, 2004). Regardless of the specifics of how corporations were formed (e.g., in the first part of the nineteenth century, it required a legislative act by state government), or the degree to which shareholder interests are privileged over the interests of other stakeholders (this has varied historically), the broad notion that corporations should create economic value has remained consistent. Acknowledgment of this reality, although relatively uncontroversial, represents an important premise that will anchor subsequent arguments.

Premise 2: Economic value, once created, flows to one or more of three societal groups: capital, consumers, or labor.

This premise can be conceptualized as a conservation rule, like the conservation of energy or the conversation of heat in the physical sciences, although a bit messier (given that social processes are involved). Economic value, once created, can be destroyed by organizations prior to distribution, through bad investments or so on, but an abundance of care is usually exercised to ensure that this doesn't happen. Organizations may also warehouse or store economic value for extended periods of time in the form of shareholder equity. To simplify things, the possibility of value destruction is assumed to be rare enough to be ignored for present purposes. Because corporations are legal fictions (and therefore cannot consume economic value), it is assumed that stored value will eventually flow to individuals.

Figure 3.1 is a circular flow diagram modeled after similar flow diagrams used in macroeconomics to conceptualize and track national accounts. In Figure 3.1, all firms (and all inter-firm exchanges, including all supplier and value-chain relationships) are represented by the box labeled "Firms." This simplification reflects a decision to focus only on the exchanges between individuals and economic institutions, rather than on interorganizational exchanges (exchanges that are assumed to be zero-sum

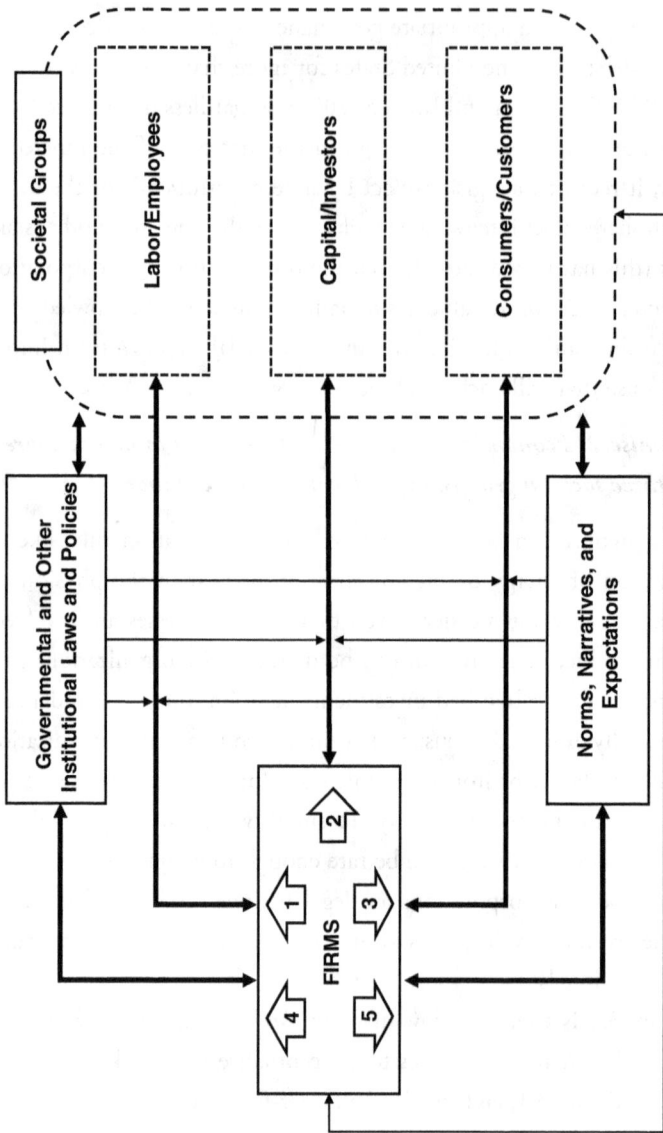

Figure 3.1 Business and society value flows and influence relationships

transactions with respect to economic value). Individuals are represented as being part of three different societal groups: (1) labor or employees, (2) capital or investors, and (3) consumers or customers. For present purposes, in the interest of simplification, only individuals in these three groups are assumed to engage in direct exchanges with firms.

Boxes representing societal groups are drawn with dotted lines that indicate that individuals often belong to all three of these different groups (e.g., they earn a paycheck, have retirement savings that is invested either directly or indirectly as capital, and routinely purchase different goods and services). Three arrows in Figure 3.1 (labeled #1, #2 and #3, respectively) represent exchange relationships with labor (or employees), capital (or investors), and consumers (or customers). The circular nature of these relationships should be evident. For example, firms exchange money (typically) for needed inputs (labor and capital), and this money circulates back to firms in their exchanges with consumers (i.e., consumers exchange money for goods and services produced by firms). From the consumer perspective, they exchange money for different goods and services, and this money circulates back to them in the form of payment for their labor.

If economic value is created by the organization, it is passed to these groups via these same exchange relationships. Understanding what it means (or what it "looks like") to distribute economic value via these exchange relationships is critical to subsequent arguments and, therefore, merits additional clarification. Imagine a scenario in which an organization creates no economic value, but no societal groups experience any loss in their respective exchanges with the organization (i.e., each group "breaks even"). By definition, in this scenario the value of all inputs is precisely equal to the value of all outputs. Let's break this down by societal group. In the case of capital or investors, this implies that the return on investment is exactly equal to the minimum they would have accepted at the outset. If, for example, suppliers of capital would have insisted on a 3 percent return, or they would have declined to provide it, then in this scenario they realize precisely a 3 percent return. Visualizing a break-even exchange relationship for consumers is more counterintuitive, but follows the same basic pattern. Consumers neither lose nor benefit from engaging in exchanges with the organization. If the organization produces TVs or t-shirts, for example, then these items are priced at precisely the value that consumers place on them. If, for example, an individual consumer believes a TV produced by the company is worth $300 dollars, then it is assumed that this consumer pays exactly $300 for it. If this consumer were to pay less for the TV, then the consumer would realize a net gain in the exchange in the form of consumer surplus (defined as the difference between the value placed on a good or service by a buyer and the value this same buyer gives up in exchange for this good or service). As is the case with capital and consumers, labor neither loses nor benefits from its exchanges with the organization. This implies that employees are paid the minimum they will accept in exchange for their labor; if they were paid any less, they would cease to work.

Although this is an odd scenario that doesn't occur often, if ever, in the real world, considering it in a hypothetical sense is instructive. In this scenario, there is no economic reason this organization should exist. Because no societal group benefits from its exchanges with the organization, this organization could disappear and no one would be worse off in an economic sense. Now let's imagine that this same company changes the way it does business. Because of improvements in the way human resources are organized, or because of more efficient resource configuration, for example, this company is now able to produce a small amount of value. To make things concrete, let's assume that this company now utilizes $10,000 in resources to produce output with a total value of $10,100. According to the perfect competition market model (Beal, 2014), competition should push marginal revenue down to marginal costs. If this were the case—in other words, if this company operated in a competitive context that approximated the perfect competition market model—where would this $100 of economic value go? Which societal group—capital, consumer, or labor—would get it? Two related questions also come to mind: (1) Which group (or groups) "should" get it, and (2) in the real world, which group actually gets it? We'll come back to these questions.

There are two additional relationships depicted in Figure 3.1, labeled #4 and #5, respectively. These relationships represent the relationship between (1) firms and governmental and institutional laws and policies, and (2) firms and norms, narratives, and expectations regarding the product role and conduct of business activities (Stone, 1975). It is important to note that these relationships are mutually defining and circular in the sense that firms collectively shape the laws, policies, and norms that subsequently circumscribe their behavior. Although only mentioned in passing in this chapter, laws and policies, and norms, narratives, and expectations constitute the legal and social context, respectively, that defines the structure and character of the direct exchange relationship between firms and societal groups. These moderating relationships are represented by gray arrows extending from these two boxes to the first three direct-exchange relationships (see Figure 3.1). Three additional gray arrows represent the direct relationship between society and (1) laws and policies; (2) norms, narratives, and expectations; and (3) firms themselves.[2]

Premise 3: Transferring value from one societal group to another is not the same as creating economic value.

Taking value from one group and *transferring* it to another can be distinguished—in theory, at least—from *creating* economic value. For example, a TV manufacturer raises its prices by $10 per unit, but despite this price increase, sells the same number of TVs. It then uses the additional revenue from this price increase to raise its annual dividend payment to shareholders. In this case, because the increase in economic value delivered to shareholders is offset by an equivalent decrease in economic value delivered to consumers in the form of consumer surplus, it should be clear that no additional economic value has been created. Other possible value-neutral transfers between societal groups could easily be envisioned. For example, a firm might negotiate a decrease in pay with its employees and then use the cost savings to lower the price of its products. In this case, economic value would be transferred from employees (or labor) to consumers (in the form of an increase in consumer surplus). Or increased competition may force a company to lower its prices, and this price decrease may be offset by a combination of lower wages and lower payments to capital.

---

[2]In order to simplify the model, Figure 1 focuses on for-profit firms and their creation (and distribution) of economic value. The creation of economic value through other mechanisms, such as collective action (e.g., government) and/or other forms of organization (nonprofits, civil society organizations, private-public partnerships, etc.), isn't represented. This isn't intended to imply that economic value can't (or isn't) created through these other mechanisms.

Circles and Ellipses

There is, at least in theory, if not in practice, a set of special circumstances under which the adoption of shareholder value maximization as the corporate objective function could be compatible with sustainable development. If all firm transactions were to take place in the context of perfectly competitive markets—that is, in markets that satisfy a number of important conditions, including fully informed participants, homogeneous products, the absence of bargaining power, costless entry and exit, no third-party effects or externalities, and so on—then it is possible to make a case that maximizing shareholder value may be compatible with sustainable development (although there may still be inherent problems with equity and the distribution of economic wealth; Walters, 1993). We need to put this in perspective, however. Economic markets that meet these basic criteria represent relatively rare and tenuous conditions under which the "knowledgeable voluntary exchange of alienable commodities" driven by self-interest are likely to produce good collective results—just as "only some ellipses are circles" (Schelling, 1978: 33).

The author of the defense of shareholder value maximization cited above acknowledges that there are "circumstances when the value-maximizing criterion does not maximize social welfare—notably, when there are monopolies or externalities" (Jensen, 2002: 11). This list needs to be expanded considerably. First, it is important to recognize that social welfare maximization (an outcome is currently treated, tentatively, as compatible with sustainable development) requires that all exchanges with capital, consumers, and labor take place in perfect or near-perfect economic markets, not just its exchanges with consumers. In other words, firms must engage with capital, consumers, and labor, in market contexts involving large numbers of participants on both sides of the exchange, and all these participants must act independently. No participant can have the ability to effect prices; in every case, there must be sufficient uniformity or homogeneity to eliminate switching costs, and entry and exit into each of these markets must be costless (i.e., no entry or exit barriers). There can be no artificial constraints on prices, each participant must be perfectly (and costlessly) informed, and there cannot be any information problems or problems with natural monopolies. There cannot be network externalities or interdependencies related to product formats or standards, and so on (this is not an exhaustive list; Bator, 1957; Beal, 2014; Lindblom, 2001; Walters, 1993). Although there are some consumer markets for some products and services that come close to meeting these conditions (e.g., commodity markets), an honest assessment of labor "markets" should demonstrate how far this hypothetical ideal is from reality.

Here are two quick tests of whether firms operate in a context that is sufficiently market-like to justify the assertion that shareholder value maximization will maximize social welfare. This is a critical point because the primary justification for the corporate objective function is that it is the best path to collective prosperity. Here's the first test. Near the end of our discussion of Premise 2 above, a scenario was proposed in which a company created a certain amount of economic value. To make things concrete, it was suggested that this company was able to generate outputs with a total value of $10,100 utilizing $10,000 in resources, and then this question was posed: If this company operated in a competitive context that approximated the perfect competition market model, where would this $100 of economic value go? To answer this question, think carefully about how ideal markets are supposed to function. In a perfectly competitive capital market, investors will compete with each other to supply capital to firms, and this competition will drive down the rate of return until the return demanded represents the minimum acceptable return, taking into the account the time value of money and the risk involved. Neither the firm nor the suppliers of capital will be able to exert any control over pricing in this exchange. The same process will occur in the consumer market, and firms, as suppliers to this market, will be forced to lower their prices until revenue is equal to marginal cost. Likewise, this same process will occur in the labor market, with potential employees competing to supply labor to the organization until the price of this labor has fallen to the minimum acceptable level. Under these conditions, based on current accounting standards, the firm will earn an accounting profit, but this profit will only be sufficient to compensate the suppliers of capital for the time value of invested resources and the accompanying risk. It will not earn any economic profit (in other words, it will not earn any abnormal return). What this means—to answer the question posed above—is that under perfect market conditions, the $100 economic value created by this hypothetical firms will go to consumers in the form of consumer surplus. In general, in properly functioning economic markets, consumers will get all the economic value created by economic organizations. One test of whether or not firms operate in properly functioning or ideal markets, therefore, is to ask this question: Are shareholders, different classes of employees (e.g., CEOs, executives, top managers), or other stakeholders able to extract economic value, defined as anything above the minimum return or payment sufficient to induce continued participation, from the firm? If the answer to this question is "yes," then the market, as a governance mechanism, is not working properly, and there is no guarantee that shareholder maximization will lead to welfare maximization (in fact, the opposite is likely true).

A second test—a test that overlaps the first test in several ways—is to ask this question: Do firms have any bargaining power in their exchange relationships with different societal groups? Asking about bargaining power exposes an irony that deserves comment. The entire field of strategic management is built on the assumption that firms can—and should—work to achieve some degree of pricing power in consumer markets. This can be achieved, according to the tenets of strategic management, in several different ways (e.g., low-cost leadership, differentiation, etc.), but the goal is the same: a sustainable competitive advantage as evidenced by the realization of abnormal shareholder returns. In other words, the entire field of strategic management is premised on an assumption that invalidates the assertion that shareholder maximization will lead to the maximization of social welfare. It is impossible, if economic theory is applied in a coherent and consistent manner, to simultaneously assert that firms can (and do) develop sustainable competitive advantages—an outcome that violates a number of necessary conditions for proper market functioning—and that shareholder value maximization will also lead to welfare maximization. The existence of the field of strategic management, in other words, is enough to undermine its claim that profit maximization by individual firms will lead to welfare maximization.

Although rarely discussed in the context of strategic management, it is also clear that firms expend a great deal of time and energy working to develop and maintain bargaining power in the labor market as well as in the consumer market. This is achieved through shaping public policy and influencing the evolution of labor market norms (see Figure 3.1, arrows #4 & #5). In practice, these efforts take the form of political lobbying, the use of temporary labor, part-time labor, off-shoring, outsourcing, different internal initiatives and practices (e.g., reengineering), and various efforts to prevent unionization (Mishel, Schmitt, and Shierholz, 2014; Morgan and Cha, 2007). In addition to these mechanisms, capital has become increasingly mobile (in a geographic sense) and particularly adept at exploiting the fact that labor's bargaining position is often undermined by biological necessity (i.e., individuals often have to work in order to secure food and shelter; Harvey, 2014). These efforts and other factors have skewed the bargaining balance between firms and labor decidedly in favor of the former (Morgan and Cha, 2007; Piketty, 2014).

The point of this section is this: We live in a world of ellipses, not circles, and understanding this reality is essential to understanding why shareholder value maximization is problematic. If markets are assumed to function perfectly—an assumption that involves a number of interrelated assertions often collectively referred to as the perfect competition market model (PCMM; Beal, 2014; Beal and Neesham, 2012), American corporate capitalism (George, 2014; Kasser et al., 2007), or neoliberalism—then firms cannot, by definition, control the flow of the economic value they create. Under perfect market conditions, competition will bring revenue in line with total cost in the consumer market, and the same will happen on the supply side for both the capital and labor markets. This implies that firms have no freedom to transfer economic value from one societal group to another. The "market" makes this decision, and the verdict is that all economic value created by an organization goes to consumers in the form of consumer surplus. When it is asserted that we live in a world of ellipses, not circles, what is meant is that firms, in reality, *do* have the capacity to make allocation decisions with regard to the economic value they create, and they exercise this capacity on a daily basis. This implies that managers of modern economic organizations play two roles: (1) They are tasked with the responsibility of organizing and directing the productive activities of their organizations in order to create as much economic value as possible and (2) they make decisions that influence how the economic value they create is distributed across the three societal groups depicted in Figure 3.1.

Shareholder Value Maximization and
Sustainable Development

There are three primary reasons why the three premises presented above lead logically to the conclusion that shareholder value maximization is fundamentally incompatible with sustainable development. The following three reasons are presented as assertions with relatively little explanation; it is left to the reader to draw on the discussion to this point to supply supporting arguments.

First, from a shareholder maximization perspective, there is no distinction between creating profit (by creating economic value) and appropriating profit (by rerouting economic value flows away from other societal groups). Second, because no distinction is made between creating profit and appropriating it, there is no guarantee that firms won't focus on the latter rather than the former. And third, firms have a clear incentive to make inefficient tradeoffs between societal groups. For example, if a firm can take a million dollars from labor by lowering compensation (because of its bargaining position), and then deliver half-a-million dollars to shareholders in the form of increased profits, if it seeks to maximize profit instead of maximizing economic value, it will do so. In this case, the missing half million—the reason that lowering wages by a million dollars doesn't increase profits by the same amount—is due to decreased employee motivation and goodwill. In other words, although this hypothetical tradeoff increases profits by half-a-million dollars, it results in the loss of half-a-million dollars in economic value (and, in this sense, it is an inefficient tradeoff).

For those who have been engaged for some time in critiquing the corporate objective function (or the shareholder model, in general), these arguments here may seem tired, redundant, and even unnecessary. Although an attempt has been made to frame these arguments in a unique and compelling way, there is very little, if anything, in this chapter that hasn't already been stated in some form by a number of other scholars (see, for example, Alvesson and Willmott, 1992, 2012; Burawoy, 1979; Dyer et al., 2014; Harvey, 2014; Parker, 2002). Regardless of how obvious these conclusions may be to many, however, the logic and reasoning behind the corporate objective function remains an integral part of the dominant ideological business paradigm on display in nearly all strategic management textbooks from major publishers used in most capstone undergraduate and graduate business courses, particularly in the United States (e.g., McGraw-Hill, Pearson Prentice Hall, South-Western Cengage Learning, and Wiley, see footnote 1).

Even if you are now convinced that the logic and assumptions that undergird the corporate objective function are likely to lead to inefficient macro-level outcomes if implemented in contexts that fall short of the market ideal (i.e., in almost all cases), it should be clear that a critical follow-up question has been left unaddressed: What should firms do about it? If finding an answer to this question seems more important or more urgent than it did before reading this, then this chapter has served its purpose. In abstract, firms need to focus on maximizing economic value while simultaneously contributing to laws, policies, and norms that contribute to a distribution of that value that reflects widespread notions of equity, fairness, and social justice. Given the complexity of economic systems, however, and the need to maintain and align incentives that lead to desired outcomes, this is much easier said than done. The emergence of multistakeholder organizations dedicated to the implementation and regulation of corporate social responsibility programs, and ongoing efforts to acknowledge, measure, and reward the creation of economic value (rather than shareholder value), such as the UN Global Compact, the International Standards Organization 26,000 corporate social responsibility standards, and the Global Reporting Initiative's sustainability reporting framework, all represent important steps in the right direction (Moon, 2014).

It can be assumed that the greater the deviation between actual and ideal market functioning, the greater the bargaining power firms are likely to possess, the greater the misspent resources dedicated to transferring or appropriating economic value instead of creating it, and the greater the potential inefficiencies of ill-advised tradeoffs motivated by a singular focus on maximizing shareholder value. It is easy to see how these deficiencies have the potential to become self-reinforcing and contribute to rising income inequality, wealth concentration, and other disruptive and potentially destabilizing trends. As an article in the *Harvard Business*

Review observed: "We believe that if business does not lead the mitigation of the forces disrupting our market system, then we may well lose it" (Bower, Leonard, and Paine, 2011: 112). Another prominent management scholar put it this way: "Management theory needs to get back to management—to the understanding of how value gets created and traded—in all of its gory particularistic detail. Talking about how all value must get created, or the one and only best way to organize value creation, or the one and only stakeholder group whose prima facie rights must always win, are all intellectual moves that serve neither truth nor freedom" (Freeman, Wicks, and Parmar, 2004: 368).

Summary

This chapter argues that privileging profit maximization (i.e., focusing on maximizing profit as the "objective function" of the corporation) is incompatible with the concept of sustainable development. This incompatibility derives from the fact that profit maximization is likely to lead to inefficient tradeoffs and self-reinforcing systemic imbalances that have the potential to threaten our economic and social institutions. It is asserted that (1) the purpose of the modern corporation is to create value; (2) economic value, once created, flows to capital, consumers, and/or labor; and (3) transferring value from one societal group to another is not the same as creating economic value. Shareholder maximization is incompatible with sustainable development because (1) there is no distinction between creating value or transferring (or appropriating) it; (2) because there is no distinction between creating and transferring value, firms may focus on the latter rather than the former; and (3) when engaging in value transfer, firms can (and often do) make inefficient tradeoffs between societal groups. Problems associated with these inefficient tradeoffs have the potential to become self-reinforcing and to contribute to rising income inequality, wealth concentration, and other disruptive and potentially destabilizing trends.

Questions

1. What is sustainable development?
2. According to an article cited in the chapter (Jensen, 2002), what is the corporate purpose or objective function?

3. According the chapter, what is the purpose of the modern corporation?

4. Once created, where does economic value go?

5. Provide an example of how a corporation might transfer economic value from one societal group to another.

6. In a perfectly competitive market, who gets the economic value created by corporations? Explain.

7. What does the author mean by the assertion that we live in a "world of ellipses, not circles"?

8. According to the chapter, what are three reasons sustainable development may be incompatible with shareholder maximization.

References

Alvesson, M., and H. Willmott. eds. 1992. *Critical Management Studies.* London, UK: SAGE Publications Ltd.

Alvesson, M., and H. Willmott. 2012. *Making Sense of Management: A Critical Introduction.* 2nd ed. Thousand Oaks, CA: SAGE Publications Inc.

Bator, F.M. 1957. "The Simple Analytics of Welfare Maximization." *American Economic Review* 47, no. 1, pp. 22-59.

Beal, B.D. 2014. *Corporate Social Responsibility: Definition, Core Issues, and Recent Developments.* Thousand Oaks, CA: SAGE Publications Inc.

Beal, B.D., and C. Neesham. 2012. Systemic CSR: Insourcing the Invisible Hand, *Best Paper Proceedings of the 2012 Academy of Management Meeting.* Boston, MA. http://proceedings.aom.org/, (accessed on September 1, 2013).

Besanko, D., D. Dranove, M. Shanley, and S. Schaefer. 2010. *Economics of Strategy.* 5th ed. Hoboken, NJ: John Wiley & Sons, Inc.

Bower, J. L., H.B. Leonard, and L.S. Paine. 2011. "Global Capitalism at Risk: What Are You Doing About It?" *Harvard Business Review* 89, no. 9, pp. 104-112.

Bradley, M., C.A. Schipani, A.K. Sundaram, and J.P. Walsh. 1999. "The Purposes and Accountability of the Corporation in Contemporary Society: Corporate Governance at a Crossroads." *Law and Contemporary Problems* 62, no. 3, pp. 9-86.

Burawoy, M. 1979. *Manufacturing Consent: Changes in the Labor Process under Monopoly Capitalism*. Chicago, IL: The University of Chicago Press.

Dyer, S., M. Humphries, D. Fitzgibbons, and F. Hurd. 2014. *Understanding Management Critically: A Student Text*. Thousand Oaks, CA: SAGE Publications Inc.

Freeman, R.E., A.C. Wicks, and B. Parmar. 2004. "Stakeholder Theory and 'The Corporate Objective Revisited.'" *Organization Science* 15, no. 3, pp. 364-69.

George, J.M. 2014. "Compassion and Capitalism: Implications for Organizational Studies." *Journal of Management* 40, no. 1, pp. 5-15.

Harvey, D. 2014. *Seventeen Contradictions and the End of Capitalism*. Oxford: Oxford University Press.

Jensen, M.C. 2002. "Value Maximization, Stakeholder Theory, and the Corporate Objective Function." *Business Ethics Quarterly* 12, no. 2, pp. 235-56.

Kasser, T., S. Cohn, A.D. Kanner, and M.R. Ryan. 2007. "Some Costs of American Corporate Capitalism: A Psychological Exploration of Value and Goal Conflicts." *Psychological Inquiry* 18, no. 1, pp. 1-22.

Lindblom, C.E. 2001. *The Market System: What it Is, How It Works, and What to Make of It*. New Haven, CT: Yale University Press.

McGuire, J.W. 1963. *Business and Society*. New York, NY: McGraw-Hill Book Company, Inc.

Mishel, L., J. Schmitt, and H. Shierholz. 2014. "Wage Inequality: A Story of Policy Choices." *New Labor Forum* 23, no. 3, pp. 26-31.

Moon, J. 2014. *Corporate Social Responsibility: A Very Short Introduction*. Oxford: Oxford University Press.

Morgan, S.L., and Y. Cha. 2007. "Rent and the Evolution of Inequality in the Late Industrial United States." *American Behavioral Scientist* 50, no. 5, pp. 677-701.

Parker, M. 2002. *Against Management: Organization in the Age of Managerialism*. Cambridge, UK: Polity Press.

Piketty, T. 2014. *Capital in the Twenty-first Century*. Cambridge, MA: The Belknap Press of Harvard University Press.

Schelling, T.C. 1978. *Micromotives and Macrobehavior*. New York, NY: W. W. Norton & Company.

Stone, C.D. 1975. *Where the Law Ends: The Social Control of Corporate Behavior*. Prospect Heights, IL: Waveland Press, Inc.

Sundaram, A.K., and A.C. Inkpen. 2004. "The Corporate Objective Revisited." *Organization Science* 15, no. 3, pp. 350-63.

United Nations. 1987. *Report of the World Commission on Environment and Development: Our Common Future*. New York, NY: United Nations.

Walters, S.J.K. 1993. *Enterprise, Government, and the Public*. New York, NY: McGraw-Hill.

CHAPTER 4

Corporate Citizenship for Responsible Management

Cristian R. Loza Adaui and Giorgio Mion

Corporate Citizenship for Responsible Management

"'Citizen' and 'citizenship' are powerful words. They speak of respect, of rights, of dignity. ... [citizen] is a weighty, monumental, humanist word" (Fraser and Gordon, 1994: 90); this word, in fact, has been used during the past decades also to describe the interaction between business and society (Garriga and Melé, 2004), in the particular form of *corporate citizenship*.

Although the term *corporate citizenship* emerged in managerial environments (Altman and Vidaver-Cohen, 2000), it has become part of the academic discussion with a significant and increasing number of publications in important academic outlets: *Academy of Management Review*, *Business Ethics Quarterly*, and *Journal of Business Ethics*. Moreover, between 2001 and 2017 the *Journal of Corporate Citizenship* provided "a forum in which the tensions and practical realities of making corporate citizenship real" were addressed (Greenleaf Publishing, 2015).

In this chapter, we present the discussion about the concept of corporate citizenship, offer some information about its historical development, elaborate on the three main approaches to corporate citizenship offered by Matten and Crane (2005), present some recent developments in the discussion, and conclude by offering two examples in the form of case studies that illustrate the relevance of corporate citizenship for a responsible, sustainable, and humanistic management.

Historical Background

According to Altman and Vidaver-Cohen (2000), the term *corporate citizenship* was initially used by practitioners. As a founding milestone the document titled "*Global Business Corporate Citizenship—The Leadership Challenge for CEOs and Boards*" has frequently quoted (e.g., Altman and Vidaver-Cohen, 2000; Matten, Crane, and Chapple, 2003; Matten and Crane, 2005, Crane, Matten, and Moon, 2008), the relevance of this document relies upon its signatories—CEOs from multinational corporations gathered in the World Economic Forum in New York in 2002.

The increasing attention toward corporate citizenship furthermore evidenced in the creation of research centers dedicated to this issue. Some of the earlier ones were: the Boston College Center for Corporate Citizenship in the United States (founded in 1989), the Center for Corporate Citizenship related to Catholic University of Eichstaett-Ingolstadt (founded in 2005), the Center for Citizenship and Globalization at Deaking University in Australia (founded in 2005).

Corporate citizenship has garnered global interest, congregating different types of organizations: governmental organizations (e.g., Corporate Citizenship Center of the U.S. Chamber of Commerce), nongovernmental organizations (e.g., African Institute for Corporate Citizenship), consultancies (e.g., www.corporate-citizenship.com), and others, some of them gathered in the Global Network for Corporate Citizenship (see: www.gn-cc.org).

At present, *corporate citizenship* is a well-stablished term in the managerial discussion on business in society, as with many terms in academy, it belongs to the corpus of an ongoing discussion.

Definition and Approaches to Corporate Citizenship

According to a report about the State of Corporate Citizenship in 2014, "Executives understand the value of corporate citizenship and are putting their money where their mouths are—investing in environmental, social, and governance (ESG) processes and programs that deliver business and social value" (Boston College Center for Corporate Citizenship, 2014).

However, as it often observed in managerial sciences and particularly in topics related to business in society, there is no common accepted definition of corporate citizenship. Since the idea of citizenship is used in a metaphorical way (Moon, Crane, and Matten 2005), there are diverse descriptions of their understanding. Consequently, there are different categorizations of the approaches to corporate citizenship. Some authors identify three main approaches in the corporate citizenship literature: a limited view, an equivalent view, and an extended view (Matten, Crane, and Chapple, 2003; Matten and Crane, 2005; Crane and Matten, 2010; Crane, Matten, and Moon, 2008).

Others propose the existence of two main approaches: an expansionist approach in which corporate citizenship is understood as synonymous of corporate social responsibility and a minimalist approach in which corporate citizenship is understood as a company's philanthropic activities and also "a range of ways [in which] the company engages with the community" (Néron and Norman, 2008: 3). Based on the works of Matten and Crane (2005) and Crane, Matten, and Moon (2008), we suggest here also three different ways to understand corporate citizenship: a strategic approach, an inclusive approach, and a political approach.

A Strategic Approach to Corporate Citizenship

Corporate citizenship from this perspective is a strategic activity; strategic, because it contributes to the long-term sustainable development of business and society. It includes the voluntary assumption of responsibility toward the society and the community in which a company develops its activities. The instruments used to operationalize corporate citizenship from this perspective include: corporate philanthropy, corporate volunteering, creation and support of foundations, and donations and sponsorships.

There are several reasons that support the engagement of corporations in citizenship activities from a strategic point of view. Maybe the most discussed one is the win-win approach, which sees in corporate citizenship the opportunity to serve society and pursue economic goals at the same time, avoiding a tradeoff thinking that considers social and economic goals in a dichotomous way (Habisch, Wildner, and Wenzel, 2008; Windsor, 2001; Logsdon and Wood, 2002).

Some authors refer to this approach as "limited" or as "based in self-interest" because the strategic approach pays attention to the necessity of a potential benefit for the corporation as a consequence of their corporate citizenship activities (Crane, Matten, and Moon, 2008). This benefit can be expressed for example in terms of social capital (Habisch, Meister, and Schmidpeter, 2001; Habisch and Schwarz, 2015) or reputational capital (Fombrun, Gardberg, and Barnett, 2001).

An Inclusive Approach to Corporate Citizenship

While in the strategic approach toward corporate citizenship the main orientation of corporate citizenship activities is the society in general, the inclusive approaches involve all activities addressing the expectation of diverse stakeholders. For this reason some authors see this inclusive approach as an equivalent between corporate citizenship and corporate social responsibility (Crane, Matten, and Moon, 2008). In fact, the terms *corporate citizenship* and *corporate social responsibility* are used synonymously, which could be found not only in academic works (see McIntosh and Andriof, 2001; Maignan, Ferrell, and Hult, 1999; Maignan and Ferrell, 2000) but also and especially in practitioners. The main criticism regarding this approach is presented by Crane and colleagues (2008), who affirm that "the corporate citizenship label is simply used to rebrand and relaunch existing ideas about business-society relation, probably to make them more accessible and attractive to business audiences" (p. 30).

A Political Approach to Corporate Citizenship

One of the most elaborated approaches present in the literature about corporate citizenship is provided by Matten and colleagues (2003). They not only present the tripartite categorization of corporate citizenship in several outlets and in different configurations (see Matten, Crane, and Chapple, 2003; Matten and Crane, 2005; Crane, Matten, and Moon, 2008; Crane and Matten, 2010) but these authors also emphasize the importance of understanding the concept of citizenship when it is linked to the activities of corporations. Moreover, they address the central question regarding the possibilities of considering corporations as citizens (Moon, Crane, and Matten, 2005, see also Logsdon and Wood, 2002; Schrader, 2003; Palacios, 2004; Thompson, 2006; Néron and Norman, 2008).

From this perspective, the term *citizenship* plays a defining role. However, the understanding of citizenship is not homogenous and is changing, even more dramatically over the past decades ever since the globalization processes have accelerated. Crane and colleagues (2008) propose three elements: status, entitlements, and process as the "main issues around which mainstream debates about citizenship have taken place" (p. 34).

The status of corporations as citizens is described in a metaphorical way, considering corporations as "artificial persons" or "juridical persons" and therefore with a different citizenship status than that of a natural person. Regarding the entitlements, corporations certainly possess some entitlements; however, the novel role that corporations can play in "administering rights" for individuals is a main point of concern. According to Matten and Crane (2005), administering of rights involves diverse roles and actions that a corporation can assume and/or carry out:

"With regard to social rights, the corporation basically either supplies or does not supply individuals with social services and, hence, administers rights by taking in a *providing role*. In the case of civil right, the corporation either capacitates or constrains citizens' civil rights and, so, can be viewed as administrating through more of an *enabling role*. Finally, in the realm of political rights, the corporation is essentially an additional conduit for the exercises of individuals' political rights: hence, the corporation primarily assumes administration through a *channeling role*" (Matten and Crane, 2005: 174, original emphasis).

Thus, the political approach toward corporate citizenship adopts an rationale that comes from the political sciences, and although it has received wider acceptance, discussing the role of corporations "as governments" has been criticized as a "politicization of corporations" (Habisch, 2011). Table 4.1 offers some examples of the different roles that a corporate citizen can assume.

Table 4.1 Corporate citizens as administrators of rights

Types of rights	Corporation roles	Examples
Social rights	Provider	• Feeding homeless people • Establishing and running schools in developing countries
	Ignorer	• Outsourcing activities to sweatshops • Taking advantage of low health and security standards
Civil rights	Enabler	• Opposing racial discrimination (Apartheid) • Promoting initiatives that enhance civil rights
	Disenabler	• Supporting oppressive regimes and dictatorships • Ignoring property rights of indigenous people
Political rights	Channel	• Pushing further a global environmental agenda through cause-related marketing
	Blockage	• Lobbying governments in developing countries to avoid the improvement of labor standards

Note: Based on Matten and Crane, 2005.

Recent Developments

Probably the unique consensus in the literature relates to the fundamental role that globalization played as driver of corporate citizenship across the world. In this sense, contemporary approaches toward corporate citizenship discuss the possibilities of global corporate citizenship (Scherer and Palazzo, 2010); adding to this discussion, some studies emphasize the main challenges and particularities of corporate citizenship activities in different countries or regions (Puppin de Oliveira, 2006; Visser, McIntosh, and Middleton, 2006; Darigan and Post, 2009; Lauriano, Spitzeck, and Bueno, 2014) and also in comparative studies between countries (e.g., Fifka, 2013).

Application Cases

In what follows, we offer two small examples of applications of strategic corporate citizenship, in order to open the discussion about the reasons for a corporate citizenship strategy as an expression of responsible management.

Case 1: Corporate Citizenship at Masi Agricola

Masi Foundation is a private foundation created by an important wine producer enterprise based in Valpolicella (Italy): *Masi Agricola*. The core business of Masi Agricola is the production of great traditional Italian wines, in particular of typical Venetian wines: Amarone, Valpolicella, and Recioto. Over the past decades, the firm reached great productive dimensions (about 12 millions of bottles per years) and an international standing; "Masi" is a very well-known brand in the field of high-quality wine, and it destines most of its excellent production to international markets. In spite of its international orientation and its productive dimensions, Masi Agricola has maintained a deep-rooted relation with the Venetian territory and the typical Italian structure of a family business.

Masi Foundation, created in 2001, plays an important role in the corporate citizenship strategy of Masi Agricola, by means of a cultural activity aimed to promote and spread Venetian culture both in original territory and in the world. There is a clear and strong relationship between the foundation's cultural activity and the characteristics of production of traditional Venetian wines.

The purpose of Masi Foundation is "... to promote the territory, cultural heritage, creative genius and productive capacity of Venetian culture, picking out the people who express these values at its best in their individual fields. Particular attention is paid to the viticultural and enological practices that are most characteristic of the Venetian regions" (Fondazione Masi, 2014: 4).

Masi Foundation mainly operates delivering three annual awards: "Civiltà Veneta" Prize, "Civiltàdel Vino" International Prize, and "Grosso d'Oro Veneziano" International Prize. The first one is aimed to honor persons who have promoted Venetian culture and image in different fields: arts, letters, business, higher education, and so on; this is the historical award instituted by Masi. The other two awards are given to persons who have contributed to encourage high-quality viticulture throughout the world (Civiltà del Vino International Prize) and to promote culture as a means of peace, solidarity, and social development (Grosso d'Oro Veneziano International Prize).

Through these cultural awards and other minor activities (conferences, concerts, sponsoring of research programs, etc.), Masi Foundation promotes the values and ethos of Venetian culture: importance of traditions for social development, protection of landscape, quality in wine productions, and so on. These values are deeply related to the mission of Agricola Masi, which is the producer of high-quality wines.

Questions

1. How are Masi Agricola and Masi Foundation interrelated? Are there strategic connections between the activities of both organizations?

2. What are the benefits and risks for "Masi Agricola" by creating a foundation dedicated to the promotion of Venetian culture?

3. What are the benefits and disadvantages for the Venetian society that emerge from the activities of Masi Foundation?

Case 2: Corporate Citizenship at CMS Group

CMS Group is an international group and a leader in the field of mechanical engineering and manufacturing; the group comprises 7 companies and 14 plants, one of which is located in China. Their mission is "To offer leading companies in their sectors a worldwide partner for the design, development, production, testing, and supply of highly complex, high-precision machines and components" (CSM Group, 2015). The claim of its business is "engineering our way ... from the idea to finished product" (CSM Group, 2015): This explains its orientation to innovation and service to customers, among which there are some big international companies as Tetra Pak and Bosch. CMS group has 500 employees and has earned 100 million euros in revenue in 2013.

According to its ethical code, CMS Group "... is aware that unethical business dealings compromise the reputation of the Company and obstruct the pursuit of the company mission, identified as satisfying the customer and all legitimate stakeholders, in a market in which the principles of ability, legitimacy and fairness prevail." During 2013, to enforce its corporate citizenship strategy, CSM had started a corporate volunteering program called "VOLONTARIamo", which involved 30 employees selected from top and middle management.

The first edition of the volunteering program involved contributing about 1.700 hours of voluntary work among five-third-sector organizations that operate in social, sanitarian, first-aid, and educational sectors. Employees involved in the program could offer their voluntary services during business hours; this choice has entailed a corporate investment of among €55,000.

The aim of the corporate volunteering program was to enforce the idea of sustainable development as a part of corporate purpose and behavior; in particular, corporate volunteering has helped CSM Group to become an active part of its community by means of participating in social life. Furthermore, the corporate volunteering program has facilitated team building and development of soft skills.

Summary

The term *corporate citizenship* has been used during the last decade to explain the relationship between business and society. This concept, originated in important managerial circles, has found its place in the academic discussion. Our main purpose in this chapter is to present the concept of corporate citizenship and the discussion around its contribution to responsible, sustainable, and humanistic management. To that aim we present some historical background about the emergence of the concept; then we develop the main approaches found in the literature and conclude the discussion offering two examples that illustrate the relevance and scope of corporate citizenship in a globalized world.

Questions

1. What are the benefits and risks for "CMS Group" with regard to its efforts to promote a corporate volunteering program?

2. What are the benefits and/or disadvantages for the participants in corporate volunteering programs, especially for the employees of CMS Group and the third-sector organizations partners?

3. What benefits and/or disadvantages to the society emerge from the activities of corporate volunteering program?

References

Altman, B.W., and D. Vidaver-Cohen. 2000. "A Framework for Understanding Corporate Citizenship Introduction to the Special Edition of Business and Society Review 'Corporate Citizenship for the New Millennium.'" *Business and Society Review* 105, no. 1, pp. 1–7. doi:10.1111/0045-3609.00061.

Boston College Center for Corporate Citizenship. 2014. *The State of Corporate Citizenship*. Boston, MA. ccc.bc.edu.

Crane, A., and D. Matten. 2010. *Business Ethics: Managing Corporate Citizenship and Sustainability in the Age of Globalization*. 3rd ed. Oxford, UK: Oxford University Press.

Crane, A., D. Matten, and J. Moon. 2008. "The Emergence of Corporate Citizenship: Historical Development and Alternative Perspectives." In *Handbook of Research on Global Corporate Citizenship*, eds. A.G. Schrerer and G. Palazzo. Cheltenham, UK: Edward Elgar, pp. 25–49.

CMS Group. 2015. "Mission and Claim." http://www.gruppocms.com/en/mission-2/, (accessed March 20, 2015).

Darigan, K.H., and J.E. Post. 2009. "Corporate Citizenship in China: CSR Challenges in the 'Harmonious Society.'" *The Journal of Corporate Citizenship* 35, Autumn, pp. 39–53.

de Oliveira, J.A.P. 2006. "Corporate Citizenship in Latin America. New Challenges for Business." *Journal of Corporate Citizenship* 21, no. pp. 17–20.

Fifka, M.S. 2013. "Corporate Citizenship in Germany and the United States—Differing Perceptions and Practices in Transatlantic Comparison." *Business Ethics: A European Review* 22, no. 4, pp. 341–56. doi:10.1111/beer.12027.

Fombrun, C.J., N.A. Gardberg, and M.L. Barnett. 2001. "Opportunity Platforms and Safety Nets: Corporate Citizenship and Reputational Risk." *Business and Society Review* 105, no. 1, pp. 85–106.

Fraser, N., and L. Gordon. 1994. "Civil Citizenship against Social Citizenship?" In *The Condition of Citizenship*, ed. B. van Steenbergen. London, UK: Sage, pp. 90–107.

Fondazione Masi. 2014, November. "Profile." http://www.fondazionemasi
.com/immagini/pdf/FM_Profile2014_EN.pdf, (accessed March 20, 2015).

Garriga, E., and D. Melé. 2004. "Corporate Social Responsibility Theories: Mapping the Territory." *Journal of Business Ethics* 53, pp. 51–71.

Greenleaf Publishing. 2015. *The Journal of Corporate Citizenship.* http://
www.greenleaf-publishing.com/default.asp?ContentID=16, (accessed
March 25, 2015).

Habisch, A. 2011. "Politicization of Companies? Empirical Evidence on
Corporate Citizenship Activities in Europe." In *Corporate Citizenship
and New Governance*, eds. I. Pies and P. Koslowski, (Vol. 40). Dordrecht:
Springer Netherlands, pp. 19–38.

Habisch, A., and C. Schwarz. 2015. "CSR als Investition in Human- und
Sozialkapital." In *Corporate Social Responsibility*, eds. A. Schneider and
R. Schmidpeter. Berlin, Heidelberg: Springer, pp. 113–32.

Habisch, A., H.P. Meister, and R. Schmidpeter. 2001. *Corporate Citizenship as Investing in Social Capital.* Berlin, Germany: Logos.

Habisch, A., M. Wildner, and F. Wenzel. 2008. "Corporate Citizenship
(CC) als Bestandteil der Unternehmensstrategie." In *Handbuch Corporate Citizenship*, eds. A. Habisch, M. Neureiter, and R. Schmidpeter. Berlin, Heidelberg: Springer, pp. 3–43.

Lauriano, L.A., H. Spitzeck, and J.H.D. Bueno. 2014. "The State of Cor-
porate Citizenship in Brazil." *Corporate Governance: The International
Journal of Business in Society* 14, no. 5, pp. 598–606. doi:10.1108/
CG-02-2014-0024.

Logsdon, J.M., and D.J. Wood. 2002. "Business Citizenship: From Domestic to Global Level of Analysis." *Business Ethics Quarterly* 12, no. 2,
pp. 155–88.

Maignan, I., and O.C. Ferrell. 2000. "Measuring Corporate Citizenship in
Two Countries: The Case of the United States and France." *Journal of
Business Ethics* 23, no. 3, pp. 283–97. doi:10.1023/A:1006262325211.

Maignan, I., O.C. Ferrell, and G.T.M. Hult. 1999. "Corporate Citizenship:
Cultural Antecedents and Business Benefits." *Journal of the Academy of Marketing Science* 27, no. 4, pp. 455–69. doi:10.1177/0092070399274005.

Matten, D., and A. Crane. 2005. "Corporate Citizenship: Toward an
Extended Theoretical Conceptualization." *Academy of Management
Review* 30, no. 1, pp. 166–79. doi:10.5465/AMR.2005.15281448.

Matten, D., A. Crane, and W. Chapple. 2003. "Behind the Mask: Revealing the True Face of Corporate Citizenship." *Journal of Business Ethics* 45, no. 1–2, pp. 109–20. doi:10.1023/A:1024128730308.

McIntosh, M., and J. Andriof. 2001. *Perspectives on Corporate Citizenship.* Sheffield, UK: Greenleaf.

Moon, J., A. Crane, and D. Matten. 2005. "Can Corporations Be Citizens? Corporate Citizenship as a Metaphor for Business Participation in Society." *Business Ethics Quarterly* 15, no. 3, pp. 429–53.

Néron, P.Y., and W. Norman. 2008. "Citizenship, Inc. Do We Really Want Businesses to Be Good Corporate Citizens?" *Business Ethics Quarterly* 18, no. 01, pp. 1–26. doi:10.1017/S1052150X00008101.

Palacios, J.J. 2004. "Corporate Citizenship and Social Responsibility in a Globalized World." *Citizenship Studies* 8, no. 4, pp. 383–402. doi:10.1080/1362102052000316981.

Scherer, A.G., and G. Palazzo. 2010. "Introduction: Corporate Citizenship in a Globalized World." In *Handbook of Research on Global Corporate Citizenship.* Cheltenham: Edward Elgar Publishing Ltd., pp. 1–21.

Schrader, U. 2003. *Corporate Citizenship—Die Unternehmung als guter Bürger.* Berlin, Germany: Logos.

Thompson, G. 2006. *Tracking Global Corporate Citizenship: Some Reflections on "Lovesick" Companies* (IIIS Discussion Paper No. 192). Dublin: Institute for International Integration Studies.

Visser, W., M. McIntosh, and C. Middleton. 2006. *Corporate Citizenship in Africa.* Sheffield, UK: Greenleaf.

Windsor, D. 2001. *Corporate Citizenship: Evolution and Interpretation.* Sheffield, UK: Greenleaf Publishing.

CHAPTER 5

Corporate Impacts

Focused on Co-creating Value with Multiple Stakeholders, Simultaneously

Jennifer J. Griffin

"All of us need to accept responsibility for the damage done to the free-market system.... You have to focus on all the stakeholders. It's a new thing for us. Long term value is only achieved if growth benefits all stakeholders in a company, from owners to employees, communities and even governments."

Henry Kravis, CEO, KKR

"My bank wants to get involved with its neighborhoods. What should it do? What can it do?"

Senior Banking Executive

Corporations, the most powerful wealth creation engine in the world, co-create value with their stakeholders on a daily basis (Freeman, 1984; Freeman et al., 2007; Griffin, 2017) or they simply don't survive. Co-creating value, defined as creating win-win-wins with others, conveniently

---

Adapted substantially, with permission, from Griffin, J.J. 2016. *Managing Corporate Impacts: Co-Creating Value.* *Cambridge, UK: Cambridge University Press.
*This book received the 2017 Academy of Management Social Issues in Management (SIM) Division, 2017 Best Book Award.

delivers safe products and needed services on time and where needed, encourages loyal customers, and creates jobs for employees in safe work-places while providing adequate returns to investors (Greening and Turban, 2000; Wood, 1991). Mutual benefits reinforcing prosperity can multiply, leveraging a corporation's impacts. In short, businesses co-create value impacting a multitude of stakeholders, simultaneously, in order to exist and thrive. A rising tide of thriving businesses, in turn, builds a broader tax base, retains and attracts an ecosystem of businesses, enhances a qualified workforce, and multiplies impacts in a virtuous cycle defraying the collective community costs of high-quality education, health care, transportation, and recreation.

Co-creating value seems like a simple concept: work with employees, customers, investors, and neighbors, make a net positive difference for them and for you, improve lives, multiply the good, and repeat. Yet down-sides and exploitation exist, too. If co-creating enduring value were simple to achieve even more firms would match actions with intent, multiplying positive corporate impacts. However, the daily headline news suggests that meaningfully co-creating value benefiting multiple stakeholders—however important—is neither straightforward nor easy to implement (Henisz et al., 2014).

Companies are questioned when going beyond minimal financial ex-pectations such as paying living wages, guaranteeing premiums during crises such as Covid-19, ensuring safe workstations, changing delivery processes to remain open, or digitally transforming logistics when rivals are not. Motives are probed and outcomes scrutinized (e.g., do quarterly profits suffer). Often, authenticity is questioned. Organizations seem to be in a Catch-22. Do something with others that impact others positively and face an inquisition. Or, do nothing for others, focus the narrative on investors only, and suffer the risk of a "profits before people" headline when, not if, a hiccup occurs.

Re-imagining Catch-22 trade-offs as a persistent opportunity for in-novation is the goal of this chapter. Re-thinking *how*, not *if*, businesses co-create value with multiple stakeholders, simultaneously, can build re-siliency and adaptability while multiplying impacts rather than spiral-ing downward. This chapter focuses on connecting WHY (a firm exists) with WHAT (products, markets, and solutions it provides) and HOW (resources and resourcefulness) a firm creates value to achieve the desired IMPACTS (investors and risk, employees and workplace, products throughout the entire value chain, communities' trust, and information). Corporate impacts, the points of intersection between a business and its stakeholders such as employees, investors, suppliers, communities, and government, are the points at which an opportunity exists for value to be co-created or destroyed.

In short, this chapter argues for understanding a business's (desired) impact as more important than ever in a post-Covid-19 world. Achieving impact in concert with others (multiple stakeholders, simultaneously) requires rejiggering and reimagining the business of business (Prakash and Griffin, 2012; Taneja et al., 2016). Reconsidering heuristics including "the business of business is just business"—or, as coined by Milton Friedman (1970) a focus on making profits solely emphasizing owners—is at the heart of successfully co-creating value with and for others.

We start with the not-so-startling observation: Firms have wide-ranging impacts some of which can be easily monetized and other impacts less so (Freeman, 1984; Baron, 1995; Griffin and Vivari, 2009). Focusing first on *four value-enhancing (or value-destroying) impacts* (e.g., investors and risk, employees and workplace, products/services throughout the value chain including end users, communities' trust, and information), this chapter then introduces indirect impacts and transformative multipliers. Leveraging good impacts to multiply the positive, or prevent downward spirals, are often opportunities hidden within routine business decisions. To begin, we must first expand our notion of a corporation's impacts and what co-creating value means in modern businesses.

This chapter starts with an example of a talent development program at a small Colombian engineering firm followed by a short case study on the BP Oil Spill in The Gulf of Mexico. Both examples exemplify the inherently intertwined, good and bad, economic and noneconomic impacts of a firm on multiple stakeholders, simultaneously. We highlight the direct, intended impacts of executive leadership as well as indirect and often unintended effects that are ignored or considered externalities that multiply the harms.

Imagine the following scenario.[1] Would your senior executives go out of their way to help employees, families of the employees, and the broader community? Could this largesse (or something similar) happen in your neighborhood? Why or why not?

Case Study: Talent Development @ Garcia Engineering

An engineering and construction firm in Colombia was growing in terms of sales, size, and prestige due to the excellent performance of its teams. These success metrics, however, were not enough for the CEO, Mr. Ivan Garcia. He felt his team had not achieved 100 percent of its potential since according to an internal survey more than 70 percent of its electrical installers, including those who had been with the company for 10 years, had not received their high school diploma. Twenty percent had only primary school education. The lack of employees' formal education, in Mr. Garcia's mind, truncated the ability of the company to continuously improve itself while also limiting the development of his employees to be satisfied, have dignity, and be treated with respect to achieve the life they wished to live.

During the following months, he worked quite extensively to develop a training plan based on building dignity by developing education programs suitable for his employees. He felt that human talent was the company's most important asset as it was the chief driver for the company's future success. Mr. Garcia's *Talent Development* program was based on four short-term goals:

1. Establish a training program for all employees at all levels.
2. Engage and sensitize all levels of management to the importance of education and training. Encourage and instill in employees the need to study as the foundation for developing their own families.
3. Develop partnerships with private and public educational institutions nationwide to train and certify the skills of employees.
4. Connect basic education with technical skills and higher education through institutional educational agreements.

---

[1] With profuse thanks to Oscar Armando Henao Herrera from ICON Ingeniería y Construcción S.A.

The results were immediate. The company gave scholarships to all employees interested in completing their primary and secondary education. Other employees not interested in starting immediately had the option to finish their high school degree over the coming 2 years. Partnerships were created to study technical and technological careers, certified by the Ministry of Education of Colombia, with flexible hours made available to all employees.

In a depressed sector south of the city, a laboratory for electricity and electronics was created training college students during the day and employees of the firm on weekends and in the evenings. With this lab, 40 high school graduates were certified in electricity.

One of the company's training rooms was transformed on Saturdays and Sundays from 8 a.m. to 4 p.m. into math, Castilian, basic sciences, chemistry, and physics classes. In other classrooms, teachers with expertise in adult basic education created content building on the employees' experiences to improve the employees' elementary-level reading and writing.

The Talent Development program was so successful that motivated the wives and children of employees to join in the classes. Families with economic problems understood the importance of training to improve their quality of life and were willing to make the continuous commitment.

The company, as it expanded its training and development programs, created a level of cooperation and commitment never before imagined in the company. Its relationships with the local communities spawned new customers, enhanced employee satisfaction, and created positive publicity as well as incalculable academic and social improvement of employees and their families who depended directly on the company and upon whom the company depends for its continued successes.

As the Garcia Engineering Talent Development program suggests, co-creating value often requires asking new questions, seeking new pathways to growth, and reexamining many, often implicit, aspects of the firm's value creation process. That is, creating economic value for customers, communities, and shareholders for Garcia Engineering required significant and sustained investments in educating, training, and developing employees—above and beyond the requirements for "doing their job"—and their families. These investments, in turn, created intangible value such as a sense of pride, new skills, and new abilities for employees and their families. Training employees to be their best possible selves is an intrinsically worthwhile goal, yet, as an organization, intangible value was created through the processes of asking and listening to workers, creating flexible hours, adapting rooms and resources, and being resourceful in redeploying underutilized spaces.

Resources across the organization were recombined and rejiggered to enable additional training beyond what the job required, creating access to earn degrees, and extend education to the children and families involved. The organization's resources and resourcefulness helped build community, new skill sets, and created more growth with more profits while also setting up employees to be their best selves, inside and outside of the business hours. The direct (employee), indirect (families), and multiplier effects (cross-training, higher productivity, more loyalty and prosperity over time) stemming from the talent development program touched employees, their teams, and their spouses, children, and families.

Extending and sustaining value creation even further, the talent development program spawned new initiatives that improved relations with customers, the press, local municipalities, the local neighborhoods, and local schools. This network of relationships—an ecosystem of mutually reinforcing relationships building mutual prosperity—in turn, positions the company and its employees to prosper in the coming years. In sum, the talent development program was a mutually beneficial win-win-win for the company, its employees and their families, prospective employees, and clients as well as numerous community members—even if all benefits cannot be monetized immediately.

In short, when Mr. Garcia highlighted the importance of his employees, it signalled the firm's intent to better understand employees' needs, and enable employees to prosper, with upskilling, increased social standing, and higher self-esteem. Mr. Garcia engaged in an ongoing dialog with his employees, who in turn implemented his vision, tweaking it to improve the business outcomes. A mutually reinforcing triumvirate of trust was created via: Think–Talk–Act. Thinking about employees as the heart of future prosperity, building a narrative centered around employees, and actively implementing new routines with continuous tweaking along the way. More experimenting led to unlocking more pathways to creating more and varied types of value. The Talent Development program simply became in Garcia Engineering's best interest to build out even though many obstacles had to be overcome.

First, all too often many stakeholders (e.g., employees, consumers, suppliers, and communities) are considered costs in the value-creating process. Employees' wages are expenses. Low-cost suppliers are prized. Taxes are a burden to be minimized. Without a monetary stake or ownership rights, these stakeholders might be seen as capturing or appropriating value. Not creating value. Reimagining employees as ambassadors, intrinsically important for the future growth of the company, innovators unlocking the firm's next generation of products, or reliable purveyors of end users' wishes, for example, rejiggers employees at the heart of value creation rather than as producers of widgets or pawns to be told what to do by the rightful owners: the shareholders.

Second, expanding the focus on impacts beyond financial impacts is a double-edged opportunity with a silver lining: More problems come to the fore due to the sheer volume of employee, product, and community impacts to consider. Organizational impacts are messy! At the same time, the possible solution sets for reconfiguring how to continuously create value expand as the potential pathways for co-creating value with and among stakeholders increase.

Third, lumping nonfinancial impacts altogether with, and prioritizing them as less important than, financial impacts suggests a false choice erring on the side of traditional, easy-to-measure, heuristics of monetized metrics. Nonfinancial intangibles, however, might be even more important during crises, such as how employees are treated (e.g., how communications were handled for laid-off, furloughed, or fired workers and suppliers) during Covid-19. Co-creating value often involves nonfinancial, intangible dimensions affecting reputation, trust, learning, resilience, and adaptability. These intangibles, in turn, affect attraction and retention of top talent (Greening and Turban, 2000), rejiggering or cross-training to enable the organization to survive the crisis, and the ability to attract top talent once the crisis is past. A one-size-fits-all heuristic emphasizing easy-to-monetize financial impacts simply misses many opportunities for talking about and creating value.

Finally, when attempting to monetize value, two second-level issues emerge. Nonfinancial impacts might be inappropriately monetized—employee safety for example might have an economic value attached to "no lost time accidents" yet becomes undervalued or accidents are inappropriately considered when a crisis such as Covid-19 occurs when temperature checks, safe distancing, and limiting expanded exposure through carpooling/public transportation become important.

Certainly, some non-monetized impacts might be overlooked or not included in a risk calculus. For example, businesses are often conducted as if pride, loyalty, learning, trustworthiness, safety, and well-being, for example, are not valued. They are simply not itemized in a balance sheet or income statement or discussed by the senior executives. Identifying, assessing, and measuring nonfinancial impacts might be quite different and prioritized differently by employees, consumers, neighbors, regulators, and/or community thought leaders.

At a minimum, effectively co-creating value enhances mutually beneficial activities while preventing harm to others. Mitigating egregious harm by installing sprinkler systems and fire escapes in case of a factory fire is simply in the firm's best interests. Preventing deaths is a reasonable investment as demonstrated in the backlash after the 2012 Bangladeshi garment mill fires that killed more than 100 workers, injuring 100s more (Greenhouse, 2005, 2013). In other words, developing and implementing measures to prevent deaths is simply in a firm's best interest as Boeing is relearning after its 737 MAX airplane crashes that killed more than 340 people in 2018 and 2019. All too often, prevention activities are passed over for higher-profile, immediate needs. When a series of preventable accidents occur over time, an unfortunate legacy is created. These legacy issues hamper future growth, damaging a firm's ability to expand in the future. Crises are going to occur. It is not if; it is when. The pertinent question becomes: Is the current crisis a hiccup for a good firm experiencing a bad event or is the perception this is a bad firm continuing to do bad things (Griffin, 2008)?

In short, firms impact multiple stakeholders every day in the process of co-creating value. In the tangle of mutually beneficial stakeholder relations lies the "sweet spot" of value co-creation as well as the "messy middle" of value destruction. Conceived often as the "messy middle," corporate impacts are not easy to address, nor are they getting any easier to address. The sheer number, and variety, of stakeholder interests impinging upon a business is growing as the number of stakeholder groups and their interests grow and morph, seemingly daily. The growth in stakeholder demands can seem a bit like managers are always chasing a moving target resulting in chaos rather than focused on WHY the firm exists and its desired impacts (Griffin et al., 2005; Griffin and Prakash, 2014).

Co-creating value is a multifaceted puzzle that is becoming increasingly important as more stakeholders are asking: What's in it for me? While financial returns create an easy-to-compare metric, emphasizing only investors creates an incomplete picture and an incomplete depiction of expectations across stakeholder groups—employees, suppliers, investors, and customers.

Let's now examine a more complex scenario focused on value destruction and the myriad ways in which many stakeholders were (mostly, negatively) impacted by the BP Oil Spill in the Gulf of Mexico in 2010.

Case Study: BP Deepwater Horizon and Corporate Impacts

On April 20, 2010, BP's Deepwater Horizon exploded and caught fire in the Gulf of Mexico, killing 11 workers and injuring 17 others (Hoffman and Jennings, 2011). Two days later the rig sank, causing the worst oil spill in U.S. history. BP eventually capped the well on July 15, 2010 after almost five billion barrels of oil—19 times more than leakage from the 1989 Exxon Valdez oil spill—contaminated the Gulf (Fahrenthold and Kindy, 2010).

The BP oil spill directly affected a variety of stakeholders, including the neighborhoods and households living near the 16,000 miles of coastline composed of Alabama, Florida, Louisiana, Mississippi, and Texas (Mackey, 2010). Thousands of animal species were killed or injured in the 6 months following the spill. The spill also had far-reaching consequences for the industry, including stricter regulation for deep-sea drilling with the potential for more regulations in the future (Goldenberg, 2010a; Webb, 2010b).

BP faced massive financial consequences: 2010 was BP's first financial loss in 19 years with $4.9 billion charged against earnings due to containing and cleaning up the oil spill in the Gulf (Webb and Bawden, 2011). BP's share price fell by over 115 percent. A week before the incident, BP, what was once Britain's most valuable company, was trading at 653 pence per share and fell to less than half of that, 303 pence per share, less than

3 months later in June 2010 (Bryant, 2011). One day in early June 2010, BP shares plummeted by 13 percent, immediately wiping £12bn off the company's value as news was released that oil well was not likely to be capped for 2 months or more. Five years after the oil spill in 2015, BP's share price hadn't returned to the pre-spill value of more than $57. Pensioners dependent upon BPs' dividend payout were acutely affected as the dividend was cut to 7 cents, less than half the level before the April 2010 Gulf Spill (Webb and Bawden, 2011). BP lost $103 billion in market value and says it faced more than $40 billion in spill-related costs with civil charges and numerous lawsuits still pending (Larino, 2015).

BP's loss of $103 billion in market value is equivalent to wiping out (in 2010 dollars) Intel, McDonalds, Visa, or Disney. The loss in shareholder value was acutely felt by both the American and British governments as yet both wanted BP to survive, and not only for financial reasons (Webb, 2010a). BP, accounting for more than 10 percent of dividends paid by UK companies, with numerous British pensioners relying on its dividend income, is headquartered in London and is a well-known British firm formerly known as British Petroleum when it was privatized from state ownership in the late 1970s (Webb, 2010a). The U.S. government was concerned that if BP went bankrupt BP would not be able to pay the potential of billions of dollars in compensation to victims leaving the U.S. government footing the bill and being responsible for implementing the cleanup activities (Webb, 2010a).

Operations were affected with production dropping to 10 percent less oil and gas being pumped compared with the prior year (Webb, 2011). And presumably, operating procedures, rig operations and oversight, deep-sea drilling protocols, as well as the reporting relationships (including the very public sacking of the BP Chairman Tony Hayward in June 2010) were significantly changed with BP taking on a laser-like focus toward safety after the oil spill. What is unknown to outsiders is the effect of the oil spill on employees. Did BP have to lay off employees due to the drop in production or were layoffs and loss of contracts outsourced, borne by suppliers of BP and their contract workers? Or did BP have to pay a premium to attract engineers or geologists to work for them and were there negative spillover effects onto franchise owners that lost money or were unable to expand?

Expectations of future production were also lowered as BP sold assets worth £17 billion to raise cash to pay for spill-related costs (Webb, 2011). BP dropped plans to drill in the Arctic owing to its tarnished reputation after the Gulf of Mexico spill (Macalaster, 2010). The reputation losses were only in part captured by the market value loss of $103 billion as the company's brand value was diminished, in part, due to how BP promoted its beyond petroleum program in the prior years and failed to execute when a disaster arose (Healy and Griffin, 2004; Sweney, 2010). With a damaged reputation, BP may find it harder to enter new markets or bid for new contracts (Sweney, 2010).

Spillover effects also included a cut in BP's credit rating—after U.S. politicians demanded the company deposit $20 billion in an escrow account to cover the cost of the Deepwater Horizon disaster making it more expensive for BP to borrow money (Wearden, 2010). Within a week, Moody's followed with a cut to BP's credit rating (Gutierrez, 2010). Months after the largest oil spill in U.S. history, speculation remained rampant in business news outlets that BP might become a takeover target, go bankrupt, or need to be significantly downsized and reorganized as the share price collapsed and was expected to drop even further (Webb and Pilkington, 2010; Tseng, 2010).

What about BP's competitors? Were they the primary beneficiaries of BP's stumble? Perhaps, BP's rival, ExxonMobil, was breathing a sigh of relief as the Exxon Valdez oil spill in Prince William Sound in 1989, the most notorious U.S. oil spill, suddenly became yesterday's news with the 2010 BP oil spill (Hoffman, 1999; Hoffman and Ocasio, 2001; Hoffman and Jennings, 2011).

Multiplier effects from the oil spill extended to the entire petrochemical industry with new regulatory, political, and legal challenges. The Obama administration reversed an earlier decision and stopped offshore drilling until 2017 saying it had learned a lesson from the BP oil disaster. The cost and time delays in opening up new areas of the Gulf of Mexico to drilling affected the entire industry as more stringent safety measures were now required (Goldenberg, 2010a; Webb, 2011). Royal Dutch Shell, a competitor with an approved, yet controversial drilling project in the Arctic, was required to upgrade its oil spill response plan, which delayed the planned start of the drilling until 2012 and then faced additional delays even after spending $4.5 billion in leases, equipment, and persuading government officials (Broder, 2013).

The Obama administration sued BP and its partners, Trans-Ocean and Anadarko Petroleum, in the Deepwater Horizon oil well disaster in the Gulf of Mexico. BP eventually settled with the Department of Justice in November 2012 for $4.5 billion in damages and pleaded guilty to 14 criminal charges while agreeing to pay fines to the Securities and Exchange Commission (Krauss and Schwartz, 2012). In later trials, BP was found grossly negligent with the penalties, and the appeal process, still ongoing nearly 5 years after the oil spill (Larino, 2015; Stempel, 2014). BP faces hundreds of lawsuits filed by fishing interests, hotel chains, restaurateurs, even condo owners who say the spill ruined their holidays. The state of Alabama is also suing BP and other firms connected to the disaster (Goldenberg, 2010b; Larino, 2015).

In short, BP's financial loss of $103 billion in market value, while significant, is only one aspect of how BP destroyed value for its stakeholders. Evaluating only BP's financial impacts via the share price plunge misses the many, important financial and nonfinancial impacts on pensioners, financial analysts, credit rating agencies, rivals, partners, suppliers, governmental contracts, local shrimp businesses, tourism companies, neighborhoods, employees, prospective employees, consumers, and the list goes on. BP's prospects for co-creating value in the future are now highly intertwined with its responses to the 2010 Deepwater Horizon oil spill (Helman, 2020). Interestingly, unintended consequences included investors fleeing to the oil-rich shale fields in North Dakota flooding the market, improving shale-based technologies, and depressing fossil fuel prices to well below 2010 levels, a decade later (Helman, 2020). As many oil operators discovered, bankruptcy was preferable to the increased scrutiny and regulations stemming from BP's Deepwater Horizon oil spill (Helman, 2020).

Below we highlight the financial impacts alongside three additional types of corporate impacts: personnel and workplace, products/services, and information (Evan, 1965). Discussing each of the impacts (financial, personnel, products, and information) in isolation allows us to deeply dissect each while alluding to how they might work in combination with one another. A deep, rich description of each impact allows for nuanced narratives to emerge when reimagining, and rejiggering combinations of, how a business impacts others, simultaneously.

Impacts: Financial

Often the shorthand for commercial success is financial impacts as the owners, those who provided the capital, are a critical stakeholder of the firm. Financial impacts, as seen in the BP example, are readily described and easily measured for publicly traded companies as share price and accounting returns are required disclosures. Performance measures net present value, discounted cash flows while also reflecting past investments and new ideas that are generating sales, serendipity, and risk adjusted to build financial prowess. Financial impacts are most easily monetized reflecting an accounting of risks, costs, benefits, and (perceived) market value.

Financial performance, however, is often based upon relative performance, especially for publicly listed firms. Comparisons to rivals, contributions to national growth, and projections for growth allow investors to assess publicly traded companies when deciding on whether to buy, hold, or sell company stock are commonplace. Thus, when a single firm creates a shock to an entire sector such as BP and the fossil fuels sector, the entire industry suffers (Griffin and Koerber, 2006; Griffin and Weber, 2006; Healy and Griffin, 2004; Mahon and McGowan, 1999).

A narrowly derived narrative of profit maximization, however, does not serve the interests of the business community or its stakeholders (Stout, 2012). The ostensible pursuit of short-term profits at all costs, as we saw in the BP oil spill case, can stymie businesses' growth potential, multiply risks, and ignore new opportunities. With even more stakeholders asking, "What's in it for me?," a financial pay-off may not be the best, or the only, answer. Furthermore, momentum toward patient capital is building with well-known CEOs from Apple, Microsoft, Alibaba, and Google defending long-term investment strategies (i.e., moonshots) without immediate returns (Goldman, 2015). Overall, corporate impacts certainly incorporate financial impacts. Without an adequate response to satisfice owners, the corporation may simply cease to exist.

Impacts: Employees in the Workplace

Corporations directly impact, and are impacted by, employees and through workplace facilities. How a company engages employees, builds internal feedback systems (hiring, firing, training, communications, and development processes), and creates facilities in which employees work (safety, security, remote access) increasingly help tip the balance in the competition for top talent (Turban and Greening, 1997). Employees are often the first stakeholders to identify gaps between the policies of a company evoking its aspirations with the way in which people are actually treated (Griffin, Bryant, and Koerber, 2015). Employee pride, retention, diversity, and loyalty as well as programs appropriately tailored to education, volunteering based on building skills and expertise, matching contributions, or internal training and development can contribute to employee effectiveness (Mackey and Sisodia, 2013). Workplace impacts can be numerically accounted for as workplace safety (accidents or deaths of employees and contract workers); number of regulatory violations (e.g., child labor and human trafficking policies); days since the last lost work accidents; carbon, water, or energy consumption; waste and efficiency, as well as LEED certification of facilities.

Overall, personnel and workplace impacts are a combination of both actual and perceived value. Being perceived as a trusted employer, an employer of choice, or winning "best place to work" awards alongside appropriate consumption of water, carbon, and energy or LEED certification of offices are not substitutes for headline-raising issues such as child labor, human trafficking, or unsafe workplace conditions yet can often help when workplace conditions make headline news. A steady paycheck at living wages, for example, may be valued differently than safe working conditions or policies on human trafficking by employees or NGOs specializing in human trafficking. Adopting a co-creating value mindset suggests that both types of value, actual and perceived, need to be satisfied as employee, rivals, and NGOs risks can threaten the survival of the company and its ability to continuously create value as it seeks to retain its employees or expand facilities into new markets.

Impacts: End Users and Product Based

A third way firms directly impact stakeholders is through day-to-day production and sourcing decisions of how a product is made and a service is delivered. Decisions that encourage (discourage) the use (misuse) and disposal of goods and services impact stakeholders in the value chain: suppliers, suppliers of suppliers, distribution networks, clients (product purchasers), and consumers (product users). Whether a local barber is offering free haircuts or a multinational company with production facilities, store fronts, or kiosks in many communities around the world, every organization positively, or negatively, impacts stakeholders through its products or services. Assessing product/service impacts are quite common as they can be readily measured through donations of in-kind products; carbon, water, and energy consumer per unit of product; recycling programs; traceability and accountability in the sourcing of pesticide-free or organic goods in grocery stores, for example. Consumer behavior research about perceived value, especially the use of branded products, is of particular interest in assessing product/services impacts as allegations of exploitation or misleading disclosures in nutritional labels, cigarette packaging, and mortgage loan disclosures are well documented (Perry and Blumenthal, 2012).

Branded products have unique risks as a brand promise might allude to specific aspirations, lifestyle choices, status, or prestige. If a brand promises eco-friendly manufacturing yet research uncovers unethical suppliers promoting unsafe workplace conditions, the brand can come under attack such as when Greenpeace attacked Timberland (Swartz, 2010). Decisions about sourcing, packaging, advertising via social media, return policies, or end-of-life recycling of products directly and indirectly impact others. Effectively addressing multiplier effects of products/services beyond economic impacts to include social and environmental impacts throughout the value chain is increasingly important for modern businesses.

Impacts: Communities' Trust and Information Sharing

Yet another way corporations impact others is through information sharing. Information sharing influences perceptions, shapes opinions, and/or educates stakeholders which in turn can build trust. Information disclosure can create (perceived and real) value by connecting stakeholders while, conversely, a lack of trust can destroy value (Edelman, 2020).

Information sharing comes in many forms. Finding restaurants, locating specific stores, and searching for "how to install" videos have never been easier with friends, tips, blogs, and tweets to share ratings, rankings, preferences, and "how to" instructions. Location-based apps (e.g., Yelp, Waze, and Maps), for example, and delivery services (e.g., Didi, Grubhub, Uber, or Lyft) provide unique services based on sharing information. Information sharing allows local indie bands to raise fund through crowdsourcing to produce another album. In short, easing transaction costs, connecting stakeholders, and building trust within an ecosystem is more important than ever leading to new, and transformative, ways to create value together.

Information impacts, an oft-overlooked area of corporate impacts, have ripple effects (positive and negative) across many constituencies and, in turn, can double back affecting the value creation process. The broadening and deepening of opportunities stemming from information sharing is both a challenge (misinformation) and incentive for emergent business models (digitally transformed offices, crowd funding, crowdsourcing).

Easily opining about an organization and its products and processes makes the firm's physical boundaries very permeable. Suddenly, "relevant" stakeholders might include financial analysts, potential customers, Facebook friends, regulators, the general public, and pundits of trade. Social media has enabled communities of users, new thought leaders, volumes of blogs, beta testers, friends, and partners extending beyond traditional physical communities of local neighborhoods. Information sharing shapes, in turn, stakeholders' expectations. The speed of response requires more communication more often in more channels to build stakeholder connections well beyond the traditional newsletters, intranets, technical reports, lobbying, grassroots advocacy, and political contributions.

Organizations, recognized as trusted partners, can convene forums that share, rate, rank, and exchange information. Early access to information about changing demands, consumer trends, and expectations allows firms to remain vital (Griffin and Youm, 2018) and hedge risks (Bryant, Griffin, and Perry, 2020). Being considered as more than a widget producer, trusted firms are looked to as thought leaders with critical expertise. This trust is especially important during crises.

When crises such as Covid-19 occur, the character of businesses as expressed through effective information sharing becomes critical. Exerting influence far beyond individual products and services, the impact of a firm's location and communities (e.g., potential consumers, regulatory agencies asking advice on promulgating new regulations) have far-ranging ripple effects. Intangibles such as expertise, know-how, training, and perception of an organization being reputable and a good corporate citizen reach far beyond the physical boundaries of the firm, as shown in the Garcia Electric and BP case studies. That is, firms connect, and co-create value, with stakeholders through tangible and intangible connections.

For example, during the 2011 Fukushima tsunami, the world's worst nuclear disaster since Chernobyl, when information about safe shelters, electricity availability/outages, and safe drinking water was scarce, many companies made donations ranging from road clearing equipment, logistical support, access to water or medicines, material to rebuild critical infrastructure. After the tsunami, Japan underwent a decades-long green boom, increasing rates of renewable energy, and plans to power Fukushima with 100 percent renewable energy by 2040 (McCurry, 2020).

On the flipside, disrupting information flows can harm relations with the media, regulators, industry bodies, opinion leaders, and so on with long-term ill effects. When Coca-Cola's brand promise was compromised through association with the 2015 FIFA corruption scandal, it cut its sponsorship. In short, a firm's trust and reputation are derived, in part, by the company it keeps.

In summary, Table 5.1 (below) provides generic examples of how financial impacts affect multiple stakeholders in different ways. Similarly, Table 5.1 highlights how employees and workplace conditions impact various stakeholder groups. These examples highlight the direct and indirect impacts that many stakeholder-oriented firms already take into consideration. For example, BP has created deep, and meaningful, relationships with its investors, employees, customers, government regulators, communities, as well as its suppliers and distributors. Yet the crisis tested those relationships and found them wanting. Prior to the oil spill, for example, BP's narrative focused on investors' financial and risk-based impacts (Healy and Griffin, 2004). The oil spill crisis broadened, and deepened, the focus to multiple stakeholders, simultaneously, highlighting the need for BP to actively incorporate safety (employees, production processes, as a means to rebuild trust with regulators) as a critical impact (Griffin, 2016).

Quite often, unfortunately, stakeholder impacts are simply reduced to financial contributions for its shareholders. A slightly more inclusive

Table 5.1 *A Focus on corporate impacts: co-creating value with multiple stakeholder, simultaneously*

| | | Stakeholders | | | | |
	Investors	Employees	Customers	Government	Communities	Suppliers/ Distributors
Financial and risk-based impacts	Share price; dividends; returns	Employee Stock Ownership Programs; wages	Price; cost	Taxes; oversight	Sponsorships; economic disparities	Costs; price
Employees in the workplace	Lawsuits; safety record	Safety; training; human trafficking; hours worked; benefits	Child labor; recalls	Oversight; jobs created; local content	Child labor; human rights; safety; jobs	Skills transfer; upskilling

I
M
P
A
C
T
S

narrative of creating jobs, as we saw with the Garcia Electric example, discusses benefits for the town, the employees, the firm, and consumers. Taken one step further, an impact orientation consisting of a holistic, integrative narrative of business acknowledges the many and varied impacts of business and hiring employees, as capitalism is increasingly under siege (Porter and Kramer, 2011; Crane et al., 2014a, b) with demands for reimagining for an enlightened capitalism.

Co-creating Value with Multiple Stakeholders, Simultaneously: Multiplier Effects

Imagine for a moment that your firm has just one supplier, one consumer, one regulator, and one employee. How many relationships might, theoretically, affect your ability to create value? Focusing solely on the four direct relationships would sub-optimize your effectiveness, as there are 24 possible relationships (4-factorial or in mathematical notation, 4!, which is 4 times 3 times 2 times 1) among the firm and its stakeholders.

Now think about a real-world organization. Does it focus solely on the direct relationships with stakeholders or does it look beyond the immediate relationships to examine the risks, rewards, and perceptions of other stakeholders?

Understanding the multitude of impacts is helpful when examining what's important to a wider set of constituencies such as governments, service providers, advocacy groups, or nonprofits. As even more and varied stakeholders become more involved in a firm's value creation process— in developing countries or during urban renewal and infill projects when permits for growing business are required, or when governmental oversight is required for manufacturing controversial products—what is of value may change, and change rapidly, for these relevant constituencies.

Multiplier Effects: The Sweet Spot or the Messy Middle

While direct and indirect effects of financial, employee, product, or information-based impacts are often intuitive, corporations often don't think through the impact's multiplier effects. Multiplier effects can transform firms' every-day, and headline-making, decisions affecting their future potential to grow and prosper. Multipliers leverage firms' ability to continuously co-create value with employees, investors, consumers, governments, and neighborhoods. Well-intentioned businesses narrowly focusing on financial returns, or fulfilling contracts for clients, or creating safe workplaces, is simply not sufficient for resilient, digitally transformed twenty-first-century firms.

Multiplier effects extend a firm's reach beyond its immediate stakeholder to include (a) the extended value chain, (b) across communities/geographies, and (c) over time. Multiplier effects may directly, and more importantly, indirectly spill over to the value creation process exacerbating (exponentially!) problems. Firms with global supply chains, for example, were particularly vulnerable to spillover risks during Covid-19 shutdowns. Local grocery stores, merely through the daisy chain of contracts with tiers of suppliers, is affected by those suppliers' policies, capabilities, and resilience.

After the oil spill in the Gulf of Mexico, for example, BP faced many claims from local tourism, shrimp, and fishing businesses physically affected by the oil spill. Communities further down the coast *without* oil slicks covering their beaches, however, also made claims without bearing *direct* physical impacts of the oil spill. They claimed the oil spill harmed or halted tourism in the neighboring region and, in doing so, their businesses, communities, and way of life were directly impacted financially and nonfinancially. In doing so, the impacts of BP were extended beyond direct, physical impacts upon close neighborhoods to communities further afield that also bore the brunt of the spill but did not have their neighborhoods marred by the physical impacts of an oil spill. Corporations' impacts extend beyond direct physical effects along the value chain.

Multiplier Effects along the Value Chain

Multiplier effects along the value chain extend a firm's interests to suppliers and the suppliers of suppliers as well as to clients who buy the product, consumers who use the products, and government agencies that monitor products. An extended enterprise ecosystem is a source of opportunity and challenges in a 24/7 social media–enabled world. Multiplier effects expand impact thinking to both ends of the value chain, across multiple geographies, and, over time.

Multiplier effects are important because they significantly enhance mutual benefits or rapidly accelerate the costs borne by stakeholders and, thus, the risks for the firm. A firm's extended value chain explicitly links consumers' interests with suppliers' designs. Tying consumers' recommendations for safety features for underage children with product designers reimagining the next generation of products creates a feedback loop that benefits consumers and the firm. In this way, consumers help dictate changes in design, manufacturing, or sourcing of raw materials.

After the BP Deepwater Horizon oil rig exploded killing 11 people, the ensuing oil spill in the Gulf of Mexico created a crisis for the company and the entire petrochemical industry. While BP had already established a "beyond petroleum" presence throughout many Gulf of Mexico communities and had extensive partnerships with international NGOs such as The Nature Conservancy, and deep relationships with university experts in drilling and capping wells, as well as a robust legal, media, public policy, investor relations, and operations team, missteps still occurred (Healy and Griffin, 2004; Healy, 2014), including BP CEO, Tony Haywood, being sacked.

Despite being the nation's largest oil spill, surprisingly, it took more than 2 months for BP's stock price to drop by more than 50 percent after the oil rig exploded (Stout, 2012). Exxon's stock price, on the other hand, dropped far more rapidly just a few days after the Exxon Valdez oil spill in 1989. Exxon Mobil spent days, and perhaps months or years, denying the spill and then was hamstrung with its defensive stance throughout the oil recovery process hampering its stock price and casting doubt on its ability to generate future earnings.

BP was able to recover far more rapidly because it had developed, and was able to leverage and learn from, an extensive stakeholder network developed prior to the crisis and upon whom BP relied upon as soon as the spill occurred. Leveraging myriad relationships to spearhead a multifaceted recovery effort, in the end, was applauded. The relationships forged and relatively rapid responses throughout BP's extended stakeholder network created from an extensive stakeholder network developed prior to the crisis and upon whom BP relied upon as soon as the spill occurred helped its recovery.

In addition, positive multiplier effects from the BP spill also occurred. Can you name one? Answer: Collaborative partnerships with new businesses specializing in cap-and-contain technologies were created (Figure 5.1).

Seemingly simple everyday decisions about employing local talent, for example, have potentially far-reaching impacts that can undermine (or reinforce) other stakeholder relationships thereby affecting the ability of a firm to grow. Hiring local talent can set the stage for a company in tune with the (local) community norms: attracting a larger pool of talented applicants, encouraging more consumers to buy from a "well-respected" company that treats its employees well, rather than a company perceived as doing what it wants regardless of the community in which it resides. Being culturally *insensitive* to local preferences may unwittingly stir up animosity and bitterness that extends far beyond the wages it pays, the products it offers, and its ability to compete even with the cheapest costs (today).

If a hotel, for example, deepens its relations with its employees by creating training and development programs benefitting all employers

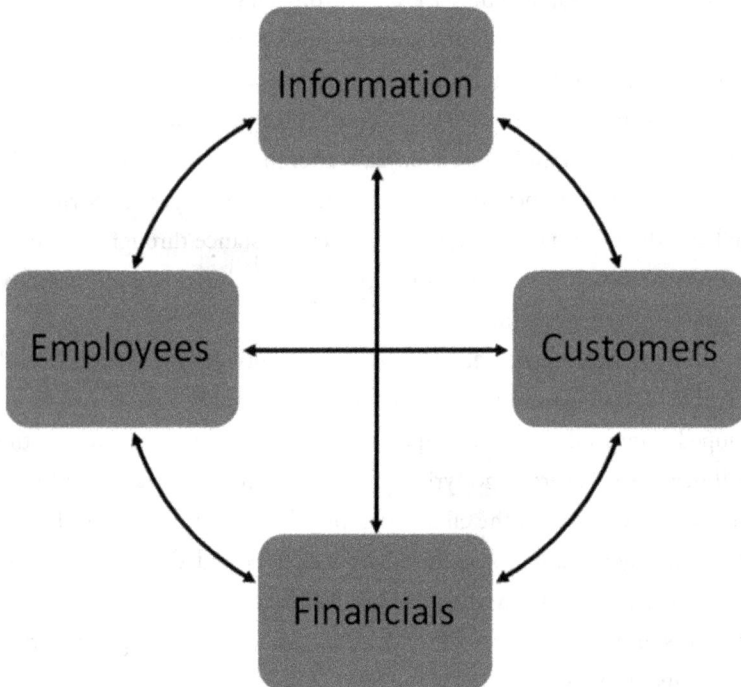

Figure 5.1 Reimagining new combinations

Griffin, J.J. 2016. *Managing Corporate Impacts: Co-creating Value.* Cambridge University Press.

in the hospitality business, value can be co-created with a ripple effect (a multiplier effect) on others. In other words, a firm is helping others help themselves. Will other communities look upon the hotel as a trusted partner and welcome it as it expands into new communities or will it just examine its potential for a tax contribution? Similarly, if the hotel obeys local laws yet voluntarily goes beyond compliance on human rights, for example, when the law is silent, does it make it a trusted partner differentiated from its rivals? Or, do the financials trump all considerations? Small contributions, in their own way, over time, make a difference. And when multiplied by a million (products, customers, employees, lives touched in the product process) the impacts can be quite astonishing! Multiply a legacy of good.

Why Now? And Why Bother?

What's different today? First, a crisis can put at risk a firm's survival (Heineman, 2008). Seemingly epiphenomenal events (e.g., Covid-19 pandemic, century floods, cyclones, and droughts) are occurring with far more frequency, testing the resilience of global relationships, worldwide supply chains, and international trade.

Yet it's not just epiphenomenal events that affect a firm's survival. Operational crises can turn a routine decision process without adequate information flows into a head-turning, top-of-the-fold newspaper story that goes viral on YouTube, blogs, Twitter, Instagram, and social media. A crisis can, if not effectively managed, affect survival (Griffin, 2008; Heineman, 2008). Lead paint in children's toys or pet food contamination, for example, leads to questioning the trustworthiness of such companies that put profit over the health and safety of kids and pets.

In addition, survival may depend on the company your firm keeps. Multiplier effects rippling through an industry are more pervasive than ever. Some beef processors went bankrupt after "pink slime," a meat-based additive to ground beef composed of fatty scraps treated with citric acid to kill bacteria. As public outcry grew, it was banned by the U.S. Department of Agriculture from school lunches for children in primary and secondary schools (Korn, 2014) resulting in closed plants and laid-off employees. Retail companies such as McDonalds and Kroger, a grocery store, said they would no longer use pink slime. Yet 2 years later, pink slime was making a comeback as beef prices climbed (Korn, 2014) while plant-based vegetarian options such as Beyond Meat patties are seeing significant growth opportunities (Petre, 2020). Cascading impacts might ebb and flow over time as public attention moves on to new topics, yet new competitors reconceiving value for customers can gain a foothold, disrupting the entire industry.

After a crisis, learning from, and systematically assessing, impacts to reimagine the business or digitally transform the value creation process is not new. Yet the stakes are now higher, especially if learning doesn't occur! What is new is the need for *rapid* learning. Learning how today's direct impacts multiply affecting tomorrow's ability to create value with multiple stakeholders is important. As Adam Smith (1776) assured us, coordination among multiple stakeholders, simultaneously, is nontrivial. Not all organizations flirt with dismissal after a crisis threatens survival. Some, such as Siemens, emerge more fortified after being tested by a crisis. Timberland, for example, changed its sourcing requirements to focus on tracing sustainable inputs once Greenpeace ran an expose (Swartz, 2010). Amazon's online delivery took off worldwide, spawning many rivals, amidst the Covid-19 pandemic.

Similarly, when the Australian government proposed a super-tax for resource-based companies during the global financial crises, the resource sector, including Rio Tinto, took out full-page advertisements to actively, and successfully, advocate for public sentiment to drop the tax (Henisz, 2014).

Corporations Are Uniquely Qualified

Companies are uniquely qualified to co-create value with multiple stakeholders due to their scale, scope, and unique resources. Large and small firms actively seek net positive impacts that create value: to make consumers happy, have productive employees, and satisfy suppliers while creating returns for investors. Satisfying multiple stakeholders continually over time is critical to survival (Griffin, 2017). So, it is in the best interests of corporations to make positive impacts on salient issues (Clark, Bryant, and Griffin, 2017) while mitigating harm.

Corporations have scale. Some corporations are larger than some governments in the post–World War II economy while governments, the traditional source for foreign direct investments as underwriters for the earliest explorers while designers of the Marshall Plan and Bretton Woods Organizations after World War II, are no longer the primary source of foreign direct investment. Foreign direct investment by private enterprise now surpasses government aid and public sector donations (Zoellick, 2011). Multinational corporations, unlike many governments, have a global scale and scope, whereas governments focus more directly on national, regional, or local populations.

Corporations, unlike many governments, often choose the products they produce, how to produce them, and in what quantity. Corporations can choose to be thought leaders as well as business leaders. Corporations are uniquely qualified to create value since they are in the business of satisfying people's needs. Providing products, goods, and services (e.g., a Tata Group commitment to build the low-cost Tata Nano automobile) in a manner that respects consumer desires, government restrictions, and is mindful of its environmental impact can create value continually over time.

Corporations are unique. Staffed with uniquely qualified personnel, companies specialize with technical experts, management expertise, and convening power. Corporations have the ability to plan, prioritize, and create performance targets (e.g., key performance indicators—KPIs) to piece together multifaceted supply chains with sophisticated distribution logistics. Corporations create jobs and employ people. Multinational corporations address challenges affecting multiple communities, with multiple points of interaction with federal, state, local regulators and administrators, and can convene multi-stakeholder discussions.

Private enterprise is innovative. A variety of governance systems embrace a wide range of desired outcomes with an equally wide-ranging variety of ownership/management models (family, publicly traded, private, social enterprise, benefit-corps, institutional pension funds, religious affiliated organizations, etc.). Organizations have continuously adapted across generations and geographies reflecting the changing mores, needs, and aspirations. If they can't, they go out of business. The chameleon-like qualities of corporations allow them to adapt to different conditions globally and across issues, industries, and nation-states to create distribution, transportation, and pricing solutions (Griffin et al., 2005).

Finally, branded businesses have unique risks. Branded, consumer-driven companies such as Cadbury, Nike, Unilever, or Matsushita must meet changing global expectations while maintaining their competitiveness to thrive. Companies whose branded products have government restrictions preventing them from selling directly to consumers (e.g., British American Tobacco or Diageo's premium drinks) have an added hurdle to meet regulatory approvals that differ from country to country due to customs, tastes, and traditions. Pharmaceutical companies—whose direct-to-consumer branded products such as Cialis, Vioxx, or Viagra rely on insurance or government reimbursements—face unique risks as they rely heavily on government and public approval to remain in business. Despite these risks, consumer-driven companies are likely to be first movers in addressing myriad financial and nonfinancial impacts.

Summary

This chapter aims to spark new conversations about the importance, and multiplicity, of corporate impacts. These impacts, in turn, affect firms' ability to co-create value with multiple stakeholders, simultaneously. We identified direct and indirect impacts (e.g., financial and risk-based, employees in the workplace; products and production; communities' trust via information sharing) as well as multiplier effects (i.e., extended value chain, across geographies, and over time) that transform HOW firms create and destroy value.

This chapter attempts to create a positive feedback loop integrating impact into business narratives. Business narratives connect WHY (a firm exists) with WHAT (products, markets, and solutions it provides) and HOW (resources and resourcefulness) a firm creates its desired IMPACTS (investors and risk, employees and workplace, products throughout the entire value chain, communities' trust, and information). Corporate impacts, the points of intersection between a business and its stakeholders (e.g., employees, investors, suppliers, communities, and government), are the points at which an opportunity exists for value to be co-created or destroyed.

Understanding a business's (desired) impact is more important than ever in a post-Covid-19 world. Yet managing impacts is harder than ever as more stakeholders are more involved than ever before. Achieving impact will require rejiggering and reimagining the business of business (Taneja et al., 2016) while reconsidering age-old heuristics, including if "the business of business is just business." Creating value with, and for, others requires a new narrative beyond solely financial value creation (Harrison and Wicks, 2012).

By expanding the means and ends desired, a firm can better withstand crises, strong regulatory headwinds, or hiccups in operations. Understanding the ways in which value is created and sustained over time with multiple stakeholders helps a firm as it encounters new economic realities, political headwinds, or social issues that inevitably emerge in modern businesses. Articulating and demonstrating multiple impacts simultaneously, modern-day firms can anticipate answers to the inevitable questions: "What's in it for me?" and "What's in it for others?" What increasingly relevant are the impacts, and the value created (or destroyed), as assessed differently by different stakeholders, in different communities/ geographies over time. A messy quagmire if the focus isn't on impacts.

The traditional, narrow view of the firm—composed of financial impacts—that focuses solely on the financial impacts leaves many other, important, aspects of the firm unaddressed and isolated from the firm's mission. Financial impacts, important in and of themselves, become even more powerful when combined with employees' wages and the firm's ability to retain loyal consumers, for example. The value creation process of businesses includes financial, employee, and consumer impacts, at a minimum. You can't have one without the other, and it is in combination that value is shared, grown, and expanded.

Overall, a focus on firm's interactions through financial, personnel and the workplace, product/services, and information impacts broaden, and deepen, what is relevant in today's value creation process. Examining information as a critical impact affecting the value creation process (e.g., an opportunity to be a thought leader) enables many and varied stakeholders while disproportionately making traditional firms vulnerable. Quite simply, systematically examining all of a corporation's impacts beyond the traditional investor-only financial emphasis highlights how cross-cutting, reciprocal relationships among multiple stakeholders, simultaneously, can multiply and transform value creation (or destruction).

Questions

1. Is your firm aware of, and appropriately addressing, all of its corporate impacts (financial with risks; employees in the workplace; products along the entire value chain, including end users; information and communities' trust)?

2. What value is co-created (destroyed or co-destroyed) with multiple stakeholders, simultaneously?

3. What direct impacts create (destroy) value? How about the multiplier effects that (exponentially) affect your corporation, for good and for ill? Have you considered the effects: over time, across geographies, and throughout the extended enterprise?

4. How can your firm best align, leverage, and learn from its customers (and stakeholders) to meaningfully create positive multiplier effects? Are you listening or telling?

References

Baron, D.P. 1995. "Integrated Strategy: Market and Nonmarket Components." *California Management Review* 37, no. 2, pp. 47–65.

Broder, J.M. 2013, February 27. "With 2 ships damaged, Shell suspends Artic drilling," *The New York Times*. www.nytimes.com/2013/02/28/business/energy-environment/shell-suspends-arctic-drilling-for-2013.html.

Bryant, A., J.J. Griffin, and V.G. Perry. 2020. "Mitigating Climate Change: A Role for Regulations and Risk-taking." *Business Strategy and the Environment* 29, pp. 605–18.

Bryant, B. 2011, April 20. "Deepwater Horizon and the Gulf Oil Spill—the Key Questions Answered," *The Guardian*. www.theguardian.com/environment/2011/apr/20/deepwater-horizon-key-questions-answered.

Clark, C., A. Bryant, and J.J. Griffin. 2017. "Firm Engagement and Social Issue Salience, Consensus and Contestation." *Business & Society* 56, no. 8, pp. 1136–1168.

Crane, A., G. Palazzo, L. Spence, and D. Matten. 2014a. "Contesting the Value of 'Creating Shared Value.'" *California Management Review* 56, no. 2, pp. 130–49.

Crane, A., G. Palazzo, L. Spence, and D. Matten. 2014b. "A Reply to 'A Response to Andrew Crane et al.'s Article by Michael E. Porter and Mark R. Kramer.'" *California Management Review* 56, no. 2, pp. 151–53.

Edelman. 2020. Edelman Trust Barometer Special Report: Brand Trust and the Coronavirus Pandemic, May.

Evan, W.M. 1965. "The Organization Set: Toward a Theory of Inter-organizational Relations." In *Approaches to Organizational Design*, ed. J.D. Thompson. Pittsburgh, PA: University of Pittsburgh Press, pp. 173–91.

Fahrenthold, D.A. and K. Kindy. 2010, October 20. "Six Months after the Spill, BP's Money is Changing the Gulf as Much as Its oil," *Washington Post*. www.washingtonpost.com/wp-dyn/content/article/2010/10/19/AR2010101907468.html.

Freeman, R.E. 1984. *Strategic Management: A Stakeholder Approach*. Marshfield, MA: Pitman Publishing.

Freeman, R.E., J.S. Harrison, and A.C. Wicks. 2007. *Managing for Stakeholders: Survival, Reputation, and Success*. New Haven, CT: Yale University Press.

Friedman, M. 1970. "Social Responsibility of Business." *The New York Times Magazine* 33, pp. 122–26.

Goldenberg, S. 2010a, . "Obama: 'No More Offshore Drilling in Gulf of Mexico Until 2017,'" *The Guardian*. www.theguardian.com/environment/2010/dec/02/obama-offshore-drilling.

Goldenberg, S. 2010b, December 15. "United States Sues BP over Gulf Oil Disaster," *The Guardian*. www.theguardian.com/business/2010/dec/16/unitedstates-sues-bp-gulf-oil?INTCMP=SRCH.

Goldman, D. 2015, January 28. "Zuckerberg has his Tim Cook Moment," *CNN Money*. http://money.cnn.com/2015/01/28/technology/social/zuckerberg-internet-cook.

Greenhouse, S. 2005, September 14. "Suit Says Wal-Mart is Lax on Labor Abuses Overseas," *New York Times Business*. www.nytimes.com/2005/09/14/business/14walmart.html?_r=0.

Greenhouse, S. 2013, May 14. "As Firms Line Up on Factories, Wal-Mart Plans solo Effort," *The New York Times*. https://www.nytimes .com/2013/05/15/business/six-retailers-join-bangladesh-factory-pact .html.

Greening, D.W. and D.B. Turban. 2000. "Corporate Social Performance as a Competitive Advantage in Attracting a Quality Workforce." *Business & Society* 39, no. 3, pp. 254–80.

Griffin, J.J. 2008. "Re-examining Corporate Community Investment: Allen's Australian Centre for Corporate Public Affairs (ACCPA) Corporate Community Involvement Report." *Journal of Public Affairs* 8, pp. 219–27.

Griffin, J.J. 2016. *Managing Corporate Impacts: Co-Creating Value.* Cambridge, UK: Cambridge University Press.

Griffin, J.J. October, 2017. "Tracing Stakeholder Terminology Then and Now: Convergence and New Pathways." *Business Ethics: A European Review* 26(4), pp. 326–46.

Griffin, J.J., A. Bryant, and C.P. Koerber. 2015. "Corporate Responsibility and Employee Relations: From External Pressure to Action." *Group & Organization Management* 20, no. 3, pp. 378–404.

Griffin, J.J., and A. Prakash. 2014. "Corporate Responsibility: Initiatives and Mechanisms." *Business & Society* 53, pp. 465–82.

Griffin, J.J., and B. Vivari. 2009. "Corporate Social Responsibility in America." In *Global Practices of Corporate Social Responsibility,* eds. S.O. Idowu and W.L. Filho. Berlin, Germany: Springer Verlag, pp. 235–50.

Griffin, J.J., and C. Koerber. August, 2006. Does industry matter when managing stakeholder relations? *Proceedings of the Annual Academy of Management Best Papers*, August 11–16, Atlanta, GA.

Griffin, J.J. and J. Weber. 2006. "Industry Social Analysis: Examining the Beer Industry." *Business & Society* 45, no. 4, pp. 413–40.

Griffin, J.J., M. McNulty, and W. Schoeffler. August-November, 2005. "Shaping Brazil's Emerging GMO Policy: Opportunities for Leadership." *Journal of Public Affairs*, 5(3–4), pp. 287–98.

Griffin, J.J. and Y.N. Youm. 2018. "Voluntarily Disclosing Prosocial Behaviors in Korean Firms." *Journal of Business Ethics* 153, no. 4, pp. 1017–1030.

Gutierrez, C. 2010, June 18. "Moody's Cuts BP Credit Rating," *Forbes*. www
.forbes.com/2010/06/18/moodys-cuts-bp-rating-markets-equities-
spill.html.

Harrison, J.S. and A.C. Wicks. 2012. "Stakeholder Theory, Value, and
Firm Performance." *Business Ethics Quarterly* 23, no. 1, pp. 97–124.

Healy, R. 2014. *Corporate Political Strategy: Why Firms do What they do*.
London, UK and New York, NY: Routledge Press.

Healy, R. and J.J. Griffin. 2004. "Building BP's Reputation: Tooting Your
Own Horn, 2001–2002." *Public Relations Quarterly* 49, no. 4.

Heineman, B.W. 2008. *High Performance with High Integrity*. Boston,
MA: Harvard Business Press.

Helman, C. 2020. "A Decade after Deepwater Horizon Oil Still Flows
from this Prolific Patch in the Gulf of Mexico," *Forbes.com*. https://
www.forbes.com/sites/christopherhelman/2020/04/23/a-decade-
after-deepwater-horizon-oil-still-flows-from-this-prolific-patch-in-
the-gulf-of-mexico/#5f0662e943a9.

Henisz, W.J. 2014. *Corporate Diplomacy: Building Reputations and Relationships with External Stakeholders*. Sheffield UK: Greenleaf
Publishing.

Henisz, W.J., S. Dorobantu, and L. Nartey. 2014. "Spinning Gold: The
Financial Returns to Stakeholder Engagement." *Strategic Management
Journal* 35, pp. 1727–1748.

Hoffman, A.J. 1999. "Institutional Evolution and Change: Environmentalism and the US Chemical Industry." *Academy of Management Journal* 42, pp. 351–71.

Hoffman, A.J. and P.D. Jennings. 2011. "The BP Oil Spill as Cultural
Anomaly? Institutional Context, Conflict and Change." *Journal of
Management Inquiry* 20, no. 2, pp. 100–112.

Hoffman, A.J. and W. Ocasio. 2001. "Not All Events are Attended
Equally: Toward a Middle-range Theory of Industry Attention to External Events." *Organization Science* 12, no. 4, pp. 414–34.

Korn, M. 2014, August 24. "High Beef Prices Force the Return of 'Pink
Slime,'" *Yahoo! Finance*. http://finance.yahoo.com/news/high-beef-
prices-force-the-return-of–pink-slime-133522348.html.

Krauss, C. and J. Schwartz. 2012, November 15. "BP will Plead
Guilty and Pay Over $4 billion," *The New York Times*. www

.nytimes.com/2012/11/16/business/global/16iht-bp16.html?
pagewanted=all&_r=0.

Larino, J. 2015. "BP Oil Spill Trial Wraps Up Nearly 2 Years after Historic Litigation Began." *The Times-Picayune*, February 2.

Macalaster, T. 2010, August 25. "BP Frozen Out of Arctic Oil Drilling Race," *The Guardian*. www.theguardian.com/environment/2010/aug/25/bp-arctic-greenland-oil-drilling.

Mackey, J. and R. Sisodia. 2013. *Conscious Capitalism: Liberating the Heroic Spirit of Business*. Cambridge, MA: Harvard Business Review Press.

Mackey, M. 2010, July 20. "Oil Spill: 90 Days Out, a Bold Look at the Big Numbers," *The Fiscal Times*. www.thefi scaltimes.com/Articles/2010/07/20/Oil-Spill-Bold-Look-Bare-Economic-Numbers.

McCurry, J. 2020, January 5. "Fukushima Unveils Plans to Become Renewable Energy Hub," *The Guardian*. www.theguardian.com/environment/2020/jan/05/fukushima-unveils-plans-to-become-renewable-energy-hub-japan.

Porter, M.E. and M.R. Kramer. 2011. "Creating Shared Value." *Harvard Business Review* 89, no. 1, pp. 2–17. www.hbr.org/2011/01/the-big-idea-creating-shared-value.

Perry, V.G. and P.M. Blumenthal. 2012. "Understanding the Fine Print: The Need for Effective Testing of Mandatory Mortgage Loan Disclosure." *Journal of Public Policy & Marketing* 31, no. 2, pp. 305–12.

Petre, A. 2020. "Impossible Burger vs. Beyond Burger: Which Is Better?" *Healthline*. https://www.healthline.com/nutrition/impossible-burger-vs-beyond-burger.

Prakash, A. and J.J. Griffin. 2012. "Corporate Responsibility, Multinationals, and Nation-States." *Business & Politics* 14, no. 3, pp. 1–10.

Smith, A. 1776. *An Inquiry into the Nature and Causes of the Wealth of Nations*. London, UK: W. Strahan and T. Cadell Publishers.

Stempel, J. 2014, November 13. "US Judge Upholds BP 'Gross Negligence' Gulf Spill Ruling," *Reuters*. www.reuters.com/article/2014/11/14/us-bp-spill-idUSKCN0IY01320141114.

Stout, L. 2012. *The Shareholder Value Myth: How Putting Shareholders First Harms Investors, Corporations, and the Public*. San Francisco, CA: Berrett-Koehler Publishers.

Swartz, J. 2010, September. "Timberland's CEO on Standing up to 65,000 Angry Activists." *Harvard Business Review*, pp. 39–43.

Sweney, M. 2010, September 16. "BP Falls Out of Index of Top 100 Brands after *Deepwater Horizon* Oil Spill," *The Guardian*. www .theguardian.com/media/2010/sep/16/apple-iphone-interbrand.

Taneja, S.S., J.J. Griffin, R.R. Sharma, P.K. Taneja, D.K. Davidson, and R.S. Ray. 2016. "A Multi-stakeholder Approach to Understanding Success: Empirical Tests in Indian Businesses." In *Corporate Behavior and Sustainability: Doing Well by Being Good*, eds. G. Aras and C. Ingley. Farnham, UK: Ashgate (Taylor and Francis Group), pp. 21–41.

Tseng, N.H. 2010, June 7. "BP after the Spill: Bankrupt, Bought or Business as Usual?" *Fortune*. http://archive.fortune.com/2010/06/04/news/companies/gulf_coast_BP_bankruptcy_odds.fortune/index .htm.

Turban, D.B. and D.W. Greening. 1997. "Corporate Social Performance and Organizational Attractiveness to Prospective Employees." *Academy of Management Journal*, 40, pp. 658–72.

Wearden, G. 2010, June 15. "BP Credit Rating Slashed as Oil Spill Costs Mount," *The Guardian*. www.theguardian.com/business/2010/jun/15/bp-credit-rating-slashed-oil-spill-costs.

Webb, T. 2010a, July 18. "BP Oil Spill: Failed Safety Device on *Deepwater Horizon* Rig was Modified in China," *The Guardian*. www.theguardian .com/environment/2010/jul/18/deepwater-horizon-blow-out-preventer-china.

Webb, T. 2010b, August 3. "BP Charges Well Partner Anadarko $1bn for Its Share of Oil Spill Cleanup," *The Guardian*. www.theguardian.com/business/2010/aug/03/bp-gulf-oil-spill-costs.

Webb, T. 2011. "BP to Cut Production Amid Impact of *Deepwater Horizon* spill," *The Guardian*, January 30. www.theguardian.com/business/2011/jan/30/bp-production-targets-deepwater-horizon-spill.

Webb, T. and T. Bawden. 2011, February 1. "Court Order Halts BP Talks with Rosneft," *The Guardian*. www.theguardian.com/business/2011/feb/01/bp-loss-gulf-oil-spill-resumes-dividend.

Webb, T. and E. Pilkington. 2010, June 1. "Gulf Oil Spill: BP Could Face Ban as US Launches Criminal Investigation," *The Guardian*. www .theguardian.com/environment/2010/jun/01/gulf-oil-spill-bp-future.

Wood, D.J. 1991. "Corporate Social Performance Revisited." *Academy of Management Review* 16, no. 4, pp. 691–718.

Zoellick, R.B. 2011. *Beyond Aid.* Speech by World Bank Group President Presented at GW University.web.worldbank.org/WBSITE /EXTERNAL/NEWS/0, contentMDK:23000133~pagePK:34370~ piPK:42770~theSitePK:4607, 00.html.

CHAPTER 6

Managing Cultural Diversity

Chantal van Esch and Diana Bilimoria

This chapter focuses on managing diversity responsibly. It promotes a mindset as well as policies of inclusion that managers and companies can institute locally to impact others globally. Cultural diversity will be discussed in depth, with specific emphasis on gender diversity. It starts with an introduction to the meaning and significance of diversity and inclusion, then shifts focus to discuss key contemporary cultural diversity issues, and concludes with practical implications and recommendations for managers.

Managers' understanding of the impact of cultural diversity directly influences companies through individual recruitment, advancement, leadership, career development, and retention. Besides the general consensus that diversity issues are moral issues and that everyone deserves equal treatment, managing cultural diversity gives businesses an advantage in the marketplace since they will be able to obtain and retain the best talent regardless of identity-based characteristics such gender, sex, race, ethnicity, sexual orientation, nationality, citizenship status, religion, socioeconomic status, education, experience, physical ability, marital and parental status, or any other dimensions of cultural diversity. Specifically, research on the business cases for diversity, show the advantages that can accrue to organizations from a well-managed diverse workforce, include increased talent utilization, improved marketplace understanding, enhanced innovation and creativity, and better team problem solving (Robinson and Dechant, 1997). Both gender and racial diversity have been shown to be correlated with increased sales revenue, customers, and relative profits (Herring, 2009). Therefore, we argue that being inclusive in corporations is not just a "soft skill" that managers should ideally develop but is in fact a business imperative in today's global economy.

Cultural Diversity

Managing diversity and inclusion is defined as valuing the full talent of the workforce—by providing access, tools, and opportunities to all, appreciating individual and group differences, and creating a workplace where all stakeholders can contribute to organizational success (Bernstein and Bilimoria, 2013). While this definition is all encompassing and does not indicate specific behaviors for managers, it is important to note that how each of the previously mentioned dimensions of identity-based cultural diversity are most effectively managed will vary according to the cultural systems of countries and regions, such as the political, economic, legal, language, and value systems in which they are embedded. The UN and its member states have indicated their commitment to cultural diversity (UNESCO, 2001). Given this caveat, we focus on key contemporary areas of diversity and inclusion to highlight critical issues of which global managers should be familiar with for effectively managing the same.

Power

The cultural systems (political, economic, legal, language, and value) combine to form different systems of power. Cultural diversity is a manifestation of individual differences within a power dimension (DiTomaso, Post, and Parks-Yancy, 2007). This indicates that cultural systems tend to privilege one group over another, granting them privileges and determining who has power in any given situation (Johnson, 2001; Lenski, 1966). Since no differences inherently suggest a power differential, it is cultural systems that emphasize and maintain power variations based on group differences (Van Knippenberg, De Dreu, and Homan, 2004). In addition to being contextual, these power systems are intersectional as well, so a person may have power due to certain combinations of their identity and lack power due to others (Johnson, 2001). Some elements of the power system may be openly acknowledged in the culture while others may be less transparent, especially to those outside the culture. Some differences, visible (e.g., physical ability) or invisible (e.g., sexual orientation) may carry a stigma that is culturally assigned. Awareness of and sensitivity to differing identity-based power dynamics in cultural systems across the world are important for managers operating in the global economy as members of their teams may come from varying cultural systems.

Next, we discuss a number of cultural diversity dimensions that highlight some of the critical issues in managing diversity and inclusion that managers deal with globally. Although by no means an exhaustive list, these issues start to reveal how cultural systems designate power to specific social groups. Understanding of these cultural systems and the power differences they confer is the first step to effectively manage diversity and create more inclusive work environments.

Gender

Gender is an aspect of cultural diversity that has been recognized internationally. Gender is a social construct, which means that it is defined socially or culturally (West and Zimmerman, 1987). Gender is related to sex, a biological construct, but is not the same thing. Gender refers to the socially constructed roles of and relationships between people of different genders. Gender differences include characteristics and behaviors that are not only tied to biology, but which also originate from culture-specific perception and treatment of what different gender roles "should" be. Norms regarding gender-specific speech, movement, activities, roles, thoughts, and feelings may vary by place, time, and culture. Gender determines what is expected, socially permitted, and valued in a particular context (Bilimoria, 2011).

The UN has recently turned a great amount of attention to gender issues. Hiring Emma Watson, of Harry Potter fame, to be the Goodwill Ambassador for Women, has helped them to get younger generations involved in gender diversity issues (Duca, 2014). Watson's "He-for-She" campaign urges men to become more feminist and to support women's equality around the world (Duca, 2014). In addition, the UN has been working with corporations such as Calvert Investments to develop an understanding of gender inclusion (Calvert Group, 2004). Calvert Investments proposed Calvert Women's Principles® in 2004 in collaboration with the National Development Fund for Women, a code of conduct for all corporations worldwide focused on empowering, advancing, and investing in women (van Esch, Cooper, and Zou, 2017). Initiated by the UN Global Compact and UN Women, these principles have been adapted by the UN as the Women's Empowerment Principles (WEP)—a set of principles offering guidance on gender equality in the workplace, marketplace, and community. The principles are:

- Establish high-level corporate leadership for gender equality,
- Treat all women and men fairly at work—respect and support human rights and nondiscrimination,
- Ensure the health, safety and well-being of all women and men workers,
- Promote education, training and professional development for women,
- Implement enterprise development, supply chain and marketing practices that empower women,
- Promote equality through community initiatives and advocacy, and
- Measure and publicly report on progress to achieve gender equality (UN, 2014).

WEP speaks to the entire world as gender inequality is still pervasive throughout. Even countries with high gender parity still face wage gaps, gender clustering in professions, and glass ceilings for women, while in low-gender-parity societies, basics such as education and property ownership may be denied to women.

Race, Ethnicity, and Nationality

The concepts of race, ethnicity, and nationality are highly related although not synonymous. Race indicates racial origins and is often linked with physical characteristics (Betancourt and Lopez, 1993). Ethnicity refers to a grouping of individuals who share the same culture, nationality, and/or language (Betancourt and Lopez, 1993). Finally, one's nationality is denoted by one's country of origin or choice and, thus, is more individualistic than either race or ethnicity which is generally shared with parents and other family members. Nationality and citizenship status are increasingly coming to the attention of managers in the global economy. Some cultural systems are more homogenous on these dimensions while others are more heterogeneous. Many countries across the world have enacted antidiscrimination laws to ban racial/ethnic discrimination (particularly of their indigenous populations) and to provide equal opportunity regardless of race and ethnicity. As global teams increasingly consist of members across different races and ethnicities, managers are being called upon to acknowledge and value these differences while finding common ground, so that they can inspire diverse team members and achieve business results.

Religion

Religion is not just an issue of cultural diversity but also a cultural system in which diversity is shaped. Most managers around the world will at some point lead individuals who are of a different religious affiliation. Even in Tokelau, Morocco, and the Vatican City which are the most religiously homogeneous countries (PewResearch, 2014), global managers likely will have to work with those who do not share the dominant religious faith.

Socioeconomic Status and Education

Another issue that every cultural system deals with is differences in socioeconomic status, which is closely related to although not the same as differences in education. Individuals' ability to obtain education also influences their ability to raise their socioeconomic status. Some countries place high importance on citizens achieving tertiary (postsecondary) education. Canada is the most educated country in the world with over 51 percent of individuals having tertiary education (Sauter and Hess, 2012). Managers across the world will work with people having different levels of socioeconomic status and varying educational accomplishments. Understanding class- and education-based dynamics and implications is important for making all employees feel welcomed and able to fulfill their jobs to their fullest abilities.

Age and Experience

Age and experience are particularly important and intertwined aspects of cultural diversity. While older age in some cultures, notably Eastern Asian countries, is revered and comes with attributions of wisdom and intelligence, in other cultures such as in many Western countries, older individuals or senior citizens often have to be protected by laws to maintain their jobs and status. Often experience comes with age-someone who has been in the workforce for many years will generally have more organizational experience than those who are just entering the workforce. However, as the global economy expands, experience needs are also becoming more specialized, particularly in specific technical functions, jobs, and industries. In addition, while some cultures focus on honoring age and experience, others take an approach that values youth and new perspectives. Particularly in Western countries, as "baby boomers" (those born between 1946 and 1964) reach retirement age, managing cultural diversity implies that managers increasingly need to mentor younger individuals as they join and eventually advance to leadership in their organizations (Dohm, 2000), manage values conflicts between five generations of employees who for the first time in history are working side by side (Knight, 2014), and adjust their products and services to changing marketplace preferences as the largest age groups in societal populations change (Leventhal, 1997).

Physical Ability

Differences due to individuals' physical abilities also affect individuals in every cultural system. Disabled or differently abled individuals face higher rates of unemployment around the globe (UN, n.d.). It is important to note that disabled does not mean in-abled, as many disabled or differently-abled individuals are able to be highly productive members of organizations given the right accommodations. Systematic accommodation for the disabled varies highly among cultural systems; for example, in the United

States antidiscrimination laws indicate that "reasonable accommodations" should be made (EEOC, 2002) while Italy mandates a quota and enforces a fee for companies who fail to hire disabled individuals (EBU, 2014). Other countries have no systematic recognition available, and often disabled individuals face severe discrimination in the workforce (UN, n.d.).

Sexual Orientation

Sexual orientation has recently become of increased importance in international diversity, ranging from cultures where individuals' orientations and expressions of sexuality are systematically and legally supported to cultures where there are dire consequences for those who admit non-heterosexual preferences, including state-supported hate crimes against members of sexual minority communities. Societal and legal responses to diverse sexual orientations affect how individuals behave in the workplace. Supportive workplaces allow individuals to openly be themselves, while others (because of company or regional/national culture and laws) may force individuals to keep their sexual orientation to themselves. Recently Tim Cook, CEO of Apple, came out publicly as gay (Molina, 2014). While this led to considerable media attention in the United States, there did not seem to be any organizational consequences, yet in Russia this same announcement led to the removal of a famous Apple statue (Molina, 2014).

Marital and Parental Status

Workplace issues of marital and parental status are often tied to issues of gender. Both come down to the notion of the "ideal worker" persona which is based on the image of the industrial worker as a man who is able to go to work every day to earn money for his family while having an "invisible" wife at home who takes care of his laundry, cooking, cleaning, and childcare needs (Pateman, 1988; see also Acker, 1990, 1992). The ideal worker can engage with a single-minded, full-time focus on his work and an exclusive devotion to career only if he has a spouse at home to take care of the domestic and childcare needs (Pateman, 1988). While in parts of the world the traditional ideal worker image still persists, today in other cultures many employees are likely to be single or in dual-career households (with or without children). Yet, to this day in most societies, women still do a majority of household and childcare work in addition to employment outside the home (Eagly and Carli, 2007). Because the ideal worker as male image remains unconsciously powerful, women often have a harder job of fulfilling the "ideal worker" persona, particularly if they have children. Managers aware of the hidden operation of the ideal worker persona can become more inclusive regarding the career development of female and male employees having different marital and parental statuses.

Conclusion

While the above dimensions of cultural diversity are by no means an exhaustive list, particularly since each cultural system assigns power, privilege, and stigma differently, they are an introduction to key aspects of cultural diversity that managers in the global economy can expect to face. Understanding not only the types of cultural diversity but also how employees' social identities may unconsciously impact their recruitment, performance, advancement, leadership, and retention in organizations will help managers transform their workplaces to become more inclusive.

Through this chapter we seek to encourage emerging and practicing managers of the global economy to create more inclusive workplaces for all. Not only is this a moral and ethical imperative of the global economy—all employees deserve the dignity of being treated fairly and provided the opportunity to bring their best, authentic selves at work-but also one that makes the most business sense (Herring, 2009; Robinson and Dechant, 1997). Not harnessing the advantages of a diverse workforce limits the global talent that a company can attract and retain. Lack of managerial awareness about cultural diversity and the unconscious operation of biases and stereotypes about diverse employees in the workplace not only lead to a less talented work pool but these attitudes also increase organizational turnover costs and reduce business competitiveness.

As the recent trends toward globalization in literally every economic sector continue to persist world over, managing cultural diversity and creating inclusive work environments has become an increasingly important managerial skill. Understanding how to attract and retain top talent regardless of social identity characteristics and helping those of different social identities work together effectively, will continue to be crucial for global managers.

Summary

It is important for managers to understand the impact of cultural diversity not just for moral reasons but also because it is a business imperative. Contextual power systems lead to differences in cultural diversity across the world. However, critical issues in managing diversity and inclusion often include gender, race, ethnicity, nationality, religion, socioeconomic status, education, age and experience, physical ability, sexual orientation, and marital and parental status.

Short Diversity Case

Business owners in the German town of Wunsiedel were paying attention to how cultural issues impacted their way of life. Every year, neo-Nazis marched through their town, where Rudolf Hess, second in command to Hitler, had been buried. The cultural traditions of Germany, both rooted in and in opposition to their involvement in WWII, led to these marches but also determined business owners' negative responses against them. Business owners and local community leaders tried to end the marches multiple times to no avail. In 2014, Wunsiedel's business owners tried a new approach by turning the march into a fundraiser for Exit, a nonprofit which helps individuals leave neo-Nazi organizations. Each meter the neo-Nazis marched turned into tangible donations to the nonprofit (Noack, 2014). These town leaders used an understanding of cultural diversity to influence regional events and make their town a more inclusive environment for all.

Questions

1. Which aspects of cultural diversity impact your own career?

2. Which cultural diversity issues are most noticeable in your area?

3. What can your organization do to make your workplace an inclusive place for everyone?

References

Acker, J. 1990. "Hierarchies, Jobs, Bodies: A Theory of Gendered Organizations." *Gender and Society* 4, no. 2, pp. 139–58.

Acker, J. 1992. "Gendering Organizational Theory." In *Gendering Organizational Analysis*, eds. A.J. Mills and P. Tancred. Newbury Park, CA: Sage, pp. 248–60.

Bernstein, R.S., and D. Bilimoria. 2013. "Diversity Perspectives and Minority Nonprofit Board Member Inclusion." *Equality, Diversity and Inclusion: An International Journal* 32, no. 7, pp. 636–53.

Betancourt, H., and S.R. Lopez. 1993. "The Study of Culture, Ethnicity, and Race in American Psychology." *American Psychologist* 48, no. 6, p. 629.

Bilimoria, D. 2011. *Gender Equity in Science and Engineering: Advancing Change in Higher Education*. New York, NY: Routledge.

Calvert Group. 2004. "Calvert Investments - Calvert Women's Principles." http://www.calvert.com/womensPrinciples.html, (accessed November 10, 2014).

DiTomaso, N., C. Post, and R. Parks-Yancy. 2007. "Workforce Diversity and Inequality: Power, Status, and Numbers." *Annual Review of Sociology* 33, pp. 473–501.

Dohm, A. 2000. "Guaging the Labor Force Effects of Retiring Baby-Boomers." *Monthly Labor Review* 123, p. 17.

Duca, L. 2014, September 21. "Emma Watson Fights for Gender Equality with Powerful UN Speech." http://www.huffingtonpost.com/2014/09/21/emma-watson-gender-equality_n_5858206.html, (accessed December 8, 2014).

Eagly, A.H., and L.L. Carli. 2007. *Through the Labyrinth: The Truth about How Women Become Leaders*. Harvard Business Press. http://books.google.com/books?hl=en&lr=&id=b2kf_B_4f0kC&oi=fnd&pg=PR9&dq=eagly+carli&ots=CSzQd7xeda&sig=eYYctTEM8VMqadp8Ffwq2PDBatE.

EBU. 2014. "Italy | European Blind Union." http://www.euroblind.org/convention/article-27--work-and-employment/nr/128, (accessed November 25, 2014).

EEOC. 2002, October 17. "Enforcement Guidance: Reasonable Accommodation and Undue Hardship under the Americans with Disabilities

Act [Text]." http://www.eeoc.gov/policy/docs/accommodation.html, (accessed December 8, 2014).

Herring, C. 2009. "Does Diversity Pay? Race, Gender, and the Business Case for Diversity." *American Sociological Review* 74, no. 2, pp. 208–24.

Johnson, A.G. 2001. *Privilege, Power, and Difference.* Boston, MA: McGraw-Hill. http://2012-textbook-deals.info/wp-content/uploads/pdfs/Privilege% 20Power%20and%20Difference%20by%20Allan%20Johnson%20 -%20It%20Opened%20My%20Eyes.pdf.

Knight, R. 2014, September 25. "Managing People from 5 Generations - HBR." https://hbr.org/2014/09/managing-people-from-5-generations/, (accessed December 21, 2014).

Lenski, G.E. 1966. *Power and Privilege: A Theory of Social Stratification.* Chapel Hill, NC: UNC Press Books.

Leventhal, R.C. 1997. "Aging Consumers and Their Effects on the Marketplace." *Journal of Consumer Marketing* 14, no. 4, pp. 276–81.

Molina, B. 2014, October 30. "Apple CEO Tim Cook: 'I'm proud to be gay.'" http://www.usatoday.com/story/tech/2014/10/30/tim-cook-comes-out/18165361/, (accessed November 25, 2014).

Noack, R. 2014, November 17. "German Town Plays Prank on Neo-Nazis," *The Washington Post.* http://www.washingtonpost.com/ blogs/worldviews/wp/2014/11/17/watch-german-town-plays-prank-on-neo-nazis/, (accessed November 18, 2014).

Pateman, C. 1988. *The Sexual Contract.* Stanford University Press. http:// books.google.com/books?hl=en&lr=&id=jH2KPvZF1L0C&oi=f nd&pg=PP9&dq=pateman+sexual+contract&ots=Xnd5z9htE_& sig=YJ6wVJ7i5JRV0-ip_8JjWWBtdd8.

PewResearch. 2014. "Global Religious Diversity." http://www.pewforum. org/2014/04/04/global-religious-diversity/.

Robinson, G., and K. Dechant. 1997. "Building a Business Case for Diversity." *The Academy of Management Executive* 11, no. 3, pp. 21–31.

Sauter, M., and A. Hess. 2012, September 24. "The Most Educated Countries in the World." http://finance.yahoo.com/news/the-most-educated-countries-in-the-world.html, (accessed November 26, 2014).

UN. 2014. "Women's Empowerment Principles." http://weprinciples .org/, (accessed November 10, 2014).

UN. n.d. "Disability and Employment." http://www.un.org/disabilities/default.asp?id=255, (accessed November 25, 2014).

UNESCO. 2001. *UNESCO Universal Declaration on Cultural Diversity.*

van Esch, C., B. Cooper, and J. Zou. 2017. *Calvert Investments: Environmental, Social, and Governance Sustainability.* Ontario, Canada: Ivey Publishing Case Study.

Van Knippenberg, D., C.K. De Dreu, and A.C. Homan. 2004. "Work Group Diversity and Group Performance: An Integrative Model and Research Agenda." *Journal of Applied Psychology* 89, no. 6, p. 1008.

West, C., and D.H. Zimmerman. 1987. "Doing Gender." *Gender & Society* 1, no. 2, pp. 125–51.

CHAPTER 7

Ecopreneurship for Sustainability: Role of Entrepreneurial Bricolage, Design Thinking, and Creative Self-Efficacy

Parag Rastogi and Radha R. Sharma

The role of business practices in dealing with sustainability issues such as environmental degradation and climate change has become a centerpiece in the sustainability-related literature (Porter and Kramer, 2011). In the realm of entrepreneurship, the concepts of ecopreneurship, sustainable entrepreneurship, and social entrepreneurship are more on the lines of Austrian economist Joseph Schumpeter's concept of "creative destruction." The chapter presents a novel approach involving design thinking to develop environmentally sustainable solutions in infrastructure industry. This approach is necessary if environmental and the relevant economic and social issues are to be addressed effectively in this sector. Drawing from the emerging fields of ecopreneurship and bricolage, we recommend creation of a cadre of design ecopreneurs who would evolve a framework for its resolution.

Introduction

Entrepreneurship and its impact on the economy is an important thread in the economic discourse. Success of an entrepreneur in a resource-constrained environment spawns inspiring stories that others want to emulate. It arouses curiosity as to how some successful entrepreneurs could make the most of the opportunities that others would have given up due to resource constraints. There are three major theories in entrepreneurship, anchored in the way opportunities are identified or created: (1) causation,[1,2] (2) effectuation,[3] and (3) bricolage.[4] Fisher,[5] after comparing the three theories, has posited that there are theoretical similarities and differences among them. The causation or discovery and exploitation model of entrepreneurship[1,6] is the dominant theory in entrepreneurship. This theory suggests a linear model of entrepreneurship in which successful entrepreneurs are characterized by their ability to identify large opportunities[6] and the exploitation of the opportunities.[7] This is done by obtaining high-quality resources according to the plan and deploying these resources in a skillful and disruptive manner.[2] However, empirical research has suggested that many of the aspects of the causation theory are violated by even successful entrepreneurs.[8] This has given rise to alternative entrepreneurial theories, which include effectuation[3] and bricolage.[4]

Bricolage

The term *bricolage* was first introduced by Levi-Strauss,[9] who defined it as "making do" with current resources and creating new forms and order from tools and materials at hand. Baker and Nelson[4] introduced bricolage theory into entrepreneurship, and since then the theory has led to widespread discussion in literature. Entrepreneurial bricolage is an emerging entrepreneurial theory,[4] and boundaries are still evolving. According to Davidsson, Baker, and Senyard,[10] the most important current theme in opportunity–resource nexus theory is the emerging theory of entrepreneurial bricolage.

Bricolage has been conceptually and empirically linked to explain market creation,[4] innovation,[11,12] opportunity exploitation,[13,14] firm's performance,[15] firm's growth,[16] processes,[17] social entrepreneurship,[18] and emerging markets.[19,20] Bricolage has been considered at the individual level,[21] organizational level,[22] and interorganizational/environmental level.[23] Bricolage studies were initiated from developed countries, namely, the United States,[4] Sweden,[24] Australia (Davidsson, Baker, and Senyard, 2009), and in recent years, some studies have emanated from emerging economies like Kenya,[20] China,[25] Palestine,[19] Bangladesh,[26] Malaysia,[27] and India.[28,29]

Bricolage as a model includes entrepreneurial activities that do not seem to fit a model of only rationality and profit-maximizing engine.[4,17,30] Bricoleurs often draw from unrelated or underdeveloped resources during the opportunity-formation process, and hence, bricolage "represents a form of value creation that does not depend on the Schumpeterian assumption that assets are withdrawn from one activity for application in another".[4]

Most of the work done on entrepreneurial bricolage is focused on developed country contexts where resource scarcity is not as acute as it is in the developing world. Bricolage research in the developed economies is focused on understanding social entrepreneurship rather than the use of bricolage for-profit entrepreneurship.[20] The contextual conditions significantly differ between developing and developed economies[31]; hence, in developing countries, entrepreneurs work in institutional voids[26] and skills and knowledge scarcity.[32] Such conditions lead to entrepreneurs behaving differently from those in the developed economies.

Ecopreneurship

The term "ecopreneurship" combines "ecological" ("eco") and "entrepreneurship" and can be thought of as "entrepreneurship through an environmental lens." Ecopreneurship is distinct from other forms of corporate environmental development by a company's commitment to impact environmental progress. Ecopreneurs combine environmental considerations with their business activities in a drive to shift the basis of economic development toward a more environment-oriented basis.[33] Schlange[34] suggested that "ecologically driven entrepreneurship has sustainability as a key element to motivate its basic approach."

There is an increasing evidence of environmental degradation. Consequently, there has been emergence of new businesses "such as renewable energy, green buildings, natural foods, and other sectors, which reflects an increase in the importance for environmental entrepreneurship".[33] Hence, it is no surprise that there has been a focus on understanding entrepreneurship as a potential mechanism for sustainable development. Sustainable entrepreneurs are those entrepreneurs who combine various aspects of sustainability[35] and seek to perpetuate resources focused on sustainable development. Such entrepreneurs play an important role in bringing a paradigm shift toward a new model of development. Beveridge and Guy[36] proposed that such development models can be used to alleviate global warming and other negative environmental impacts. These entrepreneurs could possibly have business models that are counter to typical opportunity-seeking and exploitative entrepreneurial behavior.

A venture can be termed as sustainability-driven if it combines opportunities and intentions to simultaneously create value from an economic, social, and ecological perspective[34]; thus, one can observe many ecological advancements in recent years, for example, commercialization of hybrid cars, solar power, and windmills. Such technologies can also trigger evolution in institutions. As these innovations become part of the mainstream, there are frequent policy responses and initiatives.

New business forms develop when ecopreneurs seek to combine environmental awareness with business success and conventional entrepreneurial activity.[37] Schaltegger[38] proposed that "ecopreneurs destroy existing conventional production methods, products, market structures and consumption patterns and replace them with superior environmental products and services."

According to Post and Altman,[39] there are three drivers of change from an external context:

1. *Compliance-driven*, which emerge as an outcome of government regulation and legislation.
2. *Market-driven*, with environmentally beneficial behavior coming as a result of profit seeking.
3. *Value-driven*, with environmental change coming in response to end-user demands.

Challenges for Ecopreneurs

The challenge of market creation or the limited extent of the market for products and processes is true for all entrepreneurs. According to Linnanen,[40] "market creation is even more difficult for environmental business ideas than it is for non-environmental business ideas, because the financial community may not yet be mature enough to finance environmental innovations, and the role of ethical reasoning creates confusion within the mainstream business community."

Over the years, there has been an improvement in the awareness levels of green issues. There have been attempts at linking sustainability and competitive advantages for businesses and an increase in the interest levels of venture capitalists toward ecopreneurial ventures, and venture capitalists have started appreciating the benefits of funding ecopreneurs. Ecopreneurs have an additional objective/constraint toward the environment. Randjelovic, O'Rourke, and Orsato[41] pointed out that ecopreneurial development may require longer gestation periods to achieve market breakthrough than conventional entrepreneurial activity. This can deter investors who are looking for a quick return on their investment. Ecopreneurs do not operate in isolation and "will be influenced by the evolving economic and social structures around them and, in turn, are influencing those structures".[42] Interplay between individual motivations for ecopreneurial activity and the broader economic and social context within which individuals operate is important.[42]

One of the main distinctive traits of ecopreneurs is their intent to change the face of their companies.[38] Ecopreneurs, by developing innovative solutions and by impacting management practices, can change the entire business model. In doing so, some ecopreneurs experience inner tension when they have to make a choice between profits and going green.[40]

Ecopreneurs work on a larger canvas than the conventional entrepreneur with many profit-seeking and nonprofit relationships and practices[43] and the ecopreneurial environment is a contingent, undetermined space full of ideologies and desires. O'Neill and Gibbs[44] conceptualized ecopreneurial businesses as continually "made and remade" and that makes ecopreneurship vary temporally and spatially termed as "relational." Thus, ecopreneurs are constrained in their potential to substantially outperform the economy.

Furthermore, Houtbeckers[45] termed ecopreneurship as a mundane process that evolves over time. Ecopreneurs contribute to the expansion of the green economy and provide new solutions that can be adopted by the industry. Ecopreneurs' output is embedded in social relations, and environmentalism is embedded in social relations.[37] Kirkwood and Walton[46] observed that the social context that ecopreneurs experience influences their behavior.

In an Indian study on building construction ecopreneurs, Rastogi and Sharma[28] identified some of the challenges that ecopreneurs face:

- Conflict of customer requirements and available solutions
- Lack of understanding of implications of long-term use of non-sustainable designs
- Supplier base not fully equipped to support the solution/stakeholders at different levels of evolution
- Risk in the solution/technology not delivering the requirements (end-of-pipe risk)

These are summarized in Figure 7.1

Entrepreneurial Resource Management and Bricolage

Resource Scarcity

Resources are critical for the performance of a new venture, and most of the firms do not own or control the set of resources required to build a competitive advantage. Entrepreneurial resources or rather the lack of them characterizes many of the start-ups. In emerging markets, the problem of scarcity of resources is likely to be more acute than that in the developed world. Undoubtedly, resources are critical in the performance of a new venture; however, the straightforward application of the resource-based view (RBV) in predicting firm success is too simplistic.[47] Wiklund and Shepherd[7] argued that the availability of resources moderates the relationship between entrepreneurial orientation (EO) and performance. Julienti,

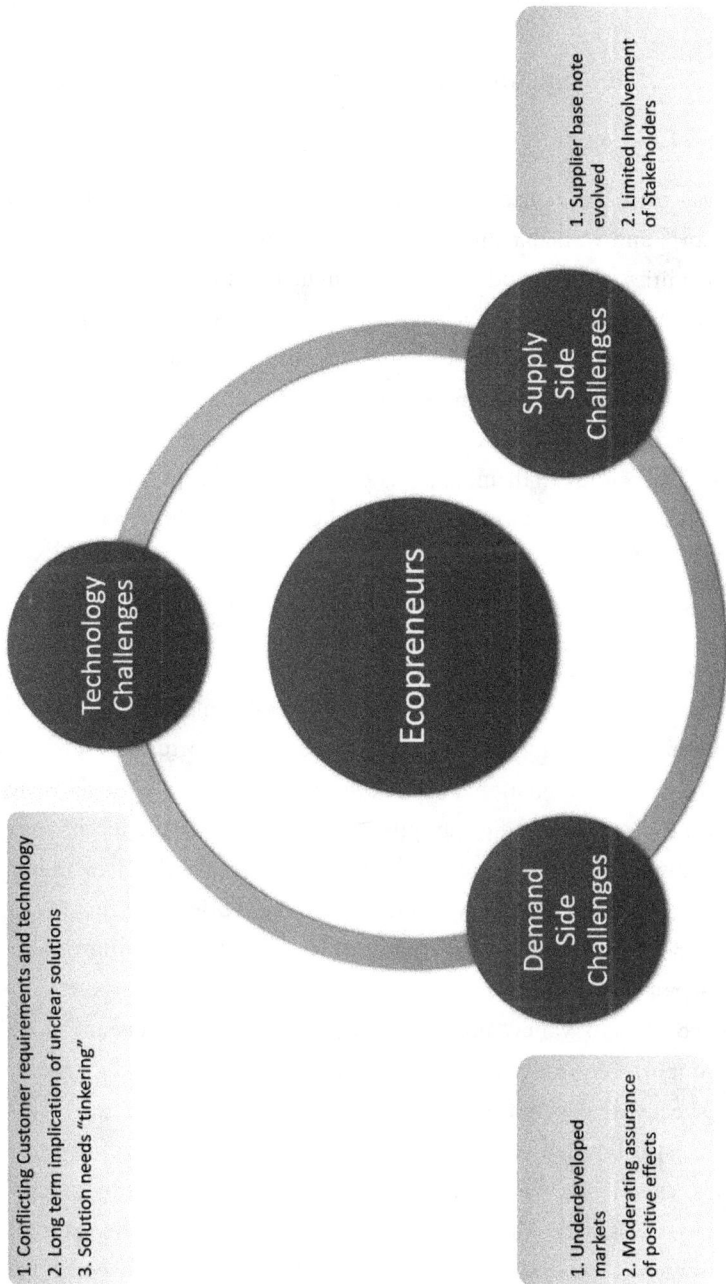

1. Conflicting Customer requirements and technology
2. Long term implication of unclear solutions
3. Solution needs "tinkering"

1. Supplier base note evolved
2. Limited Involvement of Stakeholders

1. Underdeveloped markets
2. Moderating assurance of positive effects

Technology Challenges

Ecopreneurs

Supply Side Challenges

Demand Side Challenges

Figure 7.1 Challenges faced by ecopreneurs in business

Bakar, and Ahmad[48] posited that both tangible and intangible resources contribute to the firm's product innovation performance.

Bricolage and Entrepreneurial Bricolage

Material Bricolage

Material bricolage represents the combination of resources at hand to find novel and workable approaches to overcome problems and exploit opportunities.[4] Many studies link entrepreneurial bricolage to resource-constrained environment.[4,20,49-51] Resources can be material (physical and financial), knowledge, and ideational.[4] Steffens, Senyard, and Baker[52] showed that firms have a more advantageous position if they have higher level of bricolage. Another categorization of bricolage is by Molecke and Pinkse.[53] According to them, material bricolage is the process of combination of resources to find workable approaches to exploit the opportunities.

Ideational Bricolage

Levi-Strauss[9] explained "ideational" bricolage by metaphorical reference to the bricoleur as a sort of handyman who makes his way into the world by meeting day-to-day challenges and opportunities through trial-and-error combination of whatever materials, tools, and skills he has accumulated along the way. Ideational bricolage is the mechanism through which old myths are combined in order to develop new myths that serve novel functions. Levi-Strauss[9] introduced bricolage primarily to explain how a society borrows structural elements of other cultures (e.g., elements of myths) and recombines them to suit their own purposes.

According to Vanevenhoven et al,[14] the way entrepreneurs move from opportunity recognition to exploitation depends on the type of bricolage used to combine resources. They also proposed two forms of bricolage: internal and external. Internal bricolage deals with individuals' experience, academic qualifications, and so on, and external bricolage deals with combination of resources present in the external environment. According to them, both types of bricolage are necessary for opportunity exploitation.

Dynamic Capabilities Theory

Dynamic capabilities are "processes that use resources–specifically the processes to integrate, reconfigure, gain, and release resources–to match and even create market change".[47] e Cunha and Da Cunha[54] integrated bricolage with improvisation, minimal structures, simple rules, dynamic capabilities, and organization resilience and proposed a theoretical model. While e Cunha and Da Cunha[54] proposed that bricolage is linked to dynamic capabilities, Fultz and Baker[55] showed that bricolage can indeed lead to dynamic capabilities by fostering willingness and ability to bring about alternative solutions. They also showed that there is a destructive potential of high levels of bricolage on dynamic capabilities.

Institutional Theory

While several studies[26,49] concluded that bricolage is a legitimate process for institutional change in emerging economies, they looked at it from the perspective of an institutional void. Linna[20] noted that no attention has been paid to bricolage in the context of local entrepreneurs in developing countries. Duymedjian and Ruling[22] made a theoretical attempt in laying the foundation of bricolage concept in organization and management theory. They identified social value creation, stakeholder participation, and persuasion as constructs that extend social bricolage.

Resource-Based View Theory

The RBV of the firm focuses on the role of resources in determining the strategic advantage of a firm.[56,57] Greene and Brown[58] identified human, social, physical, organizational, and financial resources as the key entrepreneurial resources in the context of RBV. The recombination of resources, activities, and processes within the firm is the implementation of the strategic choice and leads to a new set of activities, new sources of revenue, and a new business model for the firm. Penrose[59] posited that a firm achieves competitiveness not just because of its resources but also because of its competence in making better use of its resources. Traditionally, RBV scholarship has been less concerned with how these resources are acquired and developed, but the bricolage processes help us understand how entrepreneurs can "make do by applying combinations of the resources at hand to new problems and opportunities."

The question remains how in a resource-constrained environment an entrepreneur leverages his or her exploratory orientation to improve entrepreneurial outcomes using bricolage processes. As bricolage is an emerging field, there are gaps in our understanding of several bricolage processes. There are knowledge gaps in understanding the mechanisms by which resources are mobilized. There are gaps in creative use of resources as practiced by entrepreneurs.[60] Bacq et al.[18] questioned the use of bricolage as a long-term strategy. Research needs to be conducted in environments where resource constraints are different and in organizations that are not social firms.[30] Molecke and Pinkse[53] find that even for-profit entrepreneurs increasingly consider their broader impact on society.

RBV posits that a firm's success is driven by resources that possess certain special characteristics.[56] Several studies have identified entrepreneurial bricolage to be a specific knowledge process that entrepreneurs use to mitigate resource limitations and to seize and leverage market opportunities.[14,17,19,30] Steffens, Senyard, and Baker[52] tested the link between bricolage and firm's strategic resource position. Ferneley and Bell[11] studied information technology innovation in small and medium enterprises (SMEs) and concluded that bricolage fits the "can do" mentality of SMEs and exhorted that for bricolage to flourish, organizational space and management vision are required. Sarkar[61] used RBV to understand the role of bricolage in social change at bottom of the pyramid (BoP) and concluded that there are distinctive features of bricolage used to overcome resource constraints.

Most of the bricolage research deals with the start-up phase of the firms as it is during the start-up phase that they are most deprived of resources. However, in recent years, there has been a small stream of research that has examined firms that have used enhanced bricolage capabilities to augment innovation, giving them a competitive advantage and, hence, positively impacting their performance (Bacq et al., 2014).[13,21] There were also instances where bricolage has functioned as a dynamic capability under a situation of crisis or environmental turbulence.[55]

To summarize, the foregoing demonstrates that bricolage transforms the scant entrepreneurial resources into performance and that entrepreneurial bricolage is a mediating variable between entrepreneurial resources and entrepreneurial success.

EO and Bricolage

EO has become a central concept in entrepreneurial theory. The research on EO and business performance is ever increasing, and firms "pursuing high entrepreneurial orientation are faced with decisions involving risk taking and the allocation of scarce resources".[62] EO is a multidimensional construct; the three dimensions of EO identified by Miller[63] are: *innovativeness, risk taking, and proactiveness*. Later, Lumpkin and Dess[64] added two more dimensions: *competitive aggressiveness* and *autonomy*.

EO captures the behavior an entrepreneur demonstrates in terms of entrepreneurial actions and decisions. Hooi et al.[27] showed that EO is linked with sustainable entrepreneurship and is mediated by the role and degree of entrepreneurial bricolage. Phillips and Tracey[13] suggested that bricolage is an entrepreneurial capability of formation of new means–ends relationships. It is suggested that SMEs use bricolage to exploit opportunities, abuse of bricolage can have a negative impact on opportunity exploitation. One of the theories defining the nature of dimensions within the EO construct is the RBV. The premise in this theoretical construct is that certain firm resources and capabilities may lead to greater EO and that EO may give rise to an increase in a firm's resources and capabilities.[65] Wiklund and Shepherd[66] observed that there has been limited research into mediating influences in EO–outcome relationships. Rauch et al.[62] posited that substantial theoretical and empirical contributions can be made in studies that investigate the conditions in which EO–performance relationships are either strengthened or weakened.

Digan et al.[29] suggested that perceived competence and self-determination help bricolage behavior in women entrepreneurs. An et al. (2018) found that learning orientation has a positive moderating effect on the relationship between bricolage and opportunity identification. Sarkar[61] studied grassroot entrepreneurs and found that domain-specific skills and the use of spare time help bricolage behavior. Bojica, Istanbouli, and Fuentes-Fuentes[19] demonstrated the role of subjective perspectives like degree of autonomy in bricolage.

Entrepreneurial Bricolage, Design Thinking, and Creative Self-Efficacy

Bricolage and Innovation

Even before Baker and Nelson[4] demonstrated the nexus between entrepreneurship and bricolage, there have been suggestions that bricolage has a link with innovation. Garud and Karnoe[23] studied technology entrepreneurship and suggested that breakthrough and bricolage are contrasting approaches toward innovation to develop alternate technology pathways. Baker, Miner, and Eesley[16] showed that bricolage processes can permeate entrepreneurial activities to create innovative implications. Hmieleski and Corbett[67] used creative bricolage to explain that improvisation accounts for a significant amount of variance in entrepreneurial intentions. Anderson[69] chose a bottom-up perspective to explore innovations and concluded that bricolage clarifies innovations from bottom-up processes utilizing what is at hand or embedded locally. Furthermore, Anderson[68] suggested that bottom-up mobilization is pivotal to release creativity. Fuglsang and Sorensen[69] stated that there is a very close association between bricolage and innovation and innovation occurs as a small step in the context of sustainable public innovation. This has also been supported by Beckett,[50] who posited that introducing radical innovation in large organizations has been proven to be difficult and that it is better to opt for incremental innovation through the bricolage process.

Witell et al.[70] used service innovation to study bricolage and concluded that a bricolage perspective is better to explain service innovation in resource-constrained environments. Leliveld and Knorringa[71] linked bricolage and frugal innovation. Kickul et al.[72] concluded that there is a positive relationship between bricolage and catalytic innovations.

Halme, Lindeman, and Linna[73] concluded that bricolage has an impact on inclusive innovations pursued by multinational corporations to create innovative, pro-poor, or inclusive business models. Salunke, Weerawardana, and McColl-Kennedy (2013) studied project-based firms and found that higher levels of bricolage are associated with supportive service innovation and, consequently, sustainable competitive advantage.

Senyard, Baker, Davidsson, and Steffens[12] provided that bricolage improves the innovativeness of resource-constrained new firms. SMEs can promote innovation using bricolage as a given. Innovating for low-income markets is very different from high-income markets and concluded that bricolage is one of the antecedents of affordable value innovations for emerging markets.

Bricolage, Design Thinking, and Creativity

Bricolage is practiced as a means of exploring creativity within a time pressure and crisis context. An, Guo and Zhang (2016) found that bricolage is a mediator of entrepreneurial creativity and firm-level innovation in SMEs. There has been evidence that social entrepreneurs utilize resources in new and innovative ways. Studies on entrepreneurship[3,4] (Bradley et al., 2010) and creativity research (Moreau and Dahl, 2005, Ward, 2004) showed innovation can be developed efficiently despite–or even because of–resource constraints.[74] Keupp and Gassman[75] linked resource constraints and innovation.

Design thinking is a multidisciplinary field and has been described as the best way to be creative and innovate.[76] Architects employ design tools like prototyping, visualization of ideas, and user observation. Bandura[77] explained self-efficacy as "concerned not with what one has but with belief in what one can do with whatever resources one can muster." One of the most important predictors of self-efficacy is the experience of success in past performance.[78] Self-efficacy describes a person's "beliefs that he/she can perform tasks and fulfil roles, and is directly related to expectations, goals and motivations".[79] High self-efficacy is linked to work-related performance,[80] small business growth,[81] and career choice.[82]

Resource constraints can stimulate entrepreneurs to adopt creative behavior to achieve the innovation outcome. In this context, resource constraints do not inhibit innovation; in fact, they enable it.[75] New firms can generate innovations because of, not despite of, resource constraints.[74] Resource constraints cannot generate innovations automatically. Certain behaviors need to be taken to translate resource constraints into innovation outcomes. Resource constraints are an antecedent of the link between bricolage and innovation. Resource constraints can trigger bricolage and thus can trigger innovation as well. Entrepreneur's self-efficacy is an important factor in mobilizing social and financial resources as a form of cognitive resilience in opportunity exploitation. In this context, the focus is on task-specific rather than general self-efficacy, that is, creative self-efficacy, which is the extent to which a person feels confident to perform well on the creative or design aspects of the job.

Creative self-efficacy has made a significant contribution as a process variable explaining how several organizational and personal factors influence creative outcomes. Researchers have demonstrated that self-belief about one's creative ability is an important motivational factor to perform creatively.[83] Results show that an increase in creative self-efficacy corresponds to an increase in creative performance as well.[83] Self-efficacy specific to a given activity domain is most instrumental in predicting performance in that domain (Bandura, 1986). Creative self-efficacy has demonstrated associations across diverse settings.[83] Tierney and Farmer[83] found that when individuals face complex tasks, they utilize cognitive faculties and processes that generate creativity. Tierney and Farmer[83] also proposed that creative self-efficacy has an important role in solving complex tasks. Consequently, it is postulated that creative self-efficacy facilitates entrepreneurial bricolage.

Exploratory Orientation

Exploratory action and exploration as a process is embedded in psychological theories. In recent years, the word "exploration" has been widely used in the field of management, for example, exploratory innovation and exploratory learning. In a broad sense, the concept of exploration includes activities of information gathering about the environment and of investigation—inspective and inquisitive behavior.[84] The essence of exploration is about engagement with the environment and the motivation to acquire information through interaction with the world.[84] Exploration is thought to be impinged upon the concepts of self-determination theory and self-regulation.[84] Exploration is a process of discovery using trial-and-error studies in an unknown field and, thus, closely related to innovation. Organizations less well-endowed with resources are more likely to explore, especially when they operate in competitive environs. Scholars have found that enterprises with an exploratory orientation can more effectively access resources and adapt to future environmental changes.[85]

"Exploratory orientation" refers to the tendency of enterprises to engage in activities such as "search, variation, risk taking, experimentation and discovery".[85] Exploratory orientation emphasizes discarding existing technology and market trajectories, seeking new knowledge actively, and promoting the development of new products, technologies, processes, or structures. In addition, it pays attention to whether enterprises can enter new markets, meet new customer demands, and develop new sales channels. According to the RBV, the enterprise's exploratory orientation is an implicit resource owned by the entrepreneur and can help the enterprises to actively expand their business areas, carry out business activities, and enhance their business performance. From the perspective of competence, the enterprise's exploratory orientation can help to strengthen its ability to deal with future risks, identify potential business opportunities, and, by trying new business methods and development concepts, promote business model innovation.

It has been argued that enterprises with an exploratory orientation are more able to access resources and adapt to future environmental changes than others. Kollmann, Stöckmann, and Kensbock[86] sought to explain exploratory innovation as a mediating variable accounting for entrepreneurial behavior. Fultz and Baker[55] suggested that the ability to envision alternative solutions and skills in recombination of entrepreneurs fosters bricolage behavior. Refusal of limitations imposed by environment is a key behavior of bricolage entrepreneurs. Houtbeckers[45] identified "finding detours" as a key tactic used. Phillips and Tracey[13] refer to the "ability of finding new solutions" as a bricolage behavior. Turturea, Jansen, and Verheul (2014) proposed that SMEs make use of entrepreneurial bricolage to pursue ambidextrous strategies and reconcile the tension between exploration and exploitation.

Creativity, Design Thinking, and Entrepreneurship

Creativity

Creativity has been described as problem-finding, problem formulation, and problem redefinition[87] and the synthesis of information. It has been suggested that opportunity recognition process is influenced by creativity.[88] Willis, Webb, and Wilsdon[89] called the entrepreneurs who challenge established business models and user expectations to develop innovative business solutions as "disruptive innovators." Scholars have used methods from creativity research to examine opportunity recognition such as creative problem-solving, divergent-thinking, and idea-generation exercises.[90] Runco[91] suggested that Person, Product, Press (environmental pressure), and Process are the most used parameters in creative studies.

Ardichvili, Cardozo, and Ray[88] regarded creativity as a characteristic of entrepreneurs to recognize opportunities. The study suggested that creativity is one of the personality traits related to successful opportunity recognition. The study further proposed that high levels of creativity are linked to high levels of entrepreneur's alertness and self-efficacy. Scholars have also proposed creativity-based models of opportunity recognition (Dyer, Gregersen, and Christensen, 2008).[93]

Design Thinking

The origins of design thinking date back to the 1960s' works of design methodologists that drew distinctions between the science of design and the natural sciences.[93] Design was proposed as a scientific method aimed at creating new forms, artifacts, or knowledge. As natural sciences deal with the analysis of existing reality, design science deals with "the transformation of existing conditions into preferred ones".[93] Schön[94] emphasized the artistic, intuitive nature of the processes that design practitioners use to understand and solve problems in situations of uncertainty, ambiguity, and instability. Schön conceptualized these processes as "reflective practice."

Design is an applied discipline and aims at creating more meaningful experiences for customers. Design is targeted toward the creation of solutions and is not seen as the prerogative of a few. Within the concept of design understanding, it is well understood that there is no one right way. Simon[93] characterized design problems as ill-structured because they have ambiguous specification of goals. There is no determined solution path, and there is a need to integrate multiple knowledge domains. Design thinking is an approach to problems that a designer might take on the premise that businesspeople need to become designers. IDEO, a leading design firm, not only applies its design expertise to product development but also provides innovative solutions in complex organizational processes. Design thinking can also be useful when applied to situations, processes, and organization forms. The principles that designers use are more apt to apply to businesses than the background of the designer, for example, industrial design or graphic design. Such principles, or approaches, are called Designerly Thinking.[95] When applied outside of the design context, like businesses, it is called Design Thinking.[76]

According to Kolko,[96] the term "Design Thinking" undermines the act of doing, when design is actually all about doing and even learning through doing. Design thinking is a mindset to be adopted for problem-solving and requires many years of training and practice to become a natural habit of thinking and doing. Later design scholars unpacked the specifics of the designerly ways of knowing[97] in terms of the nature of the design problems and the designers' attitude to solve such problems.[98] Some scholars have proposed that managing is designing.[98] Entrepreneurship and design also extend the business model developed by the entrepreneur to create novelty and value in the market. Boland and Collopy[98] described entrepreneurs as designers and that "entrepreneurs are wonderful examples of designing managers—giving form to valuable new products, services and sometimes creating whole new industries."

Based on the review of researches and identification of gaps, a conceptual model has been developed for future research termed "Ecopreneurship for Sustainability: Role of Entrepreneurial Bricolage, Design Thinking, and Creative Self –efficacy" and is presented in Figure 7.2.

Over a period of time, interest in how designers work and think moved from the purview of designers and architects to the field of management, where scholars focused on identifying the design tools that could be used to solve management problems. Designerly problem-solving tools were advocated as effective approaches for businesses seeking to innovate. Brown[99] suggested design thinking as a loosely structured organizational process based on a set of tools that encourage innovation and the use of design thinking by business people who needed to solve abstract and multifaceted problems.

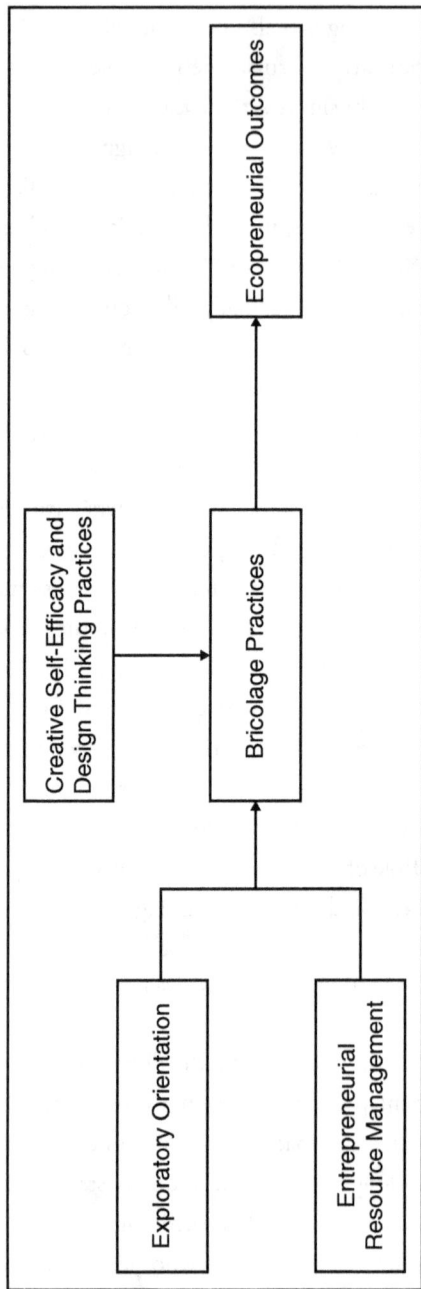

Figure 7.2 A conceptual model of ecopreneurship for sustainability: role of entrepreneurial bricolage, design thinking, and creative self-efficacy

Martin[100] proposed the metaphor of the "knowledge funnel" to describe design thinking as a way of thinking that balanced both the exploration of new knowledge (innovation) and the exploitation of current knowledge (efficiency). Martin[100] argued that this balance of innovation and efficiency helped businesses to systematically develop breakthrough innovations and to gain sustainable competitive advantages.

Sarasvathy[3] posited entrepreneurship as design and that "entrepreneurs not only design firms as instruments that adapt to their environments–and help exploit profit opportunities within those environments; but they also shape parts of their environments to more closely resemble both their personal aspirations and their firms' resource endowments."

Summary

The chapter argues that resolution of sustainability issues under resource-constrained environment can be done using design thinking and bricolage practices. The ecopreneur, who practices bricolage, is an agent of "creative destruction" and thus creates solutions that are environmentally sustainable. The chapter describes a novel approach that integrates bricolage, design thinking, and creative self-efficacy. This proposed approach can be used to address environmentally sustainable issues and thus merits further research.

Questions

1. How do we balance what is profitable and what is environmentally sustainable? What are the possible approaches to resolve this dilemma?

2. Humans cannot exist without environment, and businesses cannot exist without both. In this context, what are the arguments that support "creative destruction" as practiced by ecopreneurs?

3. In what ways have ecopreneurs practicing design thinking extended the boundaries of business? What are the issues they may face when working on these boundaries to find new solutions?

References

1. Kirzner, I.M. 1997. "Entrepreneurial Discovery and the Competitive Market Process: An Austrian Approach." *Journal of Economic Literature* 35, no. 1, pp. 60–85.

2. Schumpeter, J.A. 1934. *The Theory of Economic Development: An Inquiry into Profits, Capital, Credit, Interest, and the Business Cycle.* New Brunswick, NJ: Transaction Books.

3. Sarasvathy, S.D. 2001. "Causation and Effectuation: Toward a Theoretical Shift from Economic Inevitability to Entrepreneurial Contingency." *Academy of Management Review* 26, no. 2, pp. 243–63.

4. Baker, T., and R.E. Nelson. 2005. "Creating Something from Nothing: Resource Construction through Entrepreneurial Bricolage." *Administrative Science Quarterly* 50, no. 3, pp. 329–66.

5. Fisher, G. 2012. "Effectuation, Causation, and Bricolage: A Behavioral Comparison of Emerging Theories in Entrepreneurship Research." *Entrepreneurship: Theory and Practice* 36, no. 5, pp. 1019–1051.

6. Shane, S., and S. Venkataraman. 2000. "The Promise of Entrepreneurship as a Field of Research." *Academy of Management Perspectives* 25, no. 1, pp. 217–26.

7. Wiklund, J., and D. Shepherd. 2005. "Entrepreneurial Orientation and Small Business Performance: A Configurational Approach." *Journal of Business Venturing* 20, no. 1, pp. 71–89.

8. Alvarez, S.A., and J.B. Barney. 2007. "Discovery and Creation: Alternative Theories of Entrepreneurial Action." *Strategic Entrepreneurship Journal* 1, no. 1/2, pp. 11–26.

9. Levi-Strauss, C. 1967. *The Savage Mind.* Chicago, IL: University of Chicago Press.

10. Davidsson, P., T. Baker, and J. Senyard. 2017. "A Measure of Entrepreneurial Bricolage Behavior." *International Journal of Entrepreneurial Behaviour and Research* 23, no. 1, pp. 114–35.

11. Ferneley, E., and F. Bell. 2006. "Using Bricolage to Integrate Business and Information Technology Innovation in SMEs." *Technovation* 26, no. 2, pp. 232–41.

12. Senyard, J., T. Baker, P. Steffens and P. Davidsson. 2014. "Bricolage as a Path to Innovativeness for Resource-constrained New Firms." *Journal of Product Innovation Management* 31, pp. 211–30.

13. Phillips, N., and P. Tracey. 2007. "Opportunity Recognition, Entrepreneurial Capabilities and Bricolage: Connecting Institutional Theory and Entrepreneurship in Strategic Organization." *Strategic Organization* 5, no. 3, pp. 313–20.

14. Vanevenhoven, J., D. Winkel, D. Malewicki, W.L. Dougan, and J. Bronson. 2011. "Varieties of Bricolage and the Process of Entrepreneurship." *New England Journal of Entrepreneurship* 14, no. 2, p. 53.

15. Senyard, J., T. Baker, and P. Davidsson. 2009. "Entrepreneurial Bricolage: Towards Systematic Empirical Testing." *Frontiers of Entrepreneurship Research* 29, no. 5, Article 5.

16. Baker, T., A.S. Miner, and D.T. Eesley. 2003. "Improvising Firms: Bricolage, Account Giving and Improvisational Competencies in the Founding Process." *Research Policy* 32, no. 2, pp. 255–76.

17. Desa, G., and S. Basu. 2013. "Optimization or Bricolage? Overcoming Resource Constraints in Global Social Entrepreneurship." *Strategic Entrepreneurship Journal* 7, no. 1, pp. 26–49.

18. Bacq, S., L.F. Ofstein, J.R. Kickul, and L.K. Gundry. 2015. "Bricolage in Social Entrepreneurship: How Creative Resource Mobilization Fosters Greater Social Impact." *The International Journal of Entrepreneurship and Innovation* 16, no. 4, pp. 283–89.

19. Bojica, A.M., A. Istanbouli, and M.D.M. Fuentes-Fuentes. 2014. "Bricolage and Growth Strategies: Effects on the Performance of Palestinian Women-led Firms." *Journal of Developmental Entrepreneurship* 19, no. 4, pp. 1–234.

20. Linna, P. 2013. "Bricolage as a Means of Innovating in a Resource-Scarce Environment: A Study of Innovator-entrepreneurs at the BOP." *Journal of Developmental Entrepreneurship* 18, no. 3.

21. Stinchfield, B.T., R.E. Nelson, and M.S. Wood. 2013. "Learning from Levi-Strauss' Legacy: Art, Craft, Engineering, Bricolage, and Brokerage in Entrepreneurship." *Entrepreneurship: Theory and Practice* 37, no. 4, pp. 889–921.

22. Duymedjian, R., and C.C. Rüling. 2010. "Toward a Foundation of Bricolage in Organization and Management Theory." *Organization Studies* 31, pp. 133–51.

23. Garud, R., and P. Karnoe. 2003. "Bricolage Versus Breakthrough: Distributed and Embedded Agency in Technology Entrepreneurship." *Research Policy* 32, no. 2, pp. 277–300.

24. Kannampuzha, M.J., and M. Suoranta. 2016. "Bricolage in the Marketing Efforts of a Social Enterprise." *Journal of Research in Marketing and Entrepreneurship* 18, no. 2, pp. 176–96.

25. An, W., X. Zhao, Z. Cao, J. Zhang, and H. Liu. 2017. "How Bricolage Drives Corporate Entrepreneurship: The Roles of Entrepreneurship in China Opportunity Identification and Learning Orientation." *Journal of Product Innovation Management* 35, pp. 49–65.

26. Mair, J., and I. Marti. 2009. "Entrepreneurship in and Around Institutional Voids: A Case Study from Bangladesh." *Journal of Business Venturing* 24, pp. 419–35.

27. Hooi, H.C., N.H. Ahmad, A. Amran, S.A. Rahman, and J. Sarkis. 2016. "The Functional Role of Entrepreneurial Orientation and Entrepreneurial Bricolage in 23 Ensuring Sustainable Entrepreneurship." *Management Research Review* 39, no. 12, pp. 1616–1638.

28. Rastogi, P., and R. Sharma. 2018. "Ecopreneurship for Sustainable Development." In *Handbook of Engaged Sustainability*, eds. S. Dhiman and J. Marques. Cham, Switzerland: Springer.

29. Digan, S.P., G. K. Sahi, S. Mantok and P.C. Patel. 2019. "Women's Perceived Empowerment in Entrepreneurial Efforts: The Role of Bricolage and Psychological Capital." *Journal of Small Business Management* 57, no. 1, pp. 206–29.

30. DiDomenico, M., H. Haugh, and P. Tracey. 2010. "Social Bricolage: Theorizing Social Value Creation in Social Enterprises." *Entrepreneurship Theory and Practice* 34, pp. 681–703.

31. Bruton, G.D., D.J. Ketchen, and R.D. Ireland. 2013. "Entrepreneurship as a Solution to Poverty." *Journal of Business Venturing* 28, no. 6, pp. 683–89.

32. Schreiber, J.C. 2004. "Microenterprises in Africa: A New Viewpoint Book." *International Journal of Commerce & Management* 14, no. 2, pp. 78–79.

33. Dean, T., and J. McMullen. 2007. "Toward a Theory of Sustainable Entrepreneurship: Reducing Environmental Degradation through

Entrepreneurial Action." *Journal of Business Venturing* 22, no. 1, pp. 50–76.

34. Schlange, L.E., 2009. "Stakeholder Identification in Sustainability Entrepreneurship: The Role of Managerial and Organisational Cognition." *Greener Management International* 55, pp. 13–32.

35. Tilley, F. and B.D. Parrish. 2006. "From Poles to Wholes: Facilitating an Intergrated Approach to Sustainable Entrepreneurship." *World Review of Entrepreneurship, Management and Sustainable Development* 2, no. 4, pp. 281–94.

36. Beveridge, R., and S. Guy. 2005. "The Rise of the Ecopreneur and the Messy World of Environmental Innovation." *Local Environment* 10, no. 6, pp. 665–76.

37. Anderson, A.R. 1998. "Cultivating the Garden of Eden: Environmental Entrepreneuring." *Journal of Change Management* 11, pp. 135–44.

38. Schaltegger, S. 2002. "A Framework for Ecopreneurship. Leading Bioneers and Environmental Managers to Ecopreneurship." *Greener Management International* 38, pp. 45–58.

39. Post, J.E., and B.W. Altman. 1994. "Managing the Environmental Change Process: Barriers and Opportunities." *Journal of Organizational Change Management* 7, no. 4, pp. 64–81.

40. Linnanen, L. 2002. "An Insider's Experiences with Environmental Entrepreneurship." *Greener Management International* 38, pp. 71–80.

41. Randjelovic, J., A.R. O'Rourke and R.J. Orsato. 2003. "The Emergence of Green Venture Capital." *Business Strategy and the Environment* 12, pp. 240–53.

42. Walley, E.E., and D.W. Taylor. 2002. "Opportunists, Champions, Mavericks...?" *Greener Management International* 38, p. 31.

43. O'Rourke, A.R. 2010. "How Venture Capital Can Help." In *Making Ecopreneurs: Developing Sustainable Entrepreneurship*, ed. M. Schaper. Surrey, UK: Gower Publishing, pp. 165–78.

44. O'Neill, K., and D. Gibbs. 2016. "Rethinking Green Entrepreneurship—Fluid Narratives of the Green Economy." *Environmental Planning A: Economy and Space* 48, pp. 1727–1749.

45. Houtbeckers, E. 2016. "The Tactics of Ecopreneurs Aiming to Influence Existing Practices." *Small Entrepreneurship Research* 23, pp. 22–38.

46. Kirkwood, J., and S. Walton. 2010. "What Motivates Ecopreneurs to Start Businesses?" *International Journal of Entrepreneurial Behaviour Research* 16, pp. 204–228.

47. Eisenhardt, K.M., and J.A. Martin. 2000. "Dynamic Capabilities: What Are They?" *Strategic Management Journal* 21, no. 10–11 Special Issue, pp. 1105–1121.

48. Julienti, L., A. Bakar, and H. Ahmad. 2010. "Assessing the Relationship between Firm Resources and Product Innovation Performance." *Business Process Management Journal* 16, no. 3, pp. 420–35.

49. Desa, G. 2012. "Resource Mobilization in International Social Entrepreneurship: Bricolage as a Mechanism of Institutional Transformation." *Entrepreneurship Theory and Practice* 36, no. 4, pp. 727–51.

50. Beckett, C.R. 2016. "Entrepreneurial Bricolage – Developing Recipes to Support Innovation." *International Journal of Innovation and Management* 20, no. 5.

51. Guo, H., Z. Su, and D. Ahlstrom. 2015. "Business Model Innovation: The Effects of Exploratory Orientation, Opportunity Recognition, and Entrepreneurial Bricolage in an Emerging Economy." *Asia Pacific Journal of Management* 33, no. 2, pp. 1–17.

52. Steffens, P.R., J. Senyard, and T. Baker. 2009. *Linking Resource Acquisition and Development Processes to Resource-based Advantage: Bricolage and the Resource-Based View.* Paper Presented at 6th AGSE International Entrepreneurship Research Exchange, Adelaide, Australia.

53. Molecke, G., and J. Pinkse. 2017. "Accountability for Social Impact: A Bricolage Perspective on Impact Measurement in Social Enterprises." *Journal of Business Venturing* 32, no. 5, pp. 550–68.

54. e Cunha, M.P., and J. Viera da Cunha. 2007. "Bricolage in Organizations: Concept and Forms." In *Current Topics in Management*, ed. M.A. Rahim. Vol. 12. New Brunswick, NJ: Transaction, pp. 51–70.

55. Fultz, A.E.F., and T. Baker. 2017. "The Day of Small Beginnings: Bricolage as a Source of Dynamic Capabilities in Young Firms." *Academy of Management Annual Meeting Proceedings* 2017, no. 1.

56. Barney, J. 1991. "Firm Resources and Sustained Competitive Advantage." *Journal of Management* 17, pp. 91–120.

57. Alvarez, S.A., and J.B. Barney. 2002. Resource-Based Theory and the Entrepreneurial Firm. In *Strategic Entrepreneurship: Creating a New Mindset*, ed. M.A. Hitt, R.D. Ireland, S.M. Camp, and D.L. Sexton. Oxford: Blackwell Publishers, pp. 89–105.

58. Greene, P. and T.E. Brown. 1997. "Resources Needs and the Dynamic Capitalism Typology." *Journal of Business Venturing* 12, pp. 161–73.

59. Penrose, E.T. (1959). *The Theory of the Growth of the Firm*. Oxford: Basil BlackIll.

60. Sonenshein, S. 2014. "How Organizations Foster the Creative Use of Resources." *Academy of Management Journal* 57, pp. 814–48.

61. Sarkar, S. 2018. "Grassroots Entrepreneurs and Social Change at the Bottom of the Pyramid: The Role of Bricolage." *Entrepreneurship & Regional Development* 30, no. 3–4, pp. 421–49.

62. Rauch, A., J. Wiklund, G.T. Lumpkin, and M. Frese. 2009. "Entrepreneurial Orientation and Business Performance: An Assessment of Past Research and Suggestions for the Future." *Entrepreneurship: Theory & Practice* 33, no. 3, pp. 761–87.

63. Miller, D. 1983. "The Correlates of Entrepreneurship in Three Types of Firms." *Management Science* 29, no. 7, pp. 770–91.

64. Lumpkin, G.T., and G.G. Dess. 1996. "Clarifying the Entrepreneurial Orientation Construct and Linking It to Performance." *Academy of Management Review* 21, no. 1, pp. 135–72.

65. Covin, J.G., and G.T. Lumpkin. 2011. "Entrepreneurial Orientation Theory and Research: Reflections on a Needed Construct." *Entrepreneurship: Theory and Practice* 35, no. 5, pp. 855–72.

66. Wiklund, J., and D. Shepherd. 2011. "Where to From Here: EO-as-Experimentation, Failure and Distribution of Outcomes." *Entrepreneurship Theory and Practice* 35, no. 5, pp. 925–46.

67. Hmieleski, K.M., and A.C. Corbett. 2006. "Proclivity for Improvisation as a Predictor of Entrepreneurial Intentions." *Journal of Small Business Management* 44, no. 1, pp. 45–63.

68. Anderson, O.J. 2008. "A Bottom-Up Perspective on Innovations Mobilizing Knowledge and Social Capital through Innovative Processes of Bricolage." *Administration & Society* 40, no. 1, pp. 54–78.

69. Fuglsang, L., and F. Sørensen, F. (2011). "The Balance between Bricolage and Innovation: Management Dilemmas in Sustainable Public Innovation." *The Service Industries Journal* 31, no. 4, pp. 581–95.

70. Witell, L., H. Gebauer, E. Jaakkola, W. Hammedi, L. Patricio, and H. Perks. 2017. "A Bricolage Perspective on Service Innovation." *Journal of Business Research* 79, no. C, pp. 290–98.

71. Leliveld, A., and P. Knorringa. 2018. "Frugal Innovation and Development Research." *The European Journal of Development Research* 30, no. 1, pp. 1–16.

72. Kickul, J., M. Griffiths, S. Bacq and N. Garud. 2018. "Catalyzing Social Innovation: Is Entrepreneurial Bricolage Always Good?" *Entrepreneurship & Regional Development* 30, no. 3–4, pp. 407–20.

73. Halme, M., S. Lindeman, and P. Linna. 2012. "Innovation for Inclusive Business: Intrapreneurial Bricolage in Multinational Corporation." *Journal of Management Studies* 49, pp. 743–84.

74. Gibbert, M., M. Hoegl, and L. Välikangas. 2007. "In Praise of Resource Constraints." *Sloan Management Review* 48, no. 3, pp. 15–17.

75. Keupp, M.M. and O. Gassman. 2009. "The Past and Future of International Entrepreneurship: A Review and Suggestions for Developing the Field." *Journal of Management* 35, no. 3, pp. 600–33.

76. Johansson-Sköldberg, U., J. Woodilla, and M. Çetinkaya. 2013. "Design Thinking: Past, Present and Possible Futures." *Creativity and Innovation Management* 22, pp. 121–46.

77. Bandura, A. 2007. "Much Ado Over a Faulty Conception of Perceived Self-Efficacy Grounded in Faulty Experimentation." *Journal of Social and Clinical Psychology* 26, no. 6, pp. 641–58.

78. Bandura, A. 1997. *Self-efficacy: The Exercise of Control.* New York, NY: Freeman.

79. Bandura, A. 1993. "Perceived Self-efficacy in Cognitive Development and Functioning." *Educational Psychologist* 28(2), pp. 117–48.

80. Stajkovic, A.D., and F. Luthans. 1998. "Selfefficacy and Work-Related Performance: A Meta-Analysis." *Psychological Bulletin* 124, pp. 240–61.

81. Baum, J.R., and E.A. Locke. 2004. "The Relationship of Entrepreneurial Traits, Skill, and Motivation to Subsequent Venture Growth." *Journal of Applied Psychology* 89, pp. 587–98.

82. Lent, R.W., and G. Hackett. 1987. "Career Self-efficacy: Empirical Status and Future Directions." *Journal of Vocational Behavior* 30, pp. 347–82.

83. Tierney, P., and S.M. Farmer. 2011. "Creative Self-efficacy Development and Creative Performance Over Time." *Journal of Applied Psychology* 96, no. 2, p. 277.

84. Flum, H., and A. Kaplan. 2006. "Exploratory Orientation as an Educational Goal." *Educational Psychologist* 41, pp. 99–100.

85. March, J.G. 1991. "Exploration and Exploitation in Organizational Learning." *Organization Science* 2, no. 1, pp. 71–87.

86. Kollmann, T., C. Stöckmann, and M. Kensbock. 2017. "Fear of Failure as a Mediator of the Relationship between Obstacles and Nascent Entrepreneurial Activity—An Experimental Approach." *Journal of Business Venturing* 32, no. 3, pp. 280–301.

87. Runco, M.A. (ed.). 1994. *Problem Finding, Problem Solving, and Creativity.* Norwood, NJ: Ablex.

88. Ardichvili, A., R. Cardozo, and S. Ray. 2003. "A Theory of Entrepreneurial Opportunity Identification and Development." *Journal of Business Venturing* 18, no. 1, pp. 105–123.

89. Willis, R., M. Webb, and J. Wilsdon. 2007. *The Disrupters: Lessons for Low-Carbon Innovation from the New Wave of Environmental Pioneers.* London: NESTA.

90. Ucbasaran, D., A. Lockett, M. Wright, and P. Westhead. 2003. "Entrepreneurial Founder Teams: Factors Associated with Member Entry and Exit." *Entrepreneurship Theory and Practice* 28, no. 2, pp. 107–28.

91. Runco, M.A. 2004. "Creativity." *Annual Review of Psychology* 55, pp. 657–87.

92. Hansen, D.J., G.T. Lumpkin, and G.E. Hills. 2011. "A Multidimensional Examination of a Creativity-Based Opportunity Recognition Model." *International Journal of Entrepreneurial Behaviour & Research* 17, no. 5, pp. 515–33.

93. Simon, H.A. 1969. *The Sciences of the Artificial.* Cambridge, MA: MIT Press.

94. Schön, D.A. 1983. *The Reflective Practitioner: How Professionals Think in Action.* New York, NY: Basic Books.

95. Cross, N. 1982. "Designerly Ways of Knowing." *Design Studies* 3, no. 4, pp. 221–27.

96. Kolko, J. 2015. "Design Thinking Comes of Age." *Harvard Business Review* 93, no. 9, pp. 66–71.

97. Cross, N. 2001. "Designerly Ways of Knowing: Design Discipline Versus Design Science." *Design Issues* 17, no. 3, pp. 49–55.

98. Boland, R. and F. Collopy (eds.). 2004. *Managing as Designing.* Stanford, CA: Stanford Business Books.

99. Brown, T. 2009. *Change by Design: How Design Thinking Transforms Organizations and Inspires Innovation.* New York, NY: HarperBusiness.

100. Martin, R. 2009. *The Design of Business: Why Design Thinking is the Next Competitive Advantage.* Boston, MA: Harvard Business School Press.

101. Davidsson, P., P. Steffens, and J. Fitzsimmons. 2009. "Growing Profitable or Growing from Profits: Putting the Horse in Front of the Cart?" *Journal of Business Venturing* 24, no. 4, pp. 388–406.

102. Katila, R., and S. Shane. 2005. "When does Lack of Resources Make New Firms Innovative?" *Academy of Management Journal* 48, pp. 814–29.

103. Porter, M.E., and M.R. Kramer. 2006. "Strategy and Society: The Link between Competitive Advantage and Corporate Social Responsibility." *Harvard Business Review* 84, pp. 78–92.

104. Salunke, S., J. Weerawardena, and J.R. McColl-Kennedy. 2011. "Towards a Model of Dynamic Capabilities in Innovation-Based

Competitive Strategy: Insights from Project-Oriented Service Firms." *Industrial Marketing Management* 40, no. 8, pp. 1251–1263.

105. Schyns, B., and G. von Collani. 2002. "A New Occupational Self-Efficacy Scale and Its Relation to Personality Constructs and Organizational Variables." *European Journal of Work and Organizational Psychology* 11, pp. 219–41.

106. Turturea, R., J. Jansen, and I. Verheul. 2015. "Top Management Team Attributes, Bricolage and Ambidexterity in SMEs." *Academy of Management Annual Meeting Proceedings* 1.

CHAPTER 8

Walking a Tightrope between Business and Sustainable Development: A Social Enterprise Marketing Perspective

Chinmoy Bandyopadhyay and Subhasis Ray

Social entrepreneurs (SEs) address sustainability-related challenges by adopting appropriate revenue-generating business models. However, combining sustainability and business-related aspects poses unique challenges for them. While these challenges are well documented, research has not adequately described the role of marketing in achieving sustainable development goals through social entrepreneurship. In this chapter, we discuss how marketing is important for social enterprises, what challenges it poses, and how they are addressed. Using information from past literature on social enterprise marketing, we present a summary model on the strategies that social enterprises adopt to counter these challenges. The chapter adds to the discussion on sustainable development and social enterprise marketing by illustrating that SEs (a) attract market attention by pairing up social-ecological impact stories with high-quality offerings; (b) try to empower, educate, and engage their stakeholders to make their own choice; and (c) maintain transparency by sharing details of their business. Our findings thus contribute to the discussion on how marketing and social entrepreneurial business models can help in achieving sustainable development goals.

Keywords: social entrepreneurship; marketing; sustainable development

Introduction

The 17 Sustainable Development Goals (SDGs) are set to tackle the pressing social and environmental challenges of our world by 2030. While governmental efforts to address developmental challenges in a country are expected and well recognized, it is now clear that other stakeholders like business and nonprofit organizations need to come forward to address the SDGs.[1-3] However, many such approaches are often short-lived and rarely succeed in achieving the desired results.[4,5] This is partly because many development projects rely on donor-dependent and time-bound grants or donations. Reliance on such external funding also limits the scalability (growth potential) of the solution. For example, a donor-funded project to provide solar-powered machines to village artisans often fails to consider maintenance and servicing of such machines beyond the life of the project. Such machines, once damaged, lie unused due to lack of (affordable) spare parts. Moreover, the recipient community loses trust in such interventions, making future projects unviable in such a region. Hence, organizations are increasingly shifting from nonprofit approaches to financially self-sufficient approaches.[6] Researchers have pointed out that many unresolved social and environmental issues present business opportunities for entrepreneurs to create both shareholder and sustainable value. According to them, businesses should address sustainability concerns profitably, rather than treating them as legal requirements.[7-9] However, business organizations are still treating sustainability initiatives as a way to hide their unsustainable business practices and to build a positive image among stakeholders. At the same time, those who tried their hands in combining business and SDGs failed largely because of their superficial and cherry-picking approach.[10-12]

Social entrepreneurs (SEs) are the organizations that bring social and business objectives together in their business model.[13-15] Unlike commercial organizations that typically focus on profitability, sales growth, and share-holder benefits, SEs go beyond economic returns and aim to create social and environmental values.[16,17] Past research has emphasized the role of SEs in addressing social issues such as unemployment and poverty as well as environmental issues like air pollution and waste disposal.[18-20] In the context of the example of solar-powered machines explained earlier, an SE may build an affordable subscription model for supplying such machines to rural artisans. Artisans pay a monthly subscription to use the solar-powered machines for their work. Such a model allows the SE to generate long-term working capital to provide for machine maintenance while en-suring community members' understanding that they are responsible and accountable for safeguarding and maintaining their assets.

SEs combine competing institutional logics–social and economic–and continuously balance between their profit and purpose components.[21,22] In our example, the SE cannot charge too low a subscription for renting out machines in order to be helpful to the artisans and go bankrupt in the process. On the other hand, if the subscription rate is too high, not many villagers will be interested, putting the entire business model at risk. This tension creates challenges for SEs while marketing such products and services.

Marketing is mainly defined as the creation of consumer value by ad-dressing their functional and emotional needs.[23] However, following only the mainstream marketing approaches cannot guarantee effectiveness on both sustainability and business fronts. According to the hypothetical ex-ample presented in this chapter, SEs need to do two things: (1) market their machines as useful, functional, and low cost and (2) promote the use of renewable solar power as an alternative to fossil fuel–based power gen-eration. This marketing challenge poses a threat to the continued survival of SEs in the marketplace. Although existing literature adequately cap-tures this issue, what has been ignored is how SEs address these issues.[24] We attempt to fill this gap by documenting how SEs manage the trade-offs and survive in the marketplace. This is important because similar kinds of moral dilemmas are also found in other areas like marketing of ecotourism[25,26] or sustainable fashion marketing.[27,28] Therefore, the dis-cussion on the duality between market and sustainability needs and how they are addressed in SEs is both timely and relevant.

The rest of the chapter proceeds as follows. First, we turn to SE marketing literature to understand the dilemma they face while taking marketing decisions and executing them. The subsequent section presents a model demonstrating the strategies to address these dilemmas. The final section summarizes the key points of this chapter.

Social Enterprise Marketing Challenges

SEs require marketing to promote both their products and the socio-environmental aspects of their mission. Hence, marketing carries great importance for SEs.[29,30] For instance, many SEs address environmental issues by upcycling waste into marketable products. Therefore, the survival of SEs appears to reside in their capability to adopt a marketing strategy that can generate sales revenue. However, SEs faces a dilemma between remaining mission-consistent and being professional, market driven, and competent. Some SEs think marketing activities go against the values of SEs and are intrusive and exploitative, which dissuades them from pursuing marketing activities wholeheartedly.[31,32] At the same time, too much involvement in marketing can also cause mission drift or might position them as businesslike or commercial among stakeholders.[33] Moreover, the existence of social and business goals in SEs poses challenges when they market their offerings to consumers. Some consumers display higher interest on aspects such as quality, price, and delivery of the products/services rather than on the social and environmental benefits espoused via marketing initiatives. Others tend to favor SEs as they see them reflecting, and in alignment with, their own worldview. SEs, therefore, find it difficult to decide which aspect to highlight and communicate more to the target audience.[34,35] In the subsequent sections, we will outline the dilemmas faced by the SEs while pursuing their marketing activities.

To Shout Out or to Whisper

The first challenge is related to the adoption of marketing activities in SEs. Marketing activities are often misunderstood and half-heartedly adopted by SEs, which often leads to suboptimal results out of the marketing activities. They do not see the need to market their offerings too

much, as they think they have carefully and responsibly produced offerings that should sell themselves. They expect consumers to find/reach
them to purchase their products. In addition, some SEs prefer keeping
a low profile and seldom market themselves as "too successful" to avoid
funders' scrutiny. Funding agencies may not be willing to provide additional second-round funding to organizations that seem to do well
by themselves. SEs would exclude themselves from rigorous marketing
activities based on the assumption that they would be commercialized
and thus might become unacceptable to the general public.[36,37] However,
marketing communication to both market and non-market stakeholders
is fundamental to SEs' survival.[38]

To Be Seen as Professional or Idealistic

SEs often lack the resources needed for running their operations–be it
financial resources or human resources. SEs often find themselves caught
between the need to be seen as professional/competent and a socially beneficial entity when communicating to customers, investors, and employees.[39] Certification or logo, depicting the social or environmental impact
of SEs, often positively influences the purchase decision of consumers.[40,41] Some consumers purchase products of SEs mainly to contribute
to social and environmental welfare. They consider it as an opportunity
to make a change in the life of the impoverished and the needy through a
purchase.[42,43] Therefore, SEs highlight they are certified, signaling to consumers they are a fully functioning and social value–creating enterprise.[41]
However, some SEs tend to hide the social and environmental aspects of
their mission because exhibiting those aspects often creates an impression
that the offerings are of poor quality.[44,45] Moreover, highlighting sustainability aspects, while it can attract prosocial-ecological consumers, cannot guarantee consumer loyalty or repeat purchase.[46] Lee, Zailani, and
Rahman[47] show how customers appreciate products made by the prison
inmates and yet their purchase or repeat purchase decisions are based on
the quality or the performance of the product.

In addition, SEs often find it difficult to motivate the employees to
appreciate the organizational objectives. This gives rise to tension and
conflicting mindsets and objectives among various stakeholder groups

within the organization and associated external entities the organization deals with in the course of business.[48,49] The tension between these groups may influence an SE's performance negatively. Battilana and Dorado[50] reported a case of a microfinance organization, where the conflict between two groups—one driven by financial and profit-maximization considerations and the other subscribing to altruistic, socially conscious aspects of the organizational goals—created problems. Without clear communication, it will be difficult for SEs to attract and retain current employees and attract new talent.

Finally, funders or investors need to be assured that they will get their money back within the stipulated timeframe for repaying the amount funded. In addition, there are impact investors who look beyond the business plan and model and evaluate SEs by their social impact model.

To Disrupt or to Play to the Gallery

The third marketing challenge relates to new product innovations and shaping consumer behavior. SEs create innovative solutions for both sustainability challenges and consumer problems. However, the majority of these radical offerings are ahead of their time and therefore do not have a readily available market. Such products are less known and mostly ignored by consumers[51,52]; for instance, shopping bags made out of waste materials are a relatively new concept for consumers and may attract fewer buyers because of the lack of visibility or awareness about such a product in the market. The survival and growth of SEs depend, on one hand, on the acceptance and support from external stakeholders who own the required resources, and, on the other, they have to remain true to their radical or disruptive values to create the intended difference in the society.[53] Therefore, SEs often take a call on whether to remain completely innovation-driven or capitulate to market signals or diktats like a regular business.

To Be a Mass or Niche Brand

This challenge refers to the issue of scaling up the sales of a socially innovative and responsible product. SEs often look to differentiate themselves through their cause and the nature of their products. However, in this process of differentiating, they often find themselves in a niche kind of positioning. Consequently, only those consumers who identify with the mission of the SE purchase their products.[54] It then becomes a challenge for SEs to come out of that niche in order to attract mainstream consumers. As SEs have a mandate to create a positive social impact on a large scale, they are expected to reach more and more people. However, SEs often do not endorse push marketing approach, which makes it more difficult for them to scale and become a mass marketer.

To Walk Alone or Walk Together

The next marketing challenge is one of partnerships for distribution and cobranding for better brand visibility. Building relationships with key stakeholders is integral in diffusing the innovative solutions that SEs offer.[55] Given the absence of internal marketing skills and a lack of financial and human resources, many SEs rely upon partnerships with other organizations. Such partnerships could be with leading retailers for better market reach or even cobranding with established market players. Such partnerships provide SEs legitimacy, credibility, and trust in a market where they are unknown entities. However, SE networking processes are different from other kinds of business relationships or networking in the sense that they often do not partner with those who are not aligned sufficiently with their social and environmental values.

To understand how SEs address these marketing dilemmas and promote their offerings and cause, we turn to the existing work on SE marketing, and based on our review we present the following summary model.

Summary Model: Toward Combining Business and Sustainability Aspects

As discussed in this chapter, SEs have to showcase their social impact to justify their existence. Some authors argue that SEs are already differentiated and branded in the sense that they are doing good to the society. The only thing they have to do is to communicate their social welfare aspect. Positioning the social welfare elements in the mind of the potential customers can be one option. However, as mentioned earlier, some customers are not that interested in the social welfare aspect. Rather, they are more concerned about the attributes and quality of the offerings. In the following model, we depict how SEs deal with the trade-offs ingrained in their marketing activities (Figure 8.1).

Consumer Advocacy Marketing

SEs try to be professional in their approach and provide quality products to remain in the marketplace while keeping sustainability as their guiding framework.[46] The value-laden nature of SEs often gives rise to challenges related to trust and credibility. Although there are consumers who can pay premium prices for the SE offerings, they are skeptical about the claims made by the SEs. Therefore, SEs continuously endeavor to prove the authenticity of their offerings to the consumers by providing information about raw materials and their producers and production processes. Some even invite consumers to see the rigorous production process and spread the word about SE offerings. Such a peer-to-peer marketing approach appears to work and sends out a credible message to consumers.[56] Engaging consumers in the production process and spreading the message through word-of-mouth help customers recognize the link between marketing and the SE's mission. Such collaboration or co-creation lowers skepticism among SEs and their clientele.[57]

Customized Marketing Communication

SEs use different marketing communication methods for customers, employees, producers, and investors. As discussed previously, different consumers respond differently to SE offerings. For some, product-related issues are far more important than the underlying sustainability issues. Others want to contribute to sustainability movements through purchases. However, in between these two groups, some consumers support the mission of the SEs but do not want to compromise with the quality of products. Therefore, the success of an SE's marketing campaign rests largely on its capability to formulate and convey messages that signal its worthiness to these different consumer groups.[24] For example, SEs with sustainable fashion products emphasize their ethical and "look and

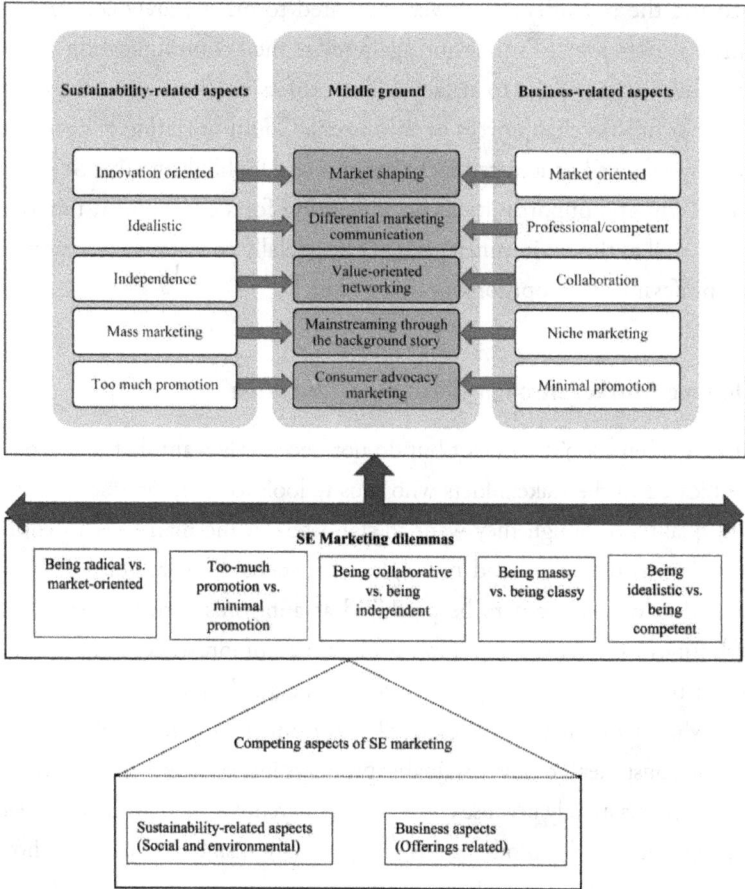

Figure 8.1 Summary model: strategies to address social enterprise marketing challenges

Source: Developed by the authors based on literature review on social enterprise marketing.

feel" aspects, or a combination of both, while targeting different types of consumers.[27]

For impact investors, SEs showcase the difference they make to the life of the beneficiaries or the quality of the environment. When it comes to traditional investors, SEs show their competence as a business entity that is socially and environmentally responsible.[58]

During recruitment, SEs look for people with skill and sensitivity to the cause they are propagating. However, it is challenging to attract skilled professionals to work for SEs given that SEs are usually of small size and the pay offered is lower compared to other purely commercial entities. Therefore, SEs time and again revise their communication strategies and hiring policies to attract skilled professionals to work with them as either full-time employees or volunteers. Communicating to potential employees a well-articulated set of benefits and highlighting that SEs offer a platform and opportunity to do something for a community, the society, as well as the environment will attract socially conscious and committed professionals to opt for working in SEs.[59]

Shaping Market through Consumer Education

SEs are often activists at heart but do not necessarily want that to be communicated to the stakeholders who mostly look for only product features and quality. Although they want to stand out in the market as an entity adhering to the values and principles of sustainable or responsible business, they do not want to be perceived as antagonistic to the key tenets of business. Consumer education is often a common strategy adopted by them: role of sustainability, how the SE is actually making a difference, and what it means to be a responsible consumer. Another problem is to get the consumers to buy sustainable products instead of existing products. This happens mainly because customers are psychologically attuned to keep buying only regular products and are generally disinclined to know how sustainable products taste, look, and feel. For example, consumers who are used to commercially produced, sugar-added honey may not know how natural honey looks or tastes and may even find the taste awkward. One way to deal with this issue is to educate consumers about authentic products. SEs repeatedly communicate the sustainability aspects to persuade their stakeholders to put in extra efforts.[60]

Mainstreaming through a Background Story

Today, customers have less time and interest in knowing the technical details about sustainability and the products and initiatives built around those technicalities. The social or environmental benefits are generally intangible and can be felt only in the long term, but consumers look for only individual-level, short-term solutions. Any promotional campaign or literature propagating the social and environmental impact that an SE wants to create has to be appealing, short, and relevant.[59] Convincing the target clientele about the impact of social and environmental problems, especially at an individual level, is no easy task. Thus, making these broader aspects personally relevant takes special skills and smart marketing communication efforts. SEs achieve this by convincing consumers that they can make a difference in someone's life or do their bit to save the environment by buying its line of products. For example, SEs selling bags made out of recycled plastic talk of how the product protects the environment and that it reduces pollution, consumes fewer natural resources, and lowers the potential of natural disasters and that all of these ultimately only benefit the customer.

Value-Oriented Networking

SEs look for partners who share the same values in regard to social and environmental welfare. As like-minded people with prosocial-ecological values are often scattered and hard to track, SEs actively use online communities and social media to reach them.[61]

Summary

Achieving SDGs will require multiparty, multisystem approaches. SEs play an important role by combining sustainable products and services with a viable business model. In doing so, they face specific marketing challenges related to communication, product quality, consumer behavior, partnerships, and scaling. This chapter aimed to highlight the tensions that SEs face while promoting their cause, the range of sustainable products they offer, and their ultimate goal of convincing potential customers that buying their products is good not only for them but also for the society and environment. We attempted to come up with possible solutions to this conundrum by asking what kind of SE marketing approach has the best chance to effectively emphasize and convince potential consumers about the sustainability-related aspects of their product offerings during marketing campaigns. After discussing the challenges, we presented a summary model, grounded in the literature related to SE marketing. Generally, consumers of SE products do not want to compromise on product quality and may be willing to even pay more. On the other hand, SEs do not want to compromise on the safety of the environment and the well-being of the society. Therefore, SEs have to balance between the present need of the consumers and the long-term needs of both the society and the environment. They achieve this goal by finding a middle ground, which entails educating customers, adopting professional marketing techniques, and creating customized communication for various stakeholders.

As sustainable consumerism is increasingly becoming a norm and many organizations are planning to create green products and services, the challenges and learnings from SE marketing will be helpful to both academicians and business owners. This chapter calls managers and entrepreneurs dealing with sustainability-related products and services to rethink their marketing strategy, keeping in mind the need to accord importance to both sustainability and market needs in business development plans.

Questions

1. What differentiates social enterprise marketing from traditional marketing approaches?

2. Thinking as a social entrepreneur or senior executive, how would you resolve the moral tensions ingrained in social enterprise marketing? Suggest the best course of option.

3. In your opinion, how can social enterprises mainstream their background (social-ecological) stories?

References

4. Sachs, J., G. Schmidt-Traub, C. Kroll, G. Lafortune, and G. Fuller. 2019. *Sustainable Development Report 2019.* New York, NY: Bertelsmann Stiftung and Sustainable Development Solutions Network (SDSN).

5. Damtoft, J.S., J. Lukasik, D. Herfort, D. Sorrentino, and E.M. Gartner. 2008. "Sustainable Development and Climate Change Initiatives." *Cement and Concrete Research* 38, no. 2, pp. 115–27.

6. Preuss, L. 2009. "Addressing Sustainable Development through Public Procurement: The Case of Local Government." *Supply Chain Management: An International Journal* 14, no. 3, pp. 213–23.

7. Dale, A., and L. Newman. 2008. "Social Capital: A Necessary and Sufficient Condition for Sustainable Community Development?" *Community Development Journal* 45, no. 1, pp. 5–21.

8. Hall, J., and H. Vredenburg. 2003. "The Challenge of Innovating for Sustainable Development." *MIT Sloan Management Review* 45, no. 1, pp. 61–68.

9. Morris, M.H., J.W. Webb, and R.J. Franklin. 2011. "Understanding the Manifestation of Entrepreneurial Orientation in the Nonprofit Context." *Entrepreneurship Theory and Practice* 35, no. 5, pp. 947–71.

10. Bocken, N.M., S.W. Short, P. Rana, and S. Evans. 2014. "A Literature and Practice Review to Develop Sustainable Business Model Archetypes." *Journal of Cleaner Production* 65, pp. 42–56.

11. Hart, S.L., and M.B. Milstein. 2003. "Creating Sustainable Value." *Academy of Management Perspectives* 17, no. 2, pp. 56–67.

12. Porter, M.E., and M.R. Kramer. 2011. "Creating Shared Value." *Harvard Business Review* 89, no. 1/2, pp. 62–77.

13. Aid, C. 2004. "Behind the Mask: The Real Face of Corporate Social Responsibility." https://baierle.files.wordpress.com/2007/11/behind-mask.pdf, (accessed January 17, 2020).

14. Ambec, S., and P. Lanoie. 2008. "Does It Pay to Be Green? A Systematic Overview." *The Academy of Management Perspectives* 22, no. 4, pp. 45–62.

15. Redman, A. 2018. "Harnessing the Sustainable Development Goals for Businesses: A Progressive Framework for Action." *Business Strategy & Development* 1, no. 4, pp. 230–43.

16. Mair, J., and I. Marti. 2006. "Social Entrepreneurship Research: A Source of Explanation, Prediction, and Delight." *Journal of World Business*, 41, no. 1, pp. 36–44.

17. Santos, F.M. 2012. "A Positive Theory of Social Entrepreneurship." *Journal of Business Ethics* 111, no. 3, pp. 335–51.

18. Zahra, S.A., and M. Wright. 2016. "Understanding the Social Role of Entrepreneurship." *Journal of Management Studies* 53, no. 4, pp. 610–29.

19. Grimes, M.G., J.S. McMullen, T.J. Vogus, and T.L. Miller. 2013. "Studying the Origins of Social Entrepreneurship: Compassion and the Role of Embedded Agency." *Academy of Management Review* 38, no. 3, pp. 460–63.

20. Perrini, F., and C. Vurro. 2006. "Social Entrepreneurship: Innovation and Social Change across Theory and Practice." In *Social Entrepreneurship*. London, UK: Palgrave Macmillan, pp. 57–85.

21. Langdon, D. and I. Burkett. 2004. "Defining Social Enterprise Enterprising Ways to Address Long-Term Unemployment", Book One: The New Mutualism Series, PI Productions, Palmwoods Queensland.

22. Seelos, C., and J. Mair. 2005. "Social Entrepreneurship: Creating New Business Models to Serve the Poor." *Business Horizons* 48, no. 3, pp. 241–46.

23. Littlewood, D., and D. Holt. 2018. "Social Entrepreneurship in South Africa: Exploring the Influence of Environment." *Business & Society* 57, no. 3, pp. 525–61.

24. Besley, T., and M. Ghatak. 2017. "Profit with Purpose? A Theory of Social Enterprise." *American Economic Journal: Economic Policy* 9, no. 3, pp. 19–58.

25. Doherty, B., H. Haugh, and F. Lyon. 2014. "Social Enterprises as Hybrid Organizations: A Review and Research Agenda." *International Journal of Management Reviews* 16, no. 4, pp. 417–36.

26. Armstrong, G.M., P. Kotler, M.J. Harker, and R. Brennan. 2018. *Marketing: An Introduction*. London, UK: Pearson.

27. Bandyopadhyay, C., and S. Ray. 2019a. "Social Enterprise Marketing: Review of Literature and Future Research Agenda." *Marketing Intelligence & Planning* 38, no. 1, pp. 121–35.

28. Font, X., and S. McCabe. 2017. "Sustainability and Marketing in Tourism: Its Contexts, Paradoxes, Approaches, Challenges and Potential." *Journal of Sustainable Tourism* 25, no.7, pp. 869–83.

29. Cowburn, B., C. Moritz, C. Birrell, G. Grimsditch, and A. Abdulla. 2018. "Can Luxury and Environmental Sustainability Co-Exist? Assessing the Environmental Impact of Resort Tourism on Coral Reefs in the Maldives." *Ocean & Coastal Management* 158, pp. 120–27.

30. Bandyopadhyay, C. and S. Ray. 2020. Finding the Sweet Spot between Ethics and Aesthetics: A Social Entrepreneurial Perspective to Sustainable Fashion Brand (Juxta) Positioning. *Journal of Global Marketing*, pp. 1–19.

31. Evans, S., and A. Peirson-Smith. 2018. "The Sustainability Word Challenge: Exploring Consumer Interpretations of Frequently Used

Words to Promote Sustainable Fashion Brand Behaviors and Imagery." *Journal of Fashion Marketing and Management* 22, no. 2, pp. 252–69.

32. Mallin, M.L., and T.A. Finkle. 2007. "Social Entrepreneurship and Direct Marketing." *Direct Marketing: An International Journal* 1, no. 2, pp. 68–77.

33. Srivetbodee, S., B. Igel, and S. Kraisornsuthasinee. 2017. "Creating Social Value Through Social Enterprise Marketing: Case Studies from Thailand's Food-Focused Social Entrepreneurs." *Journal of Social Entrepreneurship* 8, no. 2, pp. 201–24.

34. Bull, M. 2007. "'Balance': The Development of a Social Enterprise Business Performance Analysis Tool." *Social Enterprise Journal* 3, no. 1, pp. 49–66.

35. Powell, M., and S.P. Osborne. 2015. "Can Marketing Contribute to Sustainable Social Enterprise?" *Social Enterprise Journal* 11, no. 1, pp. 24–46.

36. Ramus, T., and A. Vaccaro. 2017. "Stakeholders Matter: How Social Enterprises Address Mission Drift." *Journal of Business Ethics* 143, no. 2, pp. 307–22.

37. Mitchell, A., J. Madill, and S. Chreim. 2016. "Social Enterprise Dualities: Implications for Social Marketing." *Journal of Social Marketing* 6, no. 2, pp. 169–92.

38. Roundy, P.T. 2017. "Doing Good While Serving Customers: Charting the Social Entrepreneurship and Marketing Interface." *Journal of Research in Marketing and Entrepreneurship* 19, no. 2, pp. 105–24.

39. Mitchell, A., J. Madill, and S. Chreim. 2015. "Marketing and Social Enterprises: Implications for Social Marketing." *Journal of Social Marketing* 5, no. 4, pp. 285–306.

40. Peattie, K., and A. Morley. 2008. "Eight Paradoxes of the Social Enterprise Research Agenda." *Social Enterprise Journal* 4, no. 2, pp. 91–107.

41. Hati, S.R.H., and A. Idris. 2019. "The Role of Leader vs Organisational Credibility in Islamic Social Enterprise Marketing Communication." *Journal of Islamic Marketing* 10, no. 4, pp. 1128–1150.

42. Chang, T.Y., J. Hu, and H.R. Wong. 2012. "Dual-value Driven Parallel Operating Systems and Interrelations of Resources in Social Enterprise." *International Journal of Business and Management* 7, no. 22, pp. 86–99.

43. Casidy, R., S.R.H. Hati, and A. Idris. 2014. "Antecedents of Customers' Intention to Support Islamic Social Enterprises in Indonesia." *Asia Pacific Journal of Marketing and Logistics*, 26, no. 5, pp. 707–737.

44. Choi, G.H., and J. Kim. 2016. "Effects of Displaying Social Enterprise Certification Information on Consumers' Product Evaluations and Purchase Intentions." *Journal of Global Scholars of Marketing Science* 26, no. 2, pp. 185–97.

45. Hibbert, S.A., G. Hogg, and T. Quinn. 2005. "Social Entrepreneurship: Understanding Consumer Motives for Buying the Big Issue." *Journal of Consumer Behaviour: An International Research Review* 4, no. 3, pp. 159–72.

46. Tsai, J.M., S.W. Hung, and T.T. Yang. 2020. "In Pursuit of Goodwill? The Cross-level Effects of Social Enterprise Consumer Behaviours." *Journal of Business Research* 109, pp. 350–61.

47. Bonar, I., and P.S. Karlsson. 2019. "Marketing Scottish Social Enterprises Using a Label?" *Social Enterprise Journal* 15, no. 3, pp. 339–57.

48. Ridley-Duff, R., and C. Southcombe. 2012. "The Social Enterprise Mark: A Critical Review of Its Conceptual Dimensions." *Social Enterprise Journal* 8, no. 3, pp. 178–200.

49. Casno, K., D. Šķiltere, and B. Sloka. 2019. "Factors that Motivate Latvian Consumers to Purchase Products and Services from Social Enterprises in Latvia: The Case of Socially Responsible Consumption." *European Integration Studies*, no. 13, pp. 90–99.

50. Lee, Y.N., S. Zailani, and M.K. Rahman. 2020. "Determinants of Customer Intention to Purchase Social Enterprise Products-A Structural Model Analysis." *Journal of Social Entrepreneurship*, pp. 1–22.

51. Smith, W.K., and M.W. Lewis. 2011. "Toward a Theory of Paradox: A Dynamic Equilibrium Model of Organizing." *Academy of Management Review* 36, no. 2, pp. 381–403.

52. Tracey, P., and N. Phillips. 2007. "The Distinctive Challenge of Educating Social Entrepreneurs: A Postscript and Rejoinder to the Special Issue on Entrepreneurship Education." *Academy of Management Learning & Education* 6, no. 2, pp. 264–71.

53. Battilana, J., and S. Dorado. 2010. "Building Sustainable Hybrid Organizations: The Case of Commercial Microfinance Organizations." *Academy of Management Journal* 53, no. 6, pp. 1419–1440.

54. Tkacz, M. 2016. "New Generation of Social Entrepreneurs: Exploratory Research and Cross Case Study Analysis of New Generation of Social Enterprises." *Ekonomia Społeczna* no. 2, pp. 20–37.

55. Moizer, J., and P. Tracey. 2010. "Strategy Making in Social Enterprise: The Role of Resource Allocation and Its Effects on Organizational Sustainability." *Systems Research and Behavioral Science* 27, no. 3, pp. 252–66.

56. Wilson, F. and J.E. Post. 2013. "Business Models for People, Planet (& Profits): Exploring the Phenomena of Social Business, A Market-Based Approach to Social Value Creation." *Small Business Economics* 40, no. 3, pp. 715–37.

57. Putra, F.H., and F.F. Dewanto. 2020. "Customer Perception Analysis of the Social Business Branding of Online Taxi in Jakarta." *Asian Journal of Business and Entrepreneurship*, 1, no. 1, pp. 42–52.

58. Phillips, W., E.A. Alexander, and H. Lee. 2019. "Going It Alone Won't Work! The Relational Imperative for Social Innovation in Social Enterprises." *Journal of Business Ethics* 156, no. 2, pp. 315–31.

59. Sigala, M. 2019. "A Market Approach to Social Value Co-creation: Findings and Implications from 'Mageires' the Social Restaurant." *Marketing Theory* 19, no. 1, pp. 27–45.

60. Bandyopadhyay, C., and S. Ray. 2019b. "Responsible Marketing: Can Social Enterprises Show the Way?" *Journal of Nonprofit & Public Sector Marketing* 31, no. 2, pp. 164–83.

61. Smith, B.R., M.L. Cronley, and T.F. Barr. 2012. "Funding Implications of Social Enterprise: The Role of Mission Consistency, Entrepreneurial Competence, and Attitude toward Social Enterprise on Donor Behavior." *Journal of Public Policy & Marketing* 31, no. 1, pp. 142–57.

62. Roundy, P. 2014. "Doing Good by Telling Stories: Emotion in Social Entrepreneurship Communication." *Journal of Small Business Strategy* 24, no. 2, pp. 41–68.

63. Hamby, A., M. Pierce, and D. Brinberg. 2017. "Solving Complex Problems: Enduring Solutions through Social Entrepreneurship, Community Action, and Social Marketing." *Journal of Macromarketing* 37, no. 4, pp. 369–80.

64. Abedin, B., B. Maloney, and J. Watson. 2019. "Benefits and Challenges Associated with Using Online Communities by Social Enterprises: A Thematic Analysis of Qualitative Interviews." *Journal of Social Entrepreneurship*, pp. 1–22. doi:10.1080/19420676.2019.1683879.

CHAPTER 9

Developing Positive Synergy

Daniela Ortiz

Developing strategies to create positive synergy within a team or organization entails asking from a managerial perspective, "What can be done to make the most out of the people who constitute an organization?" The search for positive synergy is also the search for efficient work processes. The way we resolve the problem of inefficiency in the use of the human factor will greatly depend on how crucial we consider the quality of human interactions to be in achieving corporate objectives. In this sense, positive synergy seems to be related to sustainability, especially if we consider the fact that the long-term performance of a company will greatly depend on the outcomes of work processes in which human beings willingly and continually interact with each other to achieve a common objective.

From a humanistic management perspective (Melé, 2003, 2009), which "emphasizes the human condition and is oriented to the development of human virtue, in all its forms, to its fullest extent" (Melé, 2003: 79), organizations are seen as communities of persons united by a common goal or purpose of the firm (Canals, 2010; Melé, 2012). Seen from this humanistic perspective, communities—as are all groups of persons and thus teams—will serve as a means to achieve a goal intrinsic to them, especially and also for the reason that they are an integral part of the social structure. In addition, such communities create real bonds between people, which as such can support or hinder the development and self-actualization of individual members of the community. In this sense, when managing groups, focus will not be solely on efficiently achieving a goal (i.e., high-quality decision-making, development of effective strate-gies, etc.) but also on quality of the bonds, or interactions, emerging from the group process. It then becomes important to ask whether these bonds support or hinder the growth and self-actualization of people who may be community members or working for an organization.

The Concept of Community of Persons and a Common Good

From a social philosophy perspective, mainly based on Christian Social Doctrine and a personalist philosophy, social structures have an element of unity (i.e., a type of bond), which is denominated as the common good. Following the definition of Russell Hittinger (2012),

> when two or more persons engage in a common structure of ac-tion for a common end, and where the common action (what Aristotle would call the 'form of order') is an intrinsic good, we have something like a common good. The union of the members in common activity is not an end that comes after some other purpose but is the good being continuously aimed at and sought. The scholastic philosophers called such a union *bonum commune*, always in the singular. The salient mark of a *bonum commune* is that it cannot, just as such, be distributed or divided in exchange but only participated by its members. (4)

The Swiss philosopher Martin Rhonheimer (2010) considers that the constitution of this bond is due to the social nature of human beings. The individual sees himself or herself in perpetual confrontation with other individuals, who, like himself or herself, are striving to satisfy their (often similar) material and spiritual needs. In this interaction, specific structures of collaboration emerge to fulfill these needs. These structures correspond to the rational, or human, way of solving material needs, a manner marked specifically by social interaction and dialogue. This ra-tional process begins with the recognition of the "other" as someone of "his or her kind" or as "his or her equal" (as another "self") and thus as someone who deserves respect and whose personal development is at least desired. The bond that thus emerges between individuals is an expression of what can be called "natural friendship or solidarity." It is the origin and the matrix of social interaction.

Managing social interactions will thus be related to formulating and discovering the common goals that constitute the work relationship and also leading every member to use his or her resources and capabilities in the best way to achieve this common objective. Seeing the firm as a community of persons implies the existence of this common objective, or business purpose, which is known and actively pursued by all the constituents of the firm, especially by the management as coordinator of resources. As Melé (2012: 98) writes, "a community has common goals which are in benefit of the whole community. They become 'common good'. Cooperating to achieve them is an ethical requirement of each member of the community. Managers should foster cooperation in common goals within the organization. This is an essential responsibility of the executive within an organization."

Creating Synergy: A Behavioral View

The Greek noun *synergya* means "joint work, working together, cooperation, assistance, help" and comes from *synergos*, that is, "working together." In modern organizational and management science, the concept describes the outcome of human interaction in work, whereas synergy is "created" when cooperation between a group of persons, or companies as in the case of M&As, results in a better outcome than the individual's effort alone. In other words, when synergy has been created, the sum of elements has created more value than each part counted individually. Larson (2010: 5) defines synergy as

> *a gain in performance that is attributable in some way to group interaction. More specifically, a group is said to exhibit synergy when it is able to accomplish collectively something that could not reasonably have been achieved by any simple combination of individual member efforts. Synergy is thus an emergent phenomenon rooted in group interaction.*

Thus, synergy describes a performance gain that is due to group interaction, that is, when individuals work together as a team. Larson stresses that this definition is in contrast to the understanding of synergy as a mere subjective concept that is based on positive feelings, emotions, or attitudes arising from group interactions. He writes, "synergy is not determined by assessing members' feelings or emotional reactions to their group experience. Nor does it depend on subjective ratings of group process." Instead, "it is determined by comparing a group's observed performance to standards derived from the performance of individuals who work alone at the same task" (348). In this understanding of human interaction, not even the existence of a real relationship between individuals performing a task is necessary, only a minimal mutual awareness of their interdependence in achieving a common goal. A group is defined as

> a collection of individuals who are mutually aware of, and at least minimally dependent upon, one another. Their mutual awareness includes being cognizant of their interdependence. This, more than anything else, is what makes a group a psychological entity, not merely a physical or statistical one. Their interdependence is rooted in a shared purpose, objective, or goal that together they are trying to achieve. It arises from the behavioral requirements of the task(s) they must perform in pursuit of the goal. (20)

Thus, what makes a group or a team working together is the common objective for which an interaction has been agreed upon, either by the members of the group themselves or by someone else, that is, higher management. Relationships are per se not considered; it only matters how behavior changes in the context of team work and how interaction leads to a desired goal. The emphasis here is on individual behavior, which is considered to be different, and more effective and productive, when that individual performs as part of a group than working alone. For Larson, and the research line following this conception of group work, synergy can be either weak or strong. Weak synergy is "a group performance that exceeds the performance of the typical group member when working alone" (6). Strong synergy is, on the other hand, "group performance that exceeds the solo performance of even the best group member" (7).

One type of experiment used to test this kind of group synergy entails comparing how individual members solve problems when working alone compared to working within a group. When it comes to decision-making activities, as Larson (2007) proposes, each individual member of a group solves a given problem according to his or her individual heuristic. Interaction consists mainly in the communication of individual outcomes, which will be adapted by other group members if considered more valuable, whereas the metrics used for value evaluation are defined in advance. By adapting these partial outcomes and introducing them into their own heuristic model, the other members "improve" and "build up" on the knowledge of other team members. The individual members continue doing what they would have done if working alone; the only difference is that the information they need to process a solution is enriched by the input of other team members. At the end of the process, the chosen alternative is the highest-value outcome. A strong synergy is said to be achieved if the same outcome would have been achieved by the "best team member," only that it is supposed that the team has done so more efficiently and in less time.

Larson's account of group synergy seems valuable because it proposes a concrete baseline by which to evaluate the additional value of group interaction. However, from an anthropological and humanistic perspective, it is unsatisfying. On the one hand, it lacks dynamism, as it reduces the content of interaction to one or just a few observable variables (communication of outcomes), and it does not consider how this interaction can actually change individual behaviors in a more significant way. Working or professional relationships per se are not considered by this approach as roles that require distinct behaviors. As Cardona and Wilkinson (2006) describe it, individual members are taken to be "working 'on their own in company', like workers on an assembly line," each fulfilling a different subtask, as "the team members' aptitudes and positions emerge but do not effectively engage with one another in pursuit of the common goal" (1). From a humanistic perspective, what is missing is the personal implication of each member in acquiring the common good.

A More Humanistic View: Quality of Personal Interactions and Interpersonal Trust as Factors of Successful Collaboration

A different contribution by Raes et al. (2011) gives importance not only to individual roles, that is, expected behaviors of each group member in a particular context, but also to the content of interaction (the relational role) for the outcome of the process. Raes et al. focus on the interaction between the Top Management Team (TMT) in rather large, complex companies and Middle Managers (MMs) in the process of strategy formulation and implementation. Their contribution describes how quality in strategic decision-making and in implementation, and thus organizational performance, can improve by managing different elements of what they call the "interface model of TMT and MM." This interface consists in episodes of contact, in which information exchange and mutual influencing take place, and periods of no contact, in which each member fulfills his or her role according to what has been experienced in the episodes of contact. In this model, organizational performance greatly depends on the behavior of the members of the group during the episodes of contact, when they enact the so-called relational role. Summarizing the authors' research paper, the quality of interpersonal interaction will depend on two basic elements, cognitive flexibility during information exchange and a mutual influencing based on integrative bargaining. These concepts are adapted from the fields of communication studies and strategic management literature.

Cognitive flexibility "describes group members' awareness of various possible options for dealing with a situation, their willingness to adapt and be flexible in new situations, and their ability to represent knowledge from different conceptual and case perspectives" (Raes et al., 2011: 111). In their model, cognitive flexibility is defined as "the extent to which the information exchange process between TMT and MMs is characterized by reflecting, reviewing information, taking different perspectives, being open to hearing from each other, being able to change opinions, and developing a large variety of interpretations" (111).

As Raes et al. state, during interaction mutual influencing also takes place, which means that each party will try to promote their own central interest in the common process. Thus, TMT will aim "to install in MMs a strong sense of organization recognition, individual ownership, and motivation for decision implementation, since this facilitates implementation of the strategy" (107). Whereas MMs "influence the TMT with the goal of receiving resources for implementation, having their input taken into account, and getting new ideas accepted." The process of mutual influencing that will lead to a better implementation quality is, according to the authors, integrative bargaining, that is, "the degree to which the mutual influencing process … is characterized by finding common or complementary interests that benefit both parties rather than just one. When integrative bargaining is high, the mutual influencing process … will be oriented toward achieving a win-win situation." In this sense, "integrative bargaining implies a way of dealing with opposing interests (between the members) that is cooperative and by which value for both parties is created" (112).

Hence, high-quality personal interaction in an organization greatly depends on cognitive flexibility, which requires specific attitudes or character traits and virtues, such as of openness toward the opinions and interpretations of the other party; respect for, and ability to adopt, different points of view concerning resolution of the same problem; and humility and willingness to learn. Integrative bargaining, on the other hand, requires a certain degree of benevolence, as it leads to searching for an alternative that makes each party better off after the collaborative transaction.

Furthermore, cognitive flexibility and integrative bargaining will increase interpersonal trust, as these attitudes increase the perceived integrity, ability, and benevolence of the parties in the eyes of their partners. Trust in this context is very positive, as it leads members to increase their collaborative behavior; that is, the top management will be willing to adopt a more participative leadership and ask the middle management for a more active participation. On the other hand, middle management will be keen to engage actively in the process. Interpersonal trust could also be considered the lubricant oil that makes it easier for the parties to interconnect.

The authors do not explicitly mention synergy when developing their model, but they do state that their interface approach will lead to better results in those cases where the complexity of organizational structure and environment makes a "stand-alone" decision-making by the TMT per se inefficient because collaboration is crucial for a better organizational performance.

The Role of Character Traits or Virtues

Although not directly intended by Raes et al., their research underlines the specific role of character and personality traits in the development of interaction. A TMT member who is open to new ideas and opinions and respects the position of middle management—that is, a humble and benevolent manager—will engage and motivate the middle management member to be more open and willing to share relevant information. Humility and benevolence lead to seeking solutions based on a shared mental model. By this, middle management will be more supportive of any emerging strategic decision. Another very valuable contribution of this research is the emphasis on the fact that group work does not only take place when people are united geographically; what is more important is the existence of moments of interaction that are well utilized to develop a positive interaction. Hence, more research is needed on the means of improving these moments, which could also be called "moments of truth," as the true willingness to collaborate will emerge here.

The management practitioner's understanding of what it means to create positive synergy is very much in line with the model presented by Raes and colleagues. Stephen Covey (2007: 263) defines synergy as follows:

> The whole is greater than the sum of its parts. It means that the relationship which the parts have to each other is a part in and of itself.

For Covey, the relational moment, that is, the moment or episode of interaction between the members of a group, is very important in the process of creating synergy. In fact, he talks of two specific habits as critically necessary to achieve synergy: (1) thinking win/win and (2) seeking first to understand the other's position and then to be understood. The latter, writes Covey, allows for the creation of a comprehensive picture of values and concerns that need to be taken into account in making a decision. Synergy is realized when a third alternative, different from the one the members of the group proposed individually, is developed together: "they communicate back and forth until they come up with a solution they both feel good about. It's better than the solutions either of them originally proposed. It's better than compromise. It's a synergistic solution" (Covey, 2007: 275). He emphasized that "it is in the relationship that creative powers are maximized" (283). Covey's proposal is strongly based on virtue and character ethics.

Summary

Synergy is the concept used to describe a gain in performance attributable to group interaction. An almost mechanistic approach will try to measure how individual behavior is influenced by interaction, whereas interaction per se is not analyzed further. A more humanistic approach, in our view, will consider that positive synergy can be created if interaction, which is the relational moment of a team working together, contains certain behaviors fostering trust. This trust can bring into active play the capabilities and resources of team members, who will be motivated to actively engage in fulfilling a common objective.

Thus, from a humanistic management perspective, creating positive energy means, first of all, acknowledging that teams are communities of persons bound together by a common objective—the common good. A positive outcome of social interaction cannot be measured solely in terms of a more or less efficient achievement of an external objective. It is also necessary to assess how members of a community are able to flourish via social interaction—something that can only happen in an organizational climate of trust.

Hence, it is important for researchers and practitioners to engage in finding ways to improve our understanding of how trust emerges and permeates organizational structures. Using the research of Raes et al., we have argued that interpersonal trust can be improved by raising the quality of interpersonal interaction. This implies that the persons interacting acquire specific character traits and personal attitudes, such as humility, benevolence, openness, and respect for one another. Further research should thus be conducted focusing on the relationship between virtuous management and positive synergy.

Research and practice should also focus on the so-called "moments of truth" or moments of interaction of team members, which can be face to face or virtual, that is, mediated by the internet and associated electronic collaboration tools. How does the quality of personal interaction impact different environments? Does positive synergy depend on external characteristics of interaction?

Last but not least, relating human flourishing to positive synergy implies also a relationship between the latter with job satisfaction. This could also be an interesting avenue for further research.

Questions

1. What is synergy? Discuss factors for successful collaboration.

2. How can synergy be created? Throw light on multiple perspectives.

3. What is the role of cognitive flexibility in integrative bargaining?

References

Canals, J. 2010. "Rethinking the Firm's Mission and Purpose." *European Management Review* 7, pp. 195–204.

Cardona, P., and H. Wilkinson. 2006. *Team Work* (IESE Occasional Paper, OP no No. 07/10-E). http://www.iese.edu/research/pdfs/OP-07-10-E.pdf.

Covey, S.R. 2007. *The 7 Habits of Highly Effective People: Powerful Lessons for Personal Change.* Norwood, MA: Soundview Executive Book Summaries.

Hittinger, F.R. 2012. "Divisible Goods and Common Good: Reflections on Caritas in Veritate: Response to Martin Rhonheimer." In *Free Markets and the Culture of Common Good*, eds. M. Schlag and J. Andrés Mercado. Dordrecht, The Netherlands: Springer, pp. 41–52.

Larson, J.R. 2007. "Deep Diversity and Strong Synergy: Modeling the Impact of Variability in Members' Problem-Solving Strategies on Group Problem-Solving Performance." *Small Group Research* 38, no. 3, pp. 413–36.

Larson, J.R. 2010. *In Search of Synergy in Small Group Performance.* New York, NY: Psychology Press.

Melé, D. 2003. "The Challenge of Humanistic Management." *Journal of Business Ethics* 44, pp. 77–88.

Melé, D. 2009. "Integrating Personalism into Virtue-Based Business Ethics: The Personalist and the Common Good Principles." *Journal of Business Ethics* 88, pp. 227–44.

Melé, D. 2012. "The Firm as a 'Community of Persons': A Pillar of Humanistic Business Ethos." *Journal of Business Ethics* 106, no. 1, pp. 89–101.

Raes, A.M.L., M.G. Heijltjes, U. Glunk, and R.A. Roe. 2011. "The Interface of the Top Management Team and Middle Managers: A Process Model." *Academy of Management Review* 36, no. 1, pp. 102–26.

CHAPTER 10

CSR Reporting: Prevalent Practices in Businesses

Kulapan Chantarasap

The prevalence and relevance of corporate social responsibility (CSR) reporting for companies in the private sector during the past two decades were limited in scope and mainly voluntary in nature, with minimal adherence to internationally accepted reporting standards that ensure transparency and integrity in reporting. According to Gray et al. (1987) in *Corporate Social Reporting—Accounting and Accountability*, CSR is the process of communicating social and environmental effects of the organization's actions to particular interest groups within and among society at large. This, in the past, entailed publicly disclosing information that had significant impact on investment decisions and the market value of trading firms' securities, and this act of disclosure had also served to keep the company's shareholders informed (Stock Exchange of Thailand, n.d.).

In addition to these drivers, the increasing awareness of climate change across the globe also led to the passing and enforcing of regulatory policies and legislations toward controlling pollution and greenhouse gas emissions that targeted both public sector and private sector companies. This in effect led to the disclosure of information on their operations and mitigation measures to the public at large as well as the regulatory and enforcement authorities. The focus on industrial safety, occupational health and safety issues, relocation and resettlement issues, employee welfare and development, and gender issues in several developed countries also propelled the popularity of CSR reporting by multinationals in order to maintain their "license to operate." This, in turn, produced a ripple effect, emphasizing the importance of CSR to government bodies, companies, investors, consumers, stakeholders, and other interest groups. The ripple effect also extended to developing and nondeveloping countries, setting examples of what types of data investors and stakeholders expected in companies' reporting, how these data are reported, and the transparency and integrity of information disclosed. The arrival of Global Reporting Initiative (GRI) in 2000 became the watershed event, a result of the pioneering efforts of the activists and interest groups of the twenty-first century (GRI, 2020). It is one of the first international nonprofit organizations to develop a comprehensive reporting framework that is globally accepted and used for disclosing information on the CSR-specific activities carried out by organizations (GRI, 2020).

Two decades later, the CSR reporting concept transcended its original meaning of "companies interacting with society and/or parts of society" to a higher level by encompassing short-, medium-, and long-term perspectives of value creation to benefit business organizations, economy, society, and the environment as a whole (Perrini and Tencati, 2006). CSR became synonymous with sustainability and expanded its scope from social responsibility to cover economic, environmental, and social impacts of the operations of business corporations. The reporting served to disclose to the public information on companies' values, governance model, linkage between business strategies and commitment to global sustainable economy targets, as well as responding to and integrating stakeholder's perception and expectations. Most Securities and Exchange Commissions that regulate the stock exchange around the world encourage listed companies to provide information beyond financial statements and reports to include info on their performances in the context of sustainability (RobecoSam, 2014).

In the oil and gas industry, where stakes are high in relation to operational disasters, accidents, fatalities, corruption cases, tax evasions, and other hazardous effects to the local community and environment, the transformation of CSR reporting into sustainability reporting and the public disclosure of relevant data have become a significant part of doing business.

It may take years for companies to gain a good reputation, and all it takes is just one day and one disaster or industrial accident to lose that reputation. In other words, public may lose faith in a company for a variety of reasons, including its mismanagement or poor handling of accidents, explosions, oil spills into the environment, heavy criticism from the social media, corruption scandals, lack of transparency of cash flows, human rights violations, and other issues, leading to the revocation of company's "license to operate" and drastic erosion of its financial securities, including its stocks and share value. These issues could have irreversible negative impacts on the company if remedial steps are not taken in time to mitigate losses all around and in a timely, transparent, and effective manner. The sustainability concept and values must be integrated into the business operations for companies to effectively and efficiently identify sustainability risks and opportunities and manage these issues to sustain long-term value for all stakeholders (RobecoSAM, 2014).

By publicly disclosing data on company's sustainability performances in compliance with international sustainability indices, standards, and practices (e.g., GRI, CDP, UN Global Compact Principles, Dow Jones Sustainability Index [DJSI], etc.), in addition to what is required by local regulators and governing bodies, companies should communicate to the public that they operate with integrity, transparency, and accountability; have the capacity to prosper in a competitive and changing global business environment; and are focused on continuous improvement in quality, innovation, and productivity to create a competitive advantage and long-term value for all stakeholders.

The transformation of CSR reporting into sustainability reporting occurs in three stages.

Stage 1

The organizational sustainability journey normally begins with tactical actions related to specific functions, issues, and/or concerns to respond to short-term business requirements and stakeholder's expectations. For example, in the past, specific function groups came together to respond to stakeholder's perceptions and expectations on certain topics, such as occupational health and safety statistics; CSR strategies, projects, and activities; and environmentally friendly/operational eco-efficiency projects. These stakeholders' expectations (which mainly include local regulators, government bodies, nongovernment organizations, and investors) included confirmation that the company complies with local regulations and legislations and is conducting business ethically, lawfully, and responsibly toward both the environment and society. The activities in the first stage mainly focus on recordable injury rates, lost time injury rates, oil spills, donations to schools and communities, as well as mitigation of environmental impacts from operations. As the company progresses along the disclosure of these elements by using international standards such as OHSAS 18001, SA 9000, ISO 14001, or ISO 26000 to benchmark and assure the company's quality of occupational health, safety, environmental and social performance, they, in fact, become obliged to adhere to these standards to continuously improve management functions and performance. Baselines statistics are collected, and both short-term and long-term targets are set within the ambit of a check-and-balance system to ensure the company is managed efficiently and its performance is improving steadily. Normally, data are collected on a monthly basis and benchmarked with past performances annually. These performances are benchmarked against other companies in the same industry for further improvement. This is still, however, a stand-alone system, where none of the specific functions are linked to or included in the business strategy development and implementation. The data at this stage have no link with the company's business strategy. Eventually, sustainability reporting guidelines and indicators help shape and evolve the separated sustainability performance targets and data by integrating them with business strategy and incorporating stakeholder's views and expectations at the early stage of operations itself.

Stage 2

Compliance is not enough to maintain a company's "license to operate" in the context of regulatory and political uncertainty, agile cultures, shift in global paradigms, and the influence of powerful social media that can drastically change public and investor's perception of the company from positive to negative or vice versa. At this stage, finding commonalities between functions, issues, and concerns is one of the major priorities for external sustainability reporting. Sustainability in this context is sometimes referred as the ESG criteria (environment, social, and governance). At this stage, sustainability risks and opportunities, measures to mitigate and minimize risks, as well as measures to capitalize on sustainability opportunities should be identified and integrated into business strategies and decision-making processes. Companies need to ensure that sustainability-related risks and opportunities are addressed and accounted for in the earliest stages of project lifecycle. This is essential for companies in the global arena to quickly respond to immediate changes such as ESG shocks (e.g., explosion, spills, or corruption scandals) or large-scale events that can lead to significant shifts in company's management, culture, and financial well-being.

Postevent management plays a pivotal role in mitigating the severity of an ESG shock, and the duration of the shock often leads to long-term measures that a company must implement to minimize the risk of future ESG events. Companies that are prepared for ESG shocks can better mitigate both short-term and long-term risks. Disclosure of measures in place for identification, assessment in terms of materiality to business value, and management of ESG risks help maintain investor confidence. Historical information on ESG outputs (e.g., reporting of emissions) is relevant because it can be used to predict future consequences (RobecoSAM, 2014).

Stage 3

The integration of sustainability strategy framework and reporting with company's business strategies and everyday decision-making occurs at this stage, and stakeholder's perceptions, expectations, and views are accounted for in business strategies to provide the right balance in creating benefits for both business and society. This is the ideal state for sustainability practices in business as it has become part of the business itself and creates value to all stakeholders (Perrini and Tencati, 2006) wherein it reinforces the following:

- Company's capacity to prosper in a competitive and changing global business environment
- Anticipating and managing current and future economic, environmental, and social opportunities and risks

- Focusing on quality, innovation, and productivity to create competitive advantage and long-term value

In addition, understanding key sustainability concerns and issues that are relevant to both the company and its stakeholders is vital for creating a complete, relevant, accurate, and transparent form of reporting. These relevant issues (material issues) are identified through the process of materiality assessment.

The most common materiality assessment process used by companies in identifying material issues to include a structured review of current and future business risks and opportunities is based on the framework developed by the GRI. The material issues include aspects that reflect significant economic, environmental, and social impacts for the company. In some companies, materiality analysis is conducted on a yearly basis as part of the reporting cycle, and in others, it is conducted only when necessary (once every 2 years), depending on the demand arising from the external dynamics of each industry.

According to the GRI framework, the materiality assessment process involves the following:

1. *Identifying and prioritizing material issues to define reporting content.* This identifies the material issues from the perspective of both business and stakeholders. The process is based on consideration of the company's business strategy and activities, risks and challenges, expectations from the society, applicable laws and regulations, future trends, and stakeholder feedback. Normally, the GRI framework addresses the full scope of sustainability issues that are specific to ESG aspects.
2. *Defining reporting boundaries.* For each material aspect, companies should consider whether the impact of that issue lies inside or outside the organization and assess and describe where the impacts end by considering the relevance to different stakeholder groups, that is, external groups such as suppliers, contractors, and communities.
3. *Prioritizing issues.* Companies should assess the level of significance of the ranks and prioritize identified issues using agreed-upon criteria (magnitude of impact and its importance to investors, society, and business). Each issue is prioritized as low, moderate, or high for

current or potential impact on the company within the specified timeframe and the degree of concern to stakeholders. Companies can use focus group meetings with relevant departments and stakeholders to identify key materiality issues. The issues and their ratings are then plotted on a "materiality matrix" with

- X (horizontal axis) as "significance to company"
- Y (vertical axis) as "significance to stakeholders"

In most cases, issues in the upper-right quadrant are considered as most material and significant to include in the sustainability report. However, companies must understand and take note that all of the issues identified in the other quadrants are essential in the materiality assessment; the position of each issue in the matrix simply represents the understanding of its relative importance to the company and its stakeholders.

4. *Validating issues.* The list of material issues identified should then be validated by the companies' management and reviewed by companies' business strategists to ensure it is included in the business strategy and aligns with business objectives. The materiality issues should be reviewed internally with all key stakeholders. All identified material issues are assessed against the reporting principle of "completeness" prior to gathering the information to be reported. The aspects identified in the prioritization step are checked against the dimensions of scope, boundary, and time.

5. *Review and continuous development.* Companies' revision process for sustainability reporting should apply the principles of stakeholder inclusiveness (Perrini and Tencati, 2006) (organization communicates info on this process to its stakeholders, including how it has responded to their reasonable expectations and interests) and sustainability context (presentation of the organization's performance in the wider context of sustainability), to ensure continuous improvement of information disclosure. Companies should be actively engaging both internal and external stakeholders to check whether the report content provides a reasonable and balanced picture of the organization's sustainability performance and whether the process by which the report content was derived reflects the company's adherence to the two reporting principles. Comments and suggestions

from external stakeholders through the annual stakeholder meeting event, interviews, surveys, and website user statistics are also considered and included in the report. The findings inform and contribute to the identification of issues that need to be considered for inclusion in the next reporting cycle.

Reporting standards advocate the use of materiality analysis within sustainability reporting to guide investors and stakeholders in identifying and prioritizing relevant sustainability aspects to be included in the report.

According to DJSI and RobecoSAM's definition of materiality of sustainability, materiality is translated in a way that reflects how different forms of capital (intellectual, customer, human, environmental, social, and financial) might have present or future impacts on company's financial performances, value drivers, competitive position, and long-term shareholder value creation. The DJSI is a tool for investors and companies to benchmark their sustainability performances against one another in the same industry and also across sectors. Investors use the DJSI index as part of their decision-making in long-term sustainability investment.

Looking Ahead

The way to go for sustainability reporting and practices is to look at the "Integrated Approach to Sustainability" by integrating material financial factors, financial key performance indicators (KPIs), and financial performances with industry value drivers and long-term intangible assets and at "Sustainability Investing"—a long-term investment approach that integrates economic, environmental, and social considerations into the selection and retention of investments. In a nutshell, corporate sustainability is driven by the idea that "the competitive position of a company ultimately determines its potential to create value" (RobecoSAM, 2014).

The global trend is heading toward integrating all forms of sustainability criteria, risks, opportunities, and strategies, as well as financial material aspects, into how companies do business in order to create long-term value for all stakeholders and create partnerships between nonprofit organizations, government bodies, and private sectors to help propel sustainability practices into the mainstream. Sustainability indices such as the DJSI, FTSE4Good, EIRIS Sustainability Ranking, CDP Leadership Indices, United Nations Global Compact, and several more will play major roles in identifying which companies are good for long-term investments and which are outstanding in their sustainability performances when benchmarked against their peers in the same industry or across different industries. Most sustainability indices seek to identify companies that demonstrate their ability to manage sustainability issues, include sustainability thinking into strategic decision-making, and also provide attractive investment opportunities. In addition, sustainability reporting trends are changing from voluntary to mandatory around the world as market regulators, government bodies, and international institutions are using sustainability reporting as a tool to screen companies with sustainability risks and identify opportunities for value creation for economy, society, and environment. To quickly conclude, in a nutshell, integrated sustainability reporting is a worldwide initiative today that is on its way to becoming tomorrow's norm for responsible reporting practices that businesses will be expected to follow.

Summary

CSR reporting for companies in the private sector during the past two decades was limited in scope and mainly voluntary in nature. The GRI is one of the first international not-for-profit organizations to develop a comprehensive reporting framework that is globally accepted and used for publicly disclosing CSR information. Two decades later, the CSR reporting concept transcended its original scope by encompassing short-, medium-, and long-term perspectives of value creation to benefit the organization, economy, society, and the environment as a whole. CSR thus became sustainable, leading to the transformation of CSR reporting into sustainability reporting, which occurs in three stages. The way forward for sustainability reporting and practices is to look at the "Integrated Approach to Sustainability" that integrates material financial factors, financial KPIs, financial performances and other industry value drivers as well as long-term intangible assets in respect to economic, environmental, and social considerations into the reporting process.

Questions

1. Discuss the pros and cons of the different approaches and standards of CSR/sustainability reporting for the private sector. (Instructor may have to look into different reporting guidelines to further this discussion.)

2. What other dimensions do you think are lacking in sustainability reports published by the private sector in a specific industry. (Instructor to select an industry for discussion.)

3. Do you think sustainability reporting should be voluntary, or do you think it should be made a mandatory requirement for the private sector? In both cases, explain why and to what extent.

References

Gray, R., D. Owen, and K. Maunders. 1987. *Corporate Social Reporting – Accounting & Accountability*. London: Prentice-Hall International.

Perrini, F., and A. Tencati. 2006. "Sustainability and Stakeholder Management: The Need for New Corporate Performance Evaluation and Reporting Systems." *Business Strategy and the Environment* 15, no. 5, pp. 296–308.

RobecoSAM Sustainability Investing Report 2014. http://www.sustainability-indices.com.

Stock Exchange of Thailand. n.d. https://www.set.or.th/en/about/annual/sd_report_p1.html.

CHAPTER 11

Organizational Transformation for Sustainability

Jyoti Bachani

Organizations, in theory and practice, are still largely defined by ideas that were developed during the industrial era. With industrialization came mechanization that required the roles of personnel to become highly specialized too, focusing on the assembly line model. With simple skills, people could do repetitive jobs and be guaranteed employment for life. The profits went to those who could control the means of production and the assets and resources. The basis of competition was the control of assets and resources. Organizations were structured in a hierarchical manner. Senior managers developed the organization's strategy to compete and kept it a well-guarded secret. Middle managers were responsible for implementing those strategies and frontline managers did the actual work in implementing those strategies.

At the end of the twentieth century, with the widespread proliferation of the Internet in business and other organizations, there was a shift away from the industrial era as we entered a new era—the information era. The first decade of the twentieth century revealed numerous problems in organizing and utilizing resources in a manner that worked better only in the industrial era and that has become increasingly obsolete or irrelevant in contemporary times. The initial economic shifts caused by the Internet companies are playing out on a daily basis. The early signs of the shift came when some Internet companies took over or wiped out established companies. Such dominance has been exemplified by America Online

(AOL) taking over Time-Warner, one of the largest and old media conglomerates, or the online bookseller and retailer Amazon.com successfully driving out of business the entire gamut of brick-and-mortar bookstores not only in the United States but across the globe. Travel agencies were wiped out with the arrival of online bookings for air travel. Organizations everywhere are facing all manner of chaos indicative of their being in the throes of a major transformation, and new ways of organizing are still emerging.

In November 2014, Sony Pictures was brought to a standstill, hacked by an anonymous group that gained control of the company's information systems and stole 100 terabytes of private data that included confidential contracts, private e-mails, passwords, executive compensation information, medical records, and social security data of over 47,000 employees (Fritz & Yadron, 2014). Over the following days and weeks, the hackers published selective data on websites while Sony struggled to defend itself. It is reported that the company may have launched counterattacks on websites that published the stolen private information to deny access, and they involved the Federal Bureau of Investigation for help in tracing the hackers.

This was one of a series of cyberattacks that have prompted a response from the U.S. government at the highest level. In February 2015, President Obama organized a Cyber Security Summit at Stanford University, calling for better practices at consumer companies. They recommended a collaborative approach between the government and private organizations, with partnerships for information sharing on cybersecurity. Even as these events play out, there is a need to reconsider the very basis of the nature of organizing. Since then, threats to the financial system, failure of companies once considered "too big to fail," debate on privacy with Edward Snowden revelations about the U.S. government surveillance of all its citizens, and many other events are pointing to the need for this transformation.

The very nature of organizing has changed due to technological innovations demanding a fundamental transformation. A quote attributed to Henry Ford, a pioneer of the industrial age and the one who introduced the radical concept of assembly line manufacturing at Ford Motor Company, is "Why is it that every time I ask for a pair of hands, they come with a brain attached?" His attitude typifies the dominant mindset and business requirements that served the industrial-age companies well. People were replaceable cogs in the capitalistic system, and uniformity and conformity were valued. In sharp contrast, in the information-age organization, uniqueness and creativity are more valued than uniformity. Uniform assembly line jobs can be standardized to such an extent that they can be performed by robots. In January 2015, at the Davos Economic Summit, leaders predicted that most of the routine jobs would go to robots that cost $3,000 or less to build and use. In the United States, it is already common to see self-check-out devices everywhere from grocery/retail stores to airports, libraries, and restaurants.

From Stable Hierarchical Organizations to Purposeful Popup Organizing

The industrial-age companies measured their success by chasing competitive advantage. These organizations were often structured hierarchically and pursued their strategic goals in a militaristic manner, with systems built to support such a style of functioning. Top management set goals and developed strategies, middle management were administrators responsible for delivering the goals set by those strategies, and frontline managers acted as functional implementers. In sharp contrast, information-age global giants are designing and selling software and technology-based customized products and services that facilitated technical expertise–based forms of organizing, often project- and team-based, that can span multiple countries and functional domains. This organizing is a dynamic and interactive process, so these corporations are much more purposeful and comfortable in the use of agile processes to deliver multiple versions of the product in rapid succession (Bachani & Vradelis, 2012). Experts who work together to accomplish this shared purpose can come together in technology-mediated ways and platforms. They don't need to be working for the same organization and they often do not reside in the same geographical area where the company is located. It may simply be a collection of individuals with nothing more in common than a shared commitment to the purpose and a willingness to come together on a collaborative platform to accomplish organizational or project goals in partnership with other individuals. One project may involve hacking and, simultaneously, another may work to resolve technical problems for a major corporation as a third-party consultant/service provider—hired help—with such jobs outsourced to them through a contract awarded by the organization; this system is typically called the gig economy, gig being a one-time work project that is based on specific deliverables. With these changes, the basis of competitive advantage is also shifting. If the industrial age rewarded those who owned resources and assets, the information age is rewarding those who have knowledge and creativity.

At the Stanford Cyber Security Summit, the president and CEO of MasterCard, Ajay Banga, said that the hackers are ahead and at every minute trying to hack into company servers housing customer data. The president and CEO of Bank of America, Brian Moynihan, said there is not enough money that he can set aside to defend the company against hacking and information stealing, a threat to his company's very existence, and that if they do not monitor their networks and systems 24/7 they would cease to exist. Former president Obama pointed out that it is not just private consumer companies but the society itself relies on information technology and infrastructure in every area of human life, including operating power plants, air traffic control, and other basic ways of organizing in industries and in areas such as military and national security; consequently, both business and the society at large have become vulnerable to cyberattacks. Control of assets is not enough because the creativity and knowledge of an expert teenage programmer in some country to hack into a vulnerable power system and unleash damages on a major scale can completely turn off the power supply for the whole city (Gorlik, 2014).

Sumantra Ghoshal and Christopher Bartlett in their call to reinvent management offered one possible road map for the renewal of the corporation (Ghoshal and Bartlett, 1997). They have argued for moving away from the purely economic basis of thinking about business organizations to include sociological aspects that pay attention to the need to work toward achieving the goal of collective welfare of the whole society. In other words, businesses are not just there to make money; they are expected to deliver something of value to society through specific strategies and goals, in addition to making profits or earning revenue. They strongly suggest reinventing the management's role that will work better in an information-age organization than in a traditional, hierarchically arranged and operated organization.

In twentieth-century organizations, the role of top management was to develop and implement strategies and control resources, with middle management acting as administrative controllers who translated the strategy for frontline managers who were responsible for implementing those strategies and supervising and managing another layer of personnel who actually implemented those strategies and did work hands-on to deliver the goals set by those strategies. In the twenty-first century, with the current climate of technology-mediated economies and society, all of these roles need to be reassessed. Ghoshal and Bartlett recommend the flipping of these roles, and their ideas seem to be better aligned with the needs of the hour (Ghoshal and Bartlett, 1997). The information-age frontline manager is not just an implementer of the strategy handed down to him or her; he or she is the seed from which creative strategy emerges. The frontline manager might be the one with the most up-to-date knowledge obtained directly from engaging with the users of their various products and services. A factory manager, for example, is more likely to know how to optimize productivity on the production floor because he or she understands the production process better than his or her bosses who only have a hands-off view or knowledge of it that is typically derived from reports that go up the chain of command. Another example is a marketing professional who is pounding the pavement meeting customers on a daily basis and meeting competitive products in proposal face-offs is best informed about the nature of competition and potential future shifts in buying preferences of consumers. Therefore, these frontline managers are best positioned to get the most precise and latest information on products, customers, and competition. They are the ones whose inputs should be the primary driver of the process of developing organizational strategies. Such a strategy best fits external needs. Frontline managers can further act, with proper incentives, as entrepreneurs, who can respond independently and quickly to seize the best opportunities in a timely manner.

With the frontline manager's role changing from that of an implementer to that of an entrepreneur, the roles for the middle and top management positions will also have to be redefined. The top management no longer needs to be chiefly responsible for developing integrated initiatives or strategies. Their role has come to focus more exclusively on the collective efforts of the organization by clearly articulating the purpose for which the organization exists. Their daily job then is to perform as the architects of organizational processes and mentor people to fulfill or achieve a shared purpose or a goal. The middle managers' role then would be to listen to the new ideas coming from the frontline managers and be personal advisors to them. Middle managers will also have the responsibility to prioritize and integrate the good ideas that they get to learn from various units, across the organization. By this integration, they may craft strategies for the firm and articulate them for both the frontline managers and the top management. Thus, middle management would play the important role of integrators. Frontline managers are opportunity creators and performance drivers. They are the ones who build new capabilities, as required, based on the immediate information collected through their engagement with consumers and external stakeholders.

Let us examine one way to use this approach, which entails reinterpreting and reframing of problems to come up with best-possible solutions. For example, the story of information breach that occurred at Sony Pictures can be reframed as follows: Instead of senior management or the government agencies trying to control the organization and secure its information infrastructure through contract-based controls and regulatory oversight, the firm needs to adopt a transparent and trust-based approach to problem-solving. The data can be considered a part of the user's online identity with each user taking ownership of their data, rather than the organization doing the job of protecting consumer data. If all data were owned by the individual consumers, then seller organizations cannot manipulate or sell such data indicating their past purchase behavior. This would free organizations from the burden of data-breaches and transfer the control of information to the customer.

Just as hackers can attack the information technology infrastructure, or more simply computer servers, from outside the firm, the solution too can come from outside in the form of a community-based, crowdsourced response to the hacker's attack. Some hackers may even find these opportunities to be a way to channel their creativity into building for and defending organizations, as not all hackers are interested in hacking into company servers and stealing information. There is an entire open-source movement where a lot of what the hackers create is shared free of cost under new public arrangements such as Creative Commons licenses. Such open-source approach is likely to be more cost-effective too, as the community ownership will likely increase the engagement due to personal skin in the game. No contracts can be as effective as a culture of belonging and a commitment to the purpose of the organization. Under such a culture, each employee is more willing to voluntarily go the distance to proactively support the purpose, be it to protect cybersecurity with high levels of due diligence, or others. This comes from a good alignment between collective organizational goals and individual goals. This is probably also good for greater commitment to the shared purpose with coordinated effort to ensure that it is achieved.

Such a reframing also implies a transformation of the relationship between the company and its external constituents. When an organization adopts transparency in its operations, there is no incentive for the hacker to break in, as operational data are already in the public domain or shared with consumers. If this comes to pass, public corporations would actually behave in a manner that shows they are answerable to both customers and the general public. The responsibility to secure the data would then be with the person who interacts and shares his or her information with the company online—it could be a customer, supplier, employee, or regulator—because he or she now owns his or her data. Since organizations currently own and have complete access and control over user data, it is not unusual for them to want to monetize such data and use that data to advertise and customize user experience to earn additional revenues. This is obviously a disservice to customers because not only are they robbed of legitimate control over data but they are also not allowed to customize data in a manner acceptable to them. Instead, customers are manipulated by highly targeted advertising that is personalized to reveal their tastes or purchase behaviors from their data.

The reframing also changes the internal relationships within the firm, and the very nature of the employee–employer relationship is fundamentally redefined. If in the earlier era the employer was likely to guarantee lifetime employment to the employees, in the new era, the employee–employer relationship shifts to the employer simply providing opportunities for the employee to contribute with their skillsets. These opportunities allow employees to grow and develop in a manner that is consistent with what they value and want to be and give them skills and experiences that will make them more employable—either with the same employer or another. An example from India illustrates this. Uber is familiar in many countries and provides the technology to connect car owners with those who need rides. Despite disrupting the taxi cab industry, Uber does not have its own fleet of vehicles. The ownership of cars rests with frontline workers, that is, those who invest in cars and often drive those cars themselves or even hire drivers to handle the rides at their behest. In India, a local company competes directly with Uber and is called Ola cabs. The car owners-cum-drivers are often operating both the apps, Uber and Ola, on their smartphones. They will accept rides from whichever app helps them connect with customers needing a ride. This is a very different model of doing business than a traditional taxi cab company.

The frontline managers are the closest to the real activities of the business, be it selling to the customers in the field or producing the goods on the factory floor. They are the ones best positioned to find new opportunities that can be grown by turning them into entrepreneurs. The person selling in the field is most likely to come across competitor's products and offerings and is best placed to decide what the most desired features to offer in products are. The factory floor manager has the best view of the shop-floor operations and knows better than anyone else about how to improve processes or when to upgrade equipment. When managers operate in an atmosphere of trust that respects and values their contributions, they will work in a more involved manner and take full ownership of their job. Instead of feeling responsible for just delivering results to satisfy someone higher up in the organizational hierarchy for the sake of rewards, they will actually want to do things that best contribute to achieving collective organizational goals. This will also nurture team spirit as they will become more supportive of and value others' work and share and improve their own knowledge as they grow. The intrinsic motivation is not based on whether or not there are external rewards; therefore, this tapping into individual creativity becomes a source of ongoing advantage.

Let us consider another company that does it differently: Pixar, the animated movie studio that has consistently delivered blockbuster films in a highly competitive market, such as Toy Story series, Ratatouille, Cars, and so on. The company relies on peer reviews where employees routinely share their work-in-progress with each other in a process called the dailies. Through the dailies, the feedback shared provides a way to get everyone's input to improve the work of each of the contributors. There are no stars or directors who are individually responsible for the creative output, as everyone's input is considered equally valuable. The openness in sharing work-in-progress takes the pressure off to deliver something perfect, and that open culture becomes conducive to really creating something that suits different tastes based on inputs received from everyone in the dailies (Catmull, 2008).

This does not mean there is consensus and no creative experts. There is a team of directors who together act as a brain-trust for the organization. Whichever project needs their help can count on their expertise. The company has redefined what a manager does by promoting a culture where a manager does not need to know what his or her direct reports are working on, because the manager is no longer someone who gets work done through managing others. Employees are allowed to self-manage and know it is okay for them to go to anyone in the organization to get what they need to do their job well. The typical organizational hierarchy and the chain of command that other organizations use, where employees have to check for boss's approval before going to talk to someone else in the company, is not a part of Pixar's culture.

Another example is Tesla Motors that produces the best electric vehicles on the road today. They did not set out to make the best electric car; instead, they wanted to make the best car. The Tesla car is so far ahead of all other competing car models on the road that the company felt confident enough to share their technology. Initially, they provided some components for certain models of Toyota electric vehicles and then they made their entire technology open source. They literally do not have the mindset of an industrial-age company that other car companies embody, where there are patents and licensing agreements to protect intellectual property. Tesla is on a mission to change the world. Toward that goal, they willingly and openly spread their technology with the zeal usually seen in missionaries spreading a new religion. Their confidence in their creative ability and innovative potential of their people is such that instead of worrying about competitors getting rich on the basis their ideas, they are so self-assured that they will have enough newer, better ideas to always stay ahead of competitors. Resting on their laurels and past success is not part of their strategy; instead, they work to offer better technology and better cars for the world.

To conclude, this chapter argues that the economics-driven approach of the industrial-era organizations is an inappropriate fit for the information-era organizing that is better understood by focusing on the sociological aspects with an emphasis on the many disparate actions by managers distributed across the various parts of the organization and the social context or ecosystem within which it operates. The industrial-era organization with hierarchy- and control-based organizing is better replaced with a flat, networked, and trust-based organizing structure where the process of identifying problems and developing solutions is democratized, leading to new roles for managers at each level of the organization. These new roles are defined in the charts provided. With examples, these ideas are illustrated to show how some firms are forging ahead and more is yet to come, as the Internet starts to go beyond the human systems to the Internet of Everything, connecting our devices and material world to the information network.

Summary

Industrial-era organizations relied on economic theories that recommended hierarchy and control-based organizing of Strategy-Structure-Systems. This approach is not appropriate in the information age. Using the examples from the twenty-first-century organizing and focusing on the sociological aspects, this chapter offers the framework for effectively organizing with an emphasis on the Purpose-Process-People. The sustainable approach is to have a flat, networked, and trust-based way of organizing where the process of problem identification and the process of developing solutions for problems are both democratized. This has implications for the new roles for managers at each level of the organization.

Questions

1. How has organizing in the industrial era been theorized and what discipline dominated and why?
2. What is the recommendation for organizing in the information era, and what discipline influences it?
3. How has the role of managers in organizations changed from the industrial era to information era?

References

Bachani, J., and M. Vradelis. 2012. *Strategy Making in Nonprofit Organizations: A Model and Case Studies*. New York, NY: Business Expert Press.

Catmull, E. September, 2008. "How Pixar Fosters Collective Creativity." *Harvard Business Review* 86, pp. 64-72, 134.

Fritz, B., and Yadron, D. 2014. "Sony Hack Exposed Personal Data of Hollywood Stars," *The Wall Street Journal*. https://www.wsj.com/articles/sony-pictures-hack-reveals-more-data-than-previously-believed-1417734425.

Gorlick, A. 2014. "Obama at Stanford: Industry Government must Cooperate on Cyber Security." https://news.stanford.edu/2015/02/13/summit-main-obama-021315/.

Ghoshal, S., and C. Bartlett. 1997. *The Individualized Corporation: A Fundamentally New Approach to Management*. New York, NY: Harper Business Books.

About the Editor & Authors

Radha R. Sharma is an executive alumnus of Harvard Business School and is certified in CSR by World Bank Institute, British Council, and New Academy of Business, UK. She is an active member of the UN Global Compact Network and international PRME working group on Sustainability Mindset. She has completed research projects supported by the World Health Organization, McClelland Centre for Research & Innovation, IDRC, Humanistic Management Network, UNESCO, and Academy of Management, among others. She is Dean, Research & Industry-Academia Linkages at New Delhi Institute of Management, New Delhi, India. Prior to this, she functioned as the Dean of the Research and Centres of Excellence at Management Development Institute (MDI) Gurgaon, India. She was chairperson of the Centre of Positive Scholarship for Organisational Sustainability, Hero MotoCorp chair professor, and professor, organizational behavior at MDI. She has served as ICCR chair professor at HHL Leipzig Graduate School Management, a visiting professor at European Business School, Germany; ESCP-Europe, Italy; University of Leipzig, Germany; and a guest professor at Wittenberg Centre for Global Ethics.

She has performed a 5-year leadership pipeline role at the International Theme Committee (ITC), Academy of Management (AOM), USA, and was recognized with a plaque for her role as ITC Chair (2018) by the president of AOM. She has received several awards and honors, including Outstanding Cutting-Edge Research Paper Award, 2005 (AHRD, USA); Best Researcher Award, 2008 (AIMS International); Best Symposium Award, Management Education Division, AOM (2018); Finalist Book Award (scholarly), 2018 International Humanistic Management Association, and Hind Rattan Award, 2015. Her research interests are emotional intelligence, executive burnout, gender equity, competencies, spirituality, sustainability and well-being. Her publications include 16 books, popular among them being *HRM for Organizational Sustainability* (2019); *Managing for Responsibility: A Sourcebook for an Alternative Paradigm* (co-ed.; Business Expert

Press, 2017); *Executive Burnout: Eastern and Western Concepts, Models and Approaches for Mitigation* (co-authored with Cary Cooper, Emerald, 2017); *Change Management and Organizational Transformation* (McGraw-Hill Co., 2012); *Reinventing Society: Search for a Paradigm* (co-ed., Macmillan, 2013); *Change Management: Concept and Applications* (McGraw-Hill Co., 2007); *360-Degree Feedback, Competency Mapping and Assessment Centers* (Tata McGraw-Hill, 2002); *Organizational Behavior* (co-authored with Steven McShane and Mary Ann Von Glinow (McGraw-Hill Co., 3 editions: 2011/08/06); and *Enhancing Academic Achievement: Role of Personality Factors* (Concept, 1985), among others. She has published a large number of research papers in peer-reviewed impact factor journals. She is associate editor, *Frontiers in Psychology* (A category journal); former editor, *Vision—The Journal of Business Perspective* (ABDC & ESCI Scopus indexed), and she is on the editorial board of *AIMS International Journal* and is reviewer for *Business Ethics: A European Review; International Journal of HRM; Journal of Management Spirituality & Religion; Journal of Management Development* (Emerald), *Cross-cultural Management—An International Journal* (Emerald), *Gender in Management: An International Journal, International Journal of Indian Culture and Business Management, Evidence-Based HRM, Current Psychology, Manpower Journal, Vikalpa* (IIMA), *Management Decision* (Emerald), *Humanistic Management Journal* (Springer), *Journal of Case Research* (XIMB), *Equality, Diversity and Inclusion, Asia-Pacific Journal of Business Administration, Management Decision, International Journal of Education Economics and Development, African Journal of Business Management, Asia Pacific Business, IIM Bangalore Review, Indian Journal of Applied Manpower Research*, and *Global Business Review*, among others. She has edited special issues of Vision on "Sustainability" (2019); Green Management and Circular Economy (2020); Recent Trends in OB Research (2020) Frontiers in Psychology on "Gender Diversity in the Workplace, Organizational Virtuousness and Well-Being" (2019); and Women and Entrepreneurship (2019).

Aard Groen is dean and professor of Entrepreneurship & Valorisation at the University of Groningen and has a broad interest in research, teaching, and business development support (in incubators and projects with companies and universities with innovation and/or business development needs). While working for more than 20 years at the University of Twente, he has established NIKOS (Netherlands Institute for

Knowledge Intensive Entrepreneurship). Since 1st of January 2020, he is fully engaged as a co-founder of the University of Groningen Centre of Entrepreneurship (UGCE). This centre contributes to building student's entrepreneurship competencies through teaching programmes. After finishing his PhD at the University of Groningen, he worked at Van Hall Institute teaching environmental management and at Fugro as a department head/consultant on environmental management.

Brent D. Beal received his PhD in management from the Lowry Mays College and Graduate School of Business at Texas A&M University and is currently a professor of management in the College of Business and Technology at the University of Texas at Tyler. He conducts research in the area of corporate social responsibility and has published articles in various journals, including in *Academy of Management Journal, Journal of Management, Journal of Philosophical Economics, Business Horizons, Journal of Managerial Issues, Case Research Journal, Business Case Journal*, and *Journal of Case Studies*, among others.

Chantal van Esch, PhD is Assistant Professor of Management at Management and Human Resources Department, California State Polytechnic University, Pomona, California.

Chinmoy Bandyopadhyay is a doctoral candidate in the area of marketing at the Xavier Institute of Management, Xavier University, Bhubaneswar, India. His doctoral work focuses on how social enterprises position their brand to multiple stakeholders. Previously, Chinmoy worked as a manager for nonprofit organizations in different parts of India. His research has appeared in academic journals such as *Journal of Nonprofit and Public Sector Marketing* and *Marketing Intelligence and Planning*.

Cristian R. Loza Adaui received his doctoral degree from the Ingolstadt School of Management of the Catholic University of Eichstätt-Ingolstadt, Germany, and is now researcher and lecturer at the Chair of Business Administration with focus on strategic and values-driven management at the Institute of Economics of the Friedrich-Alexander University Erlangen-Nürnberg, Germany. His research focuses on business ethics, strategic management, humanistic management, social responsibility, sustainability reporting, and business and society in Latin America.

Daniela Ortiz Avram is a teaching coordinator and senior researcher at the Institute for Business Ethics and Sustainable Strategy (IBES) at the FHWien der WKW, University of Applied Sciences for Management in Communication in Vienna, Austria (ibes.fh-wien.ac.at).

She studied philosophy with a specialization in ethics and anthropology at the Pontifical University of the Holy Cross (Rome), where she also completed her doctoral studies. She also holds a master's degree in business administration from the University of Innsbruck.

From 2016 to 2019, she headed the "Competence Team for Sustainable, Strategic and Opportunity-Oriented Management of SMEs" at FHWien der WKW, sponsored by the City of Vienna. Prior to this, Dr. Ortiz Avram worked as associate researcher at the Research Center Markets, Culture and Ethics (MCE) in Rome and as a research assistant at the Management Center Innsbruck (MCI).

Diana Bilimoria, Diana Bilimoria, PhD, is KeyBank Professor and Professor and Chair of Organizational Behavior at the Weatherhead School of Management, Case Western Reserve University. Her research interests focus on gender, diversity, equity, and inclusion in governance and leadership, and organizational transformation. Dr. Bilimoria has authored several books and published in leading journals and edited volumes. Recent awards she has received include the Scholarly Contributions to Educational Practice Advancing Women in Leadership Award from the Gender and Diversity in Organizations division of the Academy of Management, and the Weatherhead School of Management Enduring Research Impact Award.

Divya Bhutiani is a researcher in the areas of sustainability, organizational culture change, and business education. She obtained her doctoral degree (PhD) from the University of Twente in the Netherlands with a thesis titled "Social entrepreneurship, transformational leadership and emergence of sustainable organizations." She holds an MBA degree in human resource management from ICFAI Business School, India. She is currently working as a consultant at ERM in Houston, USA. She is a visiting assistant professor at LM Thapar School of Management.

Giorgio Mion received his PhD from the University "Ca' Foscari" of Venice, and is associate professor of business administration at the

University of Verona. He is the director of the post-graduate program in business ethics and president of the Teaching Board of the Master's Degree in Business Management and Strategy. His research interests include business ethics, hybrid organizations, and sustainability reporting.

Gregory G. Dess, presently holds the Andrew R. Cecil Endowed Chair in Applied Ethics at the University of Texas at Dallas. His research interests are in strategic management and entrepreneurship. He has published over 50 articles in many academic and practitioner journals as well as served on the editorial boards of several major journals. He has co-authored several books, including *Strategic Management: Text and Cases* (2019, 9th edition, McGraw-Hill Education), as well as two books targeted at the practitioner market: *Beyond Productivity* (AMACOM) and *Mission Critical* (Irwin Business). Dr. Dess received his Bachelor of Industrial Engineering from Georgia Tech, his M.B.A. from Georgia State University, and his Ph.D. in Business Administration from the University of Washington. He received an honorary doctorate in 2009 from the University of Bern (Switzerland).

Jennifer J. Griffin is Raymond C. Baumhart, S.J., endowed chair of business ethics and professor of strategy at Loyola University, Chicago and is an award-winning scholar and internationally recognized educator. Her book, published by Cambridge University Press, examining social impact and innovative CSR, *Managing Corporate Impacts: Co-creating Value,* won the Academy of Management SIM 2017 Best Book Award. Jenn has earned the highest educator awards, including the *Teaching Excellence Award*, the *MBA Teaching Award* at GW's School of Business, and was nominated nine times by students for the *Best PhD Teacher Award* and for the *National Inspire Integrity Award.*

Jyoti Bachani is an associate professor at Saint Mary's College of California. She earned a PhD at London Business School, a masters in management science and engineering at Stanford, and MBA and bachelor of science (physics) from the Delhi University. She serves on the editorial board of *Journal of Management Inquiry* and as an executive member of the Western Academy of Management, and the Management Spirituality and Religion interest group of the Academy of Management. Formerly, she has been a Fulbright Senior Research Scholar, the president of the

Western Casewriters Association, a board member of NACRA, and the editor-in-chief of the Emerald Emerging Markets Case Collection. She is a founding member of the U.S. and India Chapters of the International Humanistic Management Association.

Kulapan Chantarasap or Noelle is a sustainability professional with over 10 years of successful experience in the upstream oil and gas industry. With a bachelor's degree in environmental economics and masters of science in environment and natural resource economics from Thailand's most prestigious University, Kulapan is recognized consistently for performance excellence and contributions to success in corporate-wide sustainability program management and tactical execution of multiple sustainability programs. Her expertise includes understanding the industries' requirement for international sustainability assessments, sustainability reporting, namely, the GRI G4 Guideline, AA 1000 Materiality Assessment, and CDP Climate Change. Presently, she is pursuing her second graduate degree in global sustainability at Virginia Polytechnic Institute and State University, Virginia, USA.

Padmakumar Nair is the director and dean of L. M. Thapar School of Management, Thapar Institute of Engineering and Technology, Dera Bassi Campus (Punjab), India. He specializes in strategizing for sustainability, social and commercial entrepreneurship, and nanomaterials, with more than 55 publications in journals of international repute to his credit. He has worked both in academia and industry and has a combined experience of more than 30 years in various industries across the world. He has a PhD from the University of Twente in the Netherlands and a Doctor of Engineering (Dr. Engineering) degree from the University of Tokyo, Japan.

Parag Rastogi has over 25 years of industry experience. He earned his bachelor of engineering degree from BITS, Pilani, India, and MBA from XLRI, Jamshedpur, India. He has worked in leadership positions across various sectors like IT, CPG, retail, consulting, and media. He has wide-ranging interests in sustainability, entrepreneurship, and leadership development. He has to his credit three publications and one textbook.

Steven Olson is the Rollins Professor of marketing and entrepreneurship at the Gary W. Rollins College of Business, University of Tennessee–Chattanooga. He began his teaching career at Emory University's Goizueta Business School, where he cofounded the first nonprofit organization for corporate ethics in the United States and then founded and directed the programs in business and professional ethics at Emory's Center for Ethics in Public Policy and the Professions. He served as a special advisor to the White House Council for Sustainable Development and to the UN Global Compact Task Force on Anti-Corruption. A graduate of Yale University (MA) and Emory University (PhD), his doctoral dissertation on the ethics of leadership received the International Leadership Association's Jablin Award for "Best Dissertation" (2007).

Subhasis Ray is a professor of marketing at the Xavier Institute of Management, Xavier University, Bhubaneswar, India. He has more than 20 years of work experience in corporate and academia. His research interests are in sustainability, marketing, social innovation and entrepreneurship, CSR, emerging markets, and Indian philosophy and religion. He has published several articles in academic journals such as *Journal of Business Research, Marketing Intelligence and Planning, Journal of Nonprofit and Public Sector Marketing, International Journal of Health Care Quality Assurance*, and so on. He is also the chairperson of Centre for Business and Society, India.

Index

OTHER TITLES IN OUR ENVIRONMENTAL AND SOCIAL SUSTAINABILITY FOR BUSINESS ADVANTAGE COLLECTION

Robert Sroufe, Duquesne University, *Editor*

- *Sustainability Leader in a Green Business Era: A Middle East Perspective* by Amr E. Sukkar
- *Managing Sustainability: First Steps to First Class* by John Friedman
- *Climate Change Management: Special Topics in the Context of Asia* by Huong Ha
- *Change Management for Sustainability* by Huong Ha
- *The Role of Legal Compliance in Sustainable Supply Chains, Operations, and Marketing* by John Wood
- *Developing Sustainable Supply Chains to Drive Value, Volume I: Management Issues, Insights, Concepts, and Tools—Foundations* by Robert P. Sroufe
- *Developing Sustainable Supply Chains to Drive Value, Volume II: Management Issues, Insights, Concepts, and Tools—Implementation* by Robert P. Sroufe
- *Social Development Through Benevolent Busines* by Kalyan SankarMandal
- *ISO 50001 Energy Management Systems: What Managers Need to Know About Energy and Business Administration* by Johannes KalsFeasibility Analysis for Sustainable Technologie: An Engineering-Economic Perspective* by Scott R. Herriott
- *Strategy Making in Nonprofit Organizations: A Model and Case Studies* by Jyoti Bachani
- *A Primer on Sustainability: In the Business Environment* by Ronald Whitfield

Concise and Applied Business Books

The Collection listed above is one of 30 business subject collections that Business Expert Press has grown to make BEP a premiere publisher of print and digital books. Our concise and applied books are for...

- Professionals and Practitioners
- Faculty who adopt our books for courses
- Librarians who know that BEP's Digital Libraries are a unique way to offer students ebooks to download, not restricted with any digital rights management
- Executive Training Course Leaders
- Business Seminar Organizers

Business Expert Press books are for anyone who needs to dig deeper on business ideas, goals, and solutions to everyday problems. Whether one print book, one ebook, or buying a digital library of 110 ebooks, we remain the affordable and smart way to be business smart. For more information, please visit **www.businessexpertpress.com**, or contact **sales@businessexpertpress.com**.

www.ingramcontent.com/pod-product-compliance
Lightning Source LLC
Chambersburg PA
CBHW061157220326
41599CB00025B/4510